Dr. youngick Lee,

POINT OF ATTACK

Best wishes,

John Yoo

Point of Attack

PREVENTIVE WAR, INTERNATIONAL LAW, AND GLOBAL WELFARE

John Yoo

OXFORD
UNIVERSITY PRESS

OXFORD
UNIVERSITY PRESS

Oxford University Press is a department of the University of Oxford. It furthers the University's objective of excellence in research, scholarship, and education by publishing worldwide.

Oxford   New York
Auckland   Cape Town   Dar es Salaam   Hong Kong   Karachi   Kuala Lumpur   Madrid
Melbourne   Mexico City   Nairobi   New Delhi   Shanghai   Taipei   Toronto

With offices in
Argentina   Austria   Brazil   Chile   Czech Republic   France   Greece   Guatemala   Hungary
Italy   Japan   Poland   Portugal   Singapore   South Korea   Switzerland   Thailand
Turkey   Ukraine   Vietnam

Oxford is a registered trademark of Oxford University Press in the UK and certain other countries.

Published in the United States of America by
Oxford University Press
198 Madison Avenue, New York, NY 10016

Library of Congress Cataloging-in-Publication Data

Yoo, John.
   Point of attack : preventive war, international law, and global welfare / John Yoo.
      pages cm
   Includes bibliographical references and index.
   ISBN 978-0-19-934773-5 ((hardback) : alk. paper)
1. War (International law) 2. Aggression (International law) 3. Intervention (International law)
4. Humanitarian intervention. 5. Just war doctrine. 6. Security, International. 7. Preemptive attack
(Military science) I. Title.
   KZ6385.Y66 2014
   341.6—dc23
                                                    2013038114

9 8 7 6 5 4 3 2 1

Printed in the United States of America on acid-free paper

Note to Readers
This publication is designed to provide accurate and authoritative information in regard to the subject matter covered. It is based upon sources believed to be accurate and reliable and is intended to be current as of the time it was written. It is sold with the understanding that the publisher is not engaged in rendering legal, accounting, or other professional services. If legal advice or other expert assistance is required, the services of a competent professional person should be sought. Also, to confirm that the information has not been affected or changed by recent developments, traditional legal research techniques should be used, including checking primary sources where appropriate.

(Based on the Declaration of Principles jointly adopted by a Committee of the American Bar Association and a Committee of Publishers and Associations.)

To my father
John Hyun Soo Yoo, M.D. (1936–2012).

Contents

Foreword

"ONLY THE DEAD have seen the end of war," Plato wrote. Unfortunately, the last two millennia have proven him right. While the post–World War II era has witnessed a steep drop in the rate of armed conflict between states, men and women today still die in war at an alarming rate. But instead of the millions killed during the great struggles for supremacy in Europe and Asia, most today have died in more contained, more brutal, civil wars. This book seeks not just to understand these changes in war in the twenty-first century but also to develop a new set of rules to address them.

Point of Attack completes a long period of work for me on the wars that dominated the last two decades: the conflicts in Afghanistan and Iraq. That work began on September 11, 2001. As an official in the United States Department of Justice, I was involved in the debates within the United States government whether to use force in both countries. As a scholar who specialized in the American system of war powers, the right to go to war in Afghanistan did not seem to me to be a difficult call, as I explained in *The Powers of War and Peace* (2005). How to engage a terrorist enemy that did not act on behalf of a nation-state and refused to follow the laws of war posed the harder questions, ones that I sought to address in *War by Other Means* (2006). Those challenges have produced more consistency in policy between Presidents George W. Bush and Barack Obama than many critics of both would have predicted, a phenomenon I placed within a broader account of the growth in executive power in *Crisis and Command* (2010).

President Bush's decision to invade Iraq in spring 2003 posed the greatest legal problems outside the U.S. legal system, where I felt most at home. It posed no constitutional difficulties once Congress enacted an authorization to use military force in Iraq. But because the United Nations refused to authorize another war against Iraq, as it had in the 1991 Persian Gulf War, American allies as well as rivals raised grave challenges under international law to the conflict. Although I had studied and taught the U.N. Charter and the history of efforts to prohibit war, I had not devoted the kind of thought to the international law dimension that I had to American constitutional law. I believed that the United States suffered from a contradiction between a Charter written to stop the next World War and the modern challenges of authoritarian oppression, human rights disasters, terrorism, and the spread of weapons of mass destruction. The crucible of the Iraq war convinced me that the current system on the use of force had divorced the formal legal rules from the all-important goal of protecting and improving global human welfare.

Point of Attack bridges the gap between the necessity of wars in the twenty-first century and a set of international rules that are aging into obsolescence. But as I thought through the problem, I drew upon more than my personal experiences of working on the Iraq war for the U.S. government. Even before my days as an undergraduate student, I had pursued a deep interest in both war and law. The destruction that befell the country of my birth, South Korea, caused my parents and other Koreans to immigrate to the United States. I have remained ever conscious that in sacrificing its young men in battle in a country most had never heard of, the United States had saved my family and millions of others from the most evil regime on the planet. The families of those men can be proud that their bravery sheltered a people of great dynamism, both in their native land and here in the United States.

When my family arrived in the United States, the Vietnam War was reaching its peak. As a child, I watched grainy television scenes of the last helicopter leaving the U.S. embassy in Saigon in 1975. Perhaps that early vision of the most powerful nation in the world in retreat, contrasted with the rescue of my native country at its hands, prompted my long desire to understand war. Curious about my origins, I read about the Korean War as a youth. A deeper interest began when I studied Latin and Ancient Greek in middle and high school. Much of the readings were drawn from stories, real and imagined, of ancient conflict. Caesar's *Gallic Wars*, Livy's *Histories*, and Virgil's *Aeneid* presented war in a heroic light and elevated personal sacrifices for a greater national good. Thucydides' *Peloponnesian War* exposed the tragedy and senselessness of war—though at the time, reading the work in ancient Greek, I imagined I was the one suffering through a catastrophe as great as the Athenian expedition to Syracuse.

College provided me with the opportunity to study war more rigorously. As an undergraduate at Harvard, I studied American diplomatic history and government policy with Thomas Schwartz and Brian Balogh, who have since moved on to better fields. They taught me how to harness my interest in war and history to the purposes of scholarship, and I am forever grateful to them both. As we lived through the waning days of the Cold War, they introduced me to the controversies over the outbreaks of

World Wars I and II and the proxy conflicts and superpower competition of our own time. Though they did not intend it, I became an admirer of the realist way of looking at things, which caused me some cognitive dissonance when I went to Law School.

At Yale, I studied war when the collapse of the Soviet Union opened up new opportunities for international cooperation. Even as war has increased in the intensity of its destructiveness, nations have engaged in unprecedented cooperation to limit its harms. The United Nations, which sprung up from the wreckage of the last worldwide conflagration with the mission to end war, suddenly became relevant in addressing the new international disorder. The North Atlantic Treaty Organization, which had deterred war on a continent that had fueled great power conflict for three centuries, took on a policing role in areas beyond its territory. Victorious and without peer at the end of the Cold War, the United States committed to the defense of the Western Hemisphere, Europe, and Asia and nurtured a liberal international economic system that benefitted all. America's provision of security and free trade produced an unprecedented period of peace and prosperity in the world. No great power has fought another in nearly seven decades.

But even as international law should have reached the heights of its powers, it faltered. It could not stop human rights disasters in the Balkans and Africa. It shielded dictators who systematically abused their populations. Other nations used the law to constrain the most powerful nation in the international system and its allies from acting to prevent great harms to global welfare. When I returned to the University of California at Berkeley from government in 2003, I continued to work on the contradiction between international law and the change in war. *Point of Attack* brings together a decade of thinking about how to enhance human welfare by changing the international rules to respond to the challenges of this century, and not the last. In the future, I plan to explore this theme further by turning this approach to changes in military technology and the nature of modern combat.

Writing a book can appear to be a lonely endeavor. Kafka wrote: "Writing is utter solitude." However a work like this, I am glad to say, depends on a more cooperative effort. First come the institutions that provide the environment for the creation and testing of ideas. I thank Dean Christopher Edley of the Boalt Hall School of Law, University of California at Berkeley, for building the resources and maintaining the vibrant intellectual culture at the law school that is my academic home. For giving me a home in Washington, D.C., I am grateful to the leaders of the American Enterprise Institute, Christopher DeMuth and his successor Arthur Brooks, David Gerson, and Dany Pletka.

Second come the scholars and friends who have read and commented on portions of the manuscript or earlier articles that first tried out its ideas: Jesse Choper, Robert Cooter, David Caron, Dan Farber, William Eskridge, Andrew Guzman,

Sandy Kadish, Julian Ku, John Manning, John McGinnis, Jide Nzelibe, Eric Posner, Sai Prakash, Cass Sunstein, and Adrian Vermeule. Third are the excellent students at Boalt Hall who have assisted me in the preparation of this manuscript: Benjamin Bright, James Cho, Troy Housman, James Phillips, and Jonathan Sidhu.

There are three people who were indispensable in helping to prepare this book. The first is my friend, coauthor, and former colleague at the United States Department of Justice, Robert Delahunty. Robert and I first met in the summer of 2001, and we worked through the aftermath of the September 11, 2001, attacks together. He was one of those great treasures of the government who was a living repository of American foreign policy and constitutional law. Robert has helped me think through these issues and pushed me to be both more careful and more creative. The second friend is Lynn Chu, who purports to be my agent at Writers Representatives but is much more. She has gone far beyond the job of arranging publication to help me think through the initial idea for a book all the way to wielding a sharp editorial pen on the manuscript. I am fortunate that she first called me almost ten years ago to talk about writing a book and that our initial contact grew into a collaboration that even reached the editorial page of The New York Times. The third is Blake Ratcliff, an impressive young lawyer and editor at Oxford University Press who has seen this book through from beginning to end. Blake's dual interest and background in both international law and international relations were a perfect fit for this book.

I am approaching the twenty-fifth anniversary of my college graduation, which causes me to think about all of the people who have helped me along the way. Harvard gave me many things, but the most valuable was the opportunity to meet and marry my classmate, Elsa Arnett. The toxic smells and disheveled papers of the Harvard Crimson—surely the most inauspicious of surroundings—nurtured a marriage that has lasted. We've been happy living on the other end of the continent from where we met, perched on a mountainside in a house that looks like a ski chalet, looking out over a bay where it seems as if the ocean is on the wrong side of the earth. I also think about my constant and loyal companion from my youth, my brother Christopher, who has a wonderful family about him now, and my mother, Sook Hee Yoo, whose love ensured that no war ever broke out between us. But most important of all, this time causes me to miss my father, John Hyun Soo Yoo, who passed away while I was writing this book. I think this is the book that he always wanted me to write, and I dedicate it to him.

1   War and the New Millennium

WE LIVE IN a world of wars—big and small, hot and cold, seen and unseen, between nations and within nations. Over the past decade, wars have dominated American politics. In 2001, the United States suffered a direct attack by an al-Qaeda terrorist group, responded by overthrowing the existing regime in Afghanistan, launched the 2003 invasion of Iraq, and started a broad-based campaign against terrorism.

As a part of the worldwide war on terror, the United States gathers intelligence through Internet and banking networks, preemptively captures suspected terrorists and detains them at Guantanamo Bay, Cuba, tries terrorist leaders in military and civil courts, and, most controversially, uses unmanned drone aircraft to kill enemy leaders in nations with which it is not at war. American troops remained in Iraq for almost a decade after the initial 2003 invasion, and they continue to fight in Afghanistan at the time of this writing.

Conflict at the dawn of the third millennium only followed the disorder that marked the closing of the second. In the 1990s, the United States sent troops abroad into hostile environments in Somalia, Haiti, and the former Yugoslavia to end civil wars, fought a full-blown conventional war in Kuwait and Iraq, and pursued terrorists in Sudan, Afghanistan, and Yemen. The United States fought two wars against sovereign nations—Serbia and Iraq. These followed a half-century of conflicts during the Cold War, ranging from Korea and Vietnam to Grenada and Panama.

The United States is not alone on today's battlefield. Members of the North Atlantic Treaty Organization (NATO) such as Great Britain, Germany, and France fought in Afghanistan. A coalition of nations including Great Britain, Australia, Spain, and Italy joined the United States in the invasion of Iraq. In 2011, NATO nations joined forces again to help local rebels overthrow Moammar Gadhafi's regime in Libya. Israel has battled Islamic groups in Lebanon, Russia and the former Soviet republic of Georgia went to war over control of border regions; Sri Lanka finally defeated the Tamil resistance; and internal conflicts raged in Colombia, Sudan, Chad, and the Congo. African civil wars alone have killed millions and displaced millions more. Fighting in the Congo is said to have killed more than 5 million people; Sudan's civil war has resulted in more than 1 million deaths.[1]

Even greater threats to international peace and stability may loom. North Korea's repressive regime has expertise and enough nuclear material to build several atomic bombs and has successfully tested what Western experts believe is an intermediate-range ballistic missile. Despite severe international economic sanctions, Iran may soon succeed in equipping itself with nuclear weapons. Both nations are fast at work on intercontinental ballistic missile technology that could bring parts of Western Europe and the United States within range. NATO efforts to build central authority in Afghanistan continue to sputter, while nuclear Pakistan and Syria battle internal groups aligned with al-Qaeda.

International rules restrict the ability of nations that can do the most to prevent these wars, maintain the peace, and advance free-market democracy. Western democracies have responded to these challenges to peace with a number of measures short of war, such as bilateral and multilateral economic sanctions, diplomatic pressure, and development assistance. While achieving varying levels of success, these tools lose power without the threat of force behind them. Various constructions of international law, however, paint the use of any force by these nations as "illegal."

Meanwhile, international rules allow states that undermine global stability, promote authoritarianism, and systematically abuse human rights to hide behind the status quo. The United Nations Charter system gives a veto over the use of force to two nations—Russia and China—that warred with their neighbors (Russia with Georgia and China with Korea, Tibet, the Soviet Union, India, and Vietnam) and obstructed international solutions to global challenges, undercutting the ability of nations to cooperate to solve dire international challenges. Both nations maintain authoritarian regimes: in China, the Communist Party holds a monopoly on political power without competitive elections; and in Russia, analysts argue that Vladimir Putin has resurrected effective one-party rule. Both nations arguably are using their veto to protect other authoritarian regimes from Western intervention, as they have for the civil war in Syria since 2011.

This system discourages the world's most powerful nations from taking measures to stop rogue states, attack terrorist groups, and end human rights catastrophes. We need not see Russia and China as the only nations that benefit from a veto at the expense of global welfare. If one believes, for example, that climate change demands collective action to reduce carbon emissions, the United States along with China, India, and Brazil stand as obstacles to a global solution. The United States has also used its veto to protect Israel from international sanctions, which may amount to placing the national interest over an international solution, depending on one's point of view about the conflict in the Middle East. And certainly, the United States proved it is able to mobilize the UN Security Council to authorize force in the Persian Gulf War in 1991, Somalia in 1992, the Balkans in the 1990s, and Afghanistan in 2001—though it failed most spectacularly to win approval of the war in Iraq in 2003. A new approach could allow more great power intervention to stop the harms caused by the erosion of the nation-state system in the twenty-first century. But it could also open the door to wars that trigger costly unforeseen consequences, as arguably occurred with the Iraq War, or provide the pretext for aggression.

Our international law and politics must evolve to confront the threats of this century, not those of the last, without encouraging conflicts that cause more harm than good. Founded at the end of the most destructive war in history, the United Nations understandably attempted to purge all interstate conflict from the world. The United Nations vested the international legal system with the same purpose as domestic legal systems—the suppression of violence between its members. During the Cold War, the broad conflicts spanning nations gave way to what historians now describe as "the Long Peace." But it can be argued that the stability of superpower competition, in the presence of nuclear mutually assured destruction, contributed far more to the maintenance of peace than systems of global governance.[2] Today, the main threat to international peace and stability no longer comes from massive wars between superpowers or multinational alliances. Rogue nations, failed states, the proliferation of weapons of mass destruction (WMD), global terrorism, and human rights catastrophes pose a greater challenge than aggressive nation-states bent on conquest.

In today's world, war becomes less a means of oppression and more a tool to help rebuild failed states, contain rogue nations, prevent terrorist attacks, and maintain the international order that makes trade, development, and progress possible. The benefits of such wars can outweigh the loss of life and treasure by preventing even worse harms. Use of force might block a terrorist group or rogue nation from acquiring weapons of mass destruction. A first strike, for example, might cause the deaths of military and civilian lives, but it might save even more lives overall by preempting a war of conquest. An even larger invasion might free an entire people from the oppression of an authoritarian state. Intervention can help avert or even end a destructive civil war that has killed hundreds of thousands, as is the case in some of today's internal armed conflicts in Africa. As these uses of force grow increasingly intense and likely more destructive, the international system should demand greater potential benefits—as measured in human lives, natural and developed resources, and global stability—to justify them. But what international rules should not do is prohibit all nondefensive uses of force, regardless of the expected gains for international peace and security.

History provides many examples of what might *not* have been. Should France and Great Britain have invaded Nazi Germany during the latter's attack on Poland? Or even launched a preventive strike to stop Hitler's remilitarization of Germany? Should the United States have intervened earlier in World Wars I or II and shifted the balance of power in favor of the Allies? This is not just a science fiction writer's excursion into counterfactual history. Sadly, in many recent cases, an earlier use of force could have brought about a greater good. A mere 10,000 Western troops could have halted the 1990s Rwandan genocide that slaughtered 1 million people. Earlier intervention in the Balkans might have preempted Serbia's 1990s campaign of "ethnic cleansing" of neighboring Muslim enclaves. Surgical strikes in Afghanistan might have prevented al-Qaeda's rise, and the removal of Saddam Hussein might have precluded the Iran-Iraq War, the 1991 Gulf War, or the 2003 Iraq War. A few thousand troops might have prevented the hundreds of thousands of lives lost in African internal conflicts of the last decade in Congo or Sudan. Domestic imperatives no doubt discouraged nations from intervening earlier in many of these cases. But these situations also involve challenges inherent in the international system. In many of these cases, no single nation or group of nations has the incentive to intervene, because others, who bear none of the costs, will free-ride off their efforts. Without any prospect of a world government that can force burden sharing among all nations, collective action will prove difficult—if not impossible—in all cases where the world would benefit from early military intervention.

This book addresses the yawning gap between the existing rules of war and the need for force in the contemporary world. It is not a brief in favor of war to resolve political differences. Instead, it argues that armed conflict remains a relevant feature of international relations that can enable progress and improve global welfare. Like any other rules, the laws of war should encourage nations to undertake socially beneficial actions and avoid costly ones. Nations already perform cost-benefit analysis when they make decisions about everything from environmental regulation to national security. When a government decides to raise fuel efficiency standards for automobiles, for example, it has a corresponding cost in weight of the cars and fatalities from traffic accidents. Pollution limits will improve human health but will raise costs for industrial production and may reduce economic growth. Greater security at airports will decrease the probability of terrorist attack but will increase government spending and slow down travel times. Even refusing to act involves a choice that the costs of the status quo outweigh the benefits of new regulation. All government policy inherently involves trade-offs between costs and benefits.[3]

This book argues that the international system should encourage the great powers to follow a similar approach to war. The system should allow armed intervention when the expected benefits to global welfare, which include putting an end to the harmful activity in a targeted country, exceed the likely costs. There are a great number of variables that decision-makers should take into account when reaching these difficult judgments. On the benefits side are lives that would be saved, resources preserved, economic growth restored, internal governance stabilized, and regional peace. On the cost side would be the lives lost and funds spent in conflict, economic disruption, political and regional turmoil, and humanitarian harms. Nations could not be certain that intervention would bring benefits, but would have to decide based on the probability of success or failure. On the cost ledger, they would also have to enter the possibility of unintended consequences and that going to war might encourage others to do the same. Only when the benefits to global welfare—not just to that of the intervening nations—exceed the costs should nations resort to force.

In pursuing the noble goal of legislating world peace, however, the international political and legal systems produce the opposite effect. By outlawing non-defensive wars, even those where the clear benefits to the United States, its allies, and the world outweigh the costs, the current rules reduce global welfare. The prohibition on war is overinclusive; it forbids too much. It is also underinclusive: it stops too little of the aggression that is the very reason for its existence. The League of Nations and the United Nations both banned war. Both were and are ignored. When states pursue their vital interests, they will not allow international law to stand in the way of using force. This dysfunctional state of affairs stems from a foundational error in the idea of collective security, the brainchild of President Woodrow Wilson. Wilson plucked just war theory from its medieval roots and transplanted it, naked, without the surrounding soil of political thought that had nourished it for over a millennium. Once rooted in the very different conditions of great power rivalry, and now the twenty-first century's growing decentralization and disintegration, the ban on war has the perverse effect of harming international peace and stability and condoning the oppression and death of millions.

Force is merely a tool, one to be used for either good or evil. It cannot be considered an absolute evil in and of itself. Rather than strive for the utopian goal of banning all violence, the international system should permit war that advances global welfare. No one doubts that war causes steep losses in lives and destruction, but it can serve the greater good too. Because of the anarchic nature of the international system, the challenge for the next century is not to stop great power wars, where national security interests will brush aside legal and political rules. Rather, the task ahead is to build a new system that encourages the great powers to use force more often, not less, but in the right circumstances. Sometimes only intervention can stop rogue states, oppressive authoritarian regimes, and the threat from terrorism and WMD proliferation. This book points the way toward a new set of rules that gives nations more flexibility to confront these trials of the new century, rather than the problems of the last.

I. War Today

Today, war has become a tool to manage a liberal international order built on free trade and globalized networks of communications and services, integrated capital and labor markets, and quick and easy transportation of people and goods.[4] These conflicts little resemble the apocalyptic clash of powerful organized armed forces of the past. All-encompassing struggles between great alliances, with casualties in the millions, disappeared in the Cold War and its aftermath. World War III never arrived. Conflict between large draft armies fielded by the most power nations inflicted the most destruction in history, but the last war between the great powers erupted almost seventy-five years ago. Today's great powers use war to stabilize the international system, not to promote revolution as in days past.

The primary security threats to the world no longer come from nation-state rivals bent on conquest. As Philip Bobbitt observes, "control of territory no longer holds its former attraction."[5] Wars of conquest lose lives, destroy valuable property, and disrupt productive economic activity. Meanwhile, financial and human capital can quickly flee to safer havens. This stands in contrast to the wars of the twentieth century. In World War I, the rise of Germany disrupted the European balance of power. It prompted two great alliances—Germany and Austria-Hungary against Great Britain, France, and Russia—to fight over the borders of northern and central Europe. America's 1917 entry on the side of Britain and France brought victory to the Allies, the breakup of the German and Austro-Hungarian Empires, and a host of new nations in Eastern Europe. But the Peace of Versailles failed to solve "the German problem," as Henry Kissinger has called it.[6] American intervention two decades later, this time on the side of Great Britain and the Soviet Union, again frustrated Germany's renewed drive for expansion. The Soviet Union then created a sphere of influence in Eastern Europe and half of Germany, while the United States countered by rebuilding the western democracies and founding NATO.

During the half-century of the Cold War, the two superpowers continued to jockey for primacy. The United States used its military to contain the spread of the Soviet Union's control and influence—at high cost. In South Korea, the United States Armed Forces suffered 53,000 killed and 92,000 wounded in order to reverse an invasion by North Korea, a Soviet proxy state. In Vietnam, the United States suffered 58,000 killed and 153,000 wounded in a failed effort to stop the communist North from seizing control of the South. The United States also used force to maintain its own sphere in Central America, the Caribbean, and the Middle East. For its part, the Soviet Union employed troops to suppress independence efforts in Hungary in 1956 and Czechoslovakia in 1968, sent aid to Marxist regimes in Cuba, Asia, and Africa, and lost a bloody 1980s war to keep Afghanistan in its orbit. While the cost in lives was high, these smaller conflicts warned the two superpowers away from a direct conflict that could have killed billions. Paradoxically, the Cold War produced perhaps the longest period of international stability—no direct wars between the great powers—since the Peace of Westphalia in 1648.

While the Cold War's end reduced the threat of nuclear Armageddon, it opened a Pandora's box long kept shut by the bipolar balance. Regional powers such as Iran and China have sought regional hegemony. Biological, chemical, and nuclear arms technology—weapons of mass destruction—have spread to unstable nations like Pakistan and rogue states like North Korea. Some nation-states have collapsed. "Failed states" have arisen where no government institutions exercised effective authority, most of the population lived in terrible conditions of poverty, and warring groups violated human rights on a broad scale.[7] Terrorist groups unconnected with any one nation-state, but nurtured in the ungoverned territories of failed states, emerged. New channels of global commerce brought forth new means to move people and resources into positions for attack. Empowered by the global reach of modern communications and transportation, terrorists struck New York City and Washington, D.C., on September 11, 2001.

As the roll of the players grew larger, the tools for the great power contest changed. Large mechanized armies bent on territorial conquest have become less relevant because of modern technology. Iraq's 1990 invasion of Kuwait may be the last such war we will see for some time, though simmering interstate disputes over territory—contests over islands in East Asia, struggles between former provinces of the Soviet Union—might still erupt into open conflict as they did between Russia and Georgia in 2008. Still, the pace of today's most pressing international threats seems to be set by the disintegration of states and the rise of civil wars, the spread of terrorism, and the proliferation of WMD technology, as well as their negative spillover effects upon neighbors, or the international system as a whole. To be sure, the threat of more conventional conflicts always persists, although, as we will see, its reality has sharply declined in the last half-century. While the chances of great power conflict have decreased, the capability to duplicate their destructiveness has expanded because of the spread of technology into less responsible hands.

In this world of new threats, war can serve as a tool of regulation, a way to control persistent problems that reduce global welfare. Preemption can help end human rights abuses or stop dangerous terrorist groups and rogue nations. The use of force today more often prevents potential atrocities than launches wars of conquest. Indeed, the flexibility to intervene earlier may even reduce the need for full armed conflict. Although a looming threat may risk a large amount of destruction, acting earlier when its probability is lower and the causes of harm are still at a remove may justify restrained but effective uses of force. This will depend on finely tuned judgments about both the capability and intentions of potential enemies or growing threats. Limited strikes directed at al-Qaeda training camps and their leaders in the 1990s, for example, might have forestalled the September 11, 2001, terrorist attacks and the conflict in Afghanistan. Prudent intervention in Rwanda or Sudan by a small force of Western troops may have prevented the human rights catastrophes there. Use of force need not always lead to full-scale war. A limited intervention may be all that is needed to prevent a crisis from growing into the type of catastrophe or aggressive regime that demands a large-scale conflict.

War-as-management cannot fit within traditional political and legal understandings of armed conflict. In the war against Serbia, for example, the United States used air power to prevent ethnic cleansing of Muslim Albanians. When British legal advisers could not find any legal support for the conflict, U.S. Secretary of State Madeleine Albright reportedly replied: "get new lawyers."[8] Regardless of the quality of the lawyers, the United States could not claim self-defense. Serbia did not pose a threat of attack on the United States or its forces, nor did the United States have any interest in adding to its own territory. Historically, however, the Balkans had provided the kindling for wider wars. And previous conflicts had given Serbian forces the opportunity to engage in the widespread killing and expulsion of Muslims. American air power stabilized central Europe and stopped a looming humanitarian crisis. Force in Haiti and Somalia in the 1990s had similar goals—to stop human rights disasters and to shore up the global order. But they also serve as cautionary tales: intervention may have headed off humanitarian catastrophes, but both nations have struggled to restore the central authority of a nation-state. They remain mired in poverty and lawlessness, with Somalia still subject to internal fighting among warlords.

The two most controversial uses of force in the last decade—Iraq and Afghanistan— also had human rights overtones. Imposing strict sharia law in much of Afghanistan, the Taliban regime deprived women of the right to vote, practice an occupation, or attend school. In Iraq, Saddam Hussein imposed an authoritarian regime that used chemical weapons on its own people, tortured and murdered tens of thousands of political opponents, and killed thousands more during wars. In 2004, President George W. Bush announced what has been called the Bush Doctrine or the freedom agenda, which declared the intent to spread democracy and respect for human rights to nations abroad.

Human rights alone did not impel the United States and its allies to seek regime change. The United States did not invade Afghanistan because the Taliban oppressed its population, but because it allowed the al-Qaeda terrorist organization to operate freely on its territory. The Bush administration justified the 2003 invasion of Iraq by pointing to Saddam Hussein's failure to destroy his weapons of mass destruction, which both the United States and the United Nations judged a threat to international peace and security. Critics claimed that the United States launched the war in Iraq to gain control over sources of oil and to broaden its sphere of influence in the Middle East. These critics accused the United States of pursuing more traditional, realist goals than simply spreading democracy or regional stability.

When U.S. forces found no WMDs in Iraq, President Bush stressed the advancement of freedom and the reversal of the conditions that promoted terrorism. The United States succeeded in removing Saddam Hussein and helped to establish a more democratically elected government, but at a high cost in civilian and military casualties, a civil war, and a regional upheaval whose consequences are still unfolding. Still, regime change in Iraq, followed by support for the Libyan overthrow of Moammar Gadhafi, the removal of Hosni Mubarak in Egypt, the ongoing rebellion against the Assad regime in Syria, and the spread of the Arab Spring, offers the possibility of transforming the Middle East from the source of much of the world's instability into a more peaceful region. Certainly, no administration wants to station American forces permanently in Iraq or Afghanistan. Strategic gains, however, may evaporate with the U.S. exit from Iraq in 2011 and scheduled withdrawals from Afghanistan in 2014.

American wars in Iraq and Afghanistan resemble Kosovo and Somalia more than World Wars I and II. The United States and its allies intervened to protect international order, not to gain resources, population, or territory or to retune a balance of power. Social scientists would call it reducing negative externalities. Iraq and Afghanistan were inflicting costs on the rest of the world, though of different kinds. Afghanistan became a safe haven for international terrorism and the drug trade, which culminated in the September 11, 2001, terrorist attacks. Iraq threatened its neighbors through its large military and aggressive designs and its severe repression of internal ethnic groups, which a decade of sanctions had barely kept in check. Intervention forces the bad actors to "internalize" these costs, though critics of both wars might argue that the conflicts only worsened the fundamental problems in

Afghanistan and Iraq. Otherwise, nations that abuse human rights, breed terrorism, or proliferate WMDs can destabilize other nations and directly threaten global security. Only a flexible system of international rules that allows the great powers to end threats to the world order can prevent these cancers from growing out of control, though they must take care not to exacerbate the very problems they seek to cure.

II. Force Rules

International legal and political institutions, as well as many states, view these challenges very differently. As commonly interpreted by many foreign and domestic leaders and lawyers, the fundamental laws of the United Nations Charter make the wars of the last two decades illegal. Since America's attack on Serbia and Iraq were not in self-defense, nor approved by the UN, many leaders and scholars claimed the wars were illegal, just as an attack by a private citizen on another would be illegal.

The UN's basic approach to the problem of violence mimics the approach to domestic criminal law: the government enjoys a monopoly on the use of force, except in cases of individual self-defense. Substitute the UN for the government and the nation-state for the individual, and the two legal regimes mirror each other. But if the UN is the "government" and nation-states are the "individuals," no one exercises the world's police power except by unanimous consent. There is no world executive branch or world police.

Many leading international lawyers see the rise of preventive war, as with Iraq, at odds with legal doctrines restricting the use of force to self-defense. Some even view American wars of the last decade as part of an effort to destroy international law and institutions. According to Professor Thomas Franck, the United Nations Charter system "has died again, and, this time, perhaps for good." These scholars do not regard the Iraq war as a mere ad hoc disagreement about a single war, but "a much broader plan to disable all supranational institutions and the constraints of international law on national sovereignty."[9] The editors of a special Iraq issue of the *American Journal of International Law* declared the Iraq War to be "one of the few events of the UN Charter period holding the potential for fundamental transformation, or possibly even destruction, of the system of law governing the use of force that evolved during the twentieth century."[10] Antiwar activists have even attempted to file criminal charges in foreign courts against President George W. Bush, Vice President Dick Cheney, Secretary of Defense Donald Rumsfeld, and National Security Advisor Condoleeza Rice, among others, for launching an allegedly illegal war.

I question the contemporary idea that only wars in self-defense fall within the law. This criminology approach to armed conflict has no modern historical foundations;

it leaped into world politics through the League of Nations Charter and Woodrow Wilson's stillborn collective security scheme to manage the postwar peace. Many today claim the UN Charter follows the same principle, which would have come as a surprise to its drafters at the 1945 San Francisco Conference. Many diplomats, politicians, and international lawyers may consider the UN Charter a progressive evolution toward a world governed by law, but a broader perspective reveals this system to be a historical and intellectual anomaly. UN Charter rules describe the hopes, not the practices, of nations. They fail to consider international costs and benefits—what I will refer to as "global welfare"—and instead trace their lineage to a medieval just war theory that was better suited for a world of one emperor and one church. As interpreted by many officials, practitioners, and scholars today, the UN Charter creates enormous strain on the international system because it imposes rules that run directly counter to the incentives of states—to protect their most vital interests.

Believing matters like war and peace can fall beneath the firm hand of law is more than idle utopianism. Relying on the idea of "international law" to achieve national security can have dire effects. As scholar and diplomat George Kennan, the intellectual father of the American policy of containment, remarked in 1951: "I see the most serious fault of our past policy formulation to lie in something that I might call the legalistic-moralistic approach to international problems."[11] In his view, "the association of legalistic ideas with moralistic ones" has run "like a red skein through our foreign policy of the last fifty years." Kennan did not mean this as a compliment. He drew upon a long pedigree of skepticism toward international law as a means of restraining violence between states. "[I]n all times, Kings, and Persons of Sovereign authority, because of their Independency," Hobbes wrote, "are in…a posture of War." Hobbes believed "Where there is no common Power, there is no Law."[12]

But American diplomats did not necessarily reject international law because they shared Hobbes' stark realism. Rather, they thought international law and institutions simply had failed. Reliance on collective security had brought the United States to the brink of disaster in World War II. Legal rules do not stop war; they invite it. When nations rely on international law, they underinvest in the resources necessary to deter security threats. Or so Americans like Kennan, Paul Nitze, Dean Acheson, and John Foster Dulles believed when they rejected Wilsonism and formed the successful American Cold War strategy of containment. Dulles, who would become President Eisenhower's Secretary of State, wrote in 1943: "I confess to being one of those lawyers who do not regard 'international law as law at all.'"[13] Kennan believed that international law appealed to Americans' peculiar moral streak in world affairs, one that they should put aside in favor of realism if they were to compete successfully with the Soviets.[14] Judge Robert Bork similarly criticized international law as contrary to American interests today: "International law about the use of force is not even a piety; it is a net loss for Western democracies."[15] While primarily an American school of thought, such hard-headed realism could claim European adherents too, such as Charles de Gaulle, French historian Raymond Aron, and British political scientist E.H. Carr.[16]

International law's utopianism has allowed philosophy to dominate the thinking about war. Instead of a war's legality, most Americans argue over war's morality. Of course, religious leaders and philosophers have long argued over the morality of war. Just war theory, for example, traces its roots back before medieval Catholic thought to the Roman Republic.[17] But philosophizing on war is more than a historical artifact; it is another sign of the irrelevance of international rules on the use of force. John Rawls, Michael Walzer, and other thinkers in the Western liberal tradition believe that universal morality allows or even compels humanitarian intervention—the right to use force in order to stop systematic abuse of human rights.[18] On its text alone, however, the UN Charter does not permit nations to intervene in another state's internal affairs. Liberal philosophers who urge humanitarian intervention must dispense with international law as swiftly as realists who pursue pure national interest.

A good example of this tension is the International Criminal Court's (ICC) recent adoption of the "crime of aggression." Originally, the ICC deferred the criminalization of aggression until the parties to the agreement could agree on its definition and the conditions for the exercise of jurisdiction. In 2010, however, the parties finally achieved consensus: a crime of aggression would be the "planning, preparation, initiation or execution, by a person in a position effectively to exercise control or to direct the political or military action of a State, of an act of aggression."[19] An act of aggression then is the "use of armed force by a State against the sovereignty, territorial integrity or political independence of another State, or in any other manner inconsistent with the Charter of the United Nations."[20] In other words, the court could prosecute those responsible for the planning, preparation, initiation, or execution of nonsanctioned, or "illegal" wars. Although it objected to the ICC's adoption of the definition, the United States had no influence over the final outcome because of its 2002 withdrawal from the Statute of Rome Treaty establishing the court.

Adoption of an ICC definition of aggression will only worsen the conflict between the international legal system and the improvement of global welfare. Under the newly christened crime of aggression, anyone involved with a war that either was not in self-defense or was unsanctioned by the United Nations is liable for ICC investigation and prosecution.[21] The ICC could have prosecuted those involved in the planning, preparation, initiation, or execution of the Kosovo or Iraq wars, the intervention in Libya, or the raid to kill Osama bin Laden—depending on one's interpretation of international law. The ICC's crime of aggression may add legal teeth to the narrow reading of the UN Charter's provisions on force, and thus deter all wars that are nondefensive or unauthorized by the UN Security Council. This will have the effect of outlawing many wars to stop human rights disasters, remove rogue states' oppressive regimes, and prevent the spread of WMD and terrorism. At the margin, the threat of ICC prosecution will add another cost to the strong incentives against interventions that seek to maintain international peace and security. If they wish to broaden rather than suppress the rate of wars for global welfare, great powers will seek to hobble the ICC or protect their militaries from its reach. The desire of great powers to intervene but escape ICC jurisdiction will only place more pressure on the prosecutors and embroil their decisions even more deeply into politics.

It is time to replace questions of morality with concern for global welfare. The typical moral debate of ordinary criminal law cannot adequately grapple with the demands of international politics, which makes it increasingly irrelevant to international reality. This was nowhere truer than the 2003 invasion of Iraq, where the United States and its allies made a half-hearted attempt to secure UN Security Council approval. But when the council finally made clear that it would not explicitly consent, the American-led coalition went forward anyway. With the rise of non-European power centers, moral claims based on Western values may find even less purchase. China, India, and Middle Eastern and African nations may not share Western notions about humanitarian intervention—Communist China has long opposed the idea as an infringement on national sovereignty. This is not to say, as Professor Samuel Huntington predicted, that cleavages between a few great civilizations will dictate the future of international politics. Instead, states will inevitably disagree over whether certain norms are universal, which have higher authority, and which demand resources and enforcement. Of course, philosophers disagree about the foundations of moral principles and international rules as well.[22]

A more realistic approach would evaluate each war by its effect on global welfare, rather than mechanically applying a set of fixed, absolute rules. Will a conflict improve the well-being of the world's people, or will its costs exceed its benefits? Despite all the "rights" talk that infects the rhetoric of international politics, as Eric Posner has observed, many nations act based on material human welfare.[23] Wealthy countries have sent more than $2 trillion in foreign aid to poor nations over the last half-century in an effort to improve health and education, despite a recipient's authoritarian political system or repression of human rights. How to measure human welfare (should we use dollars and cents), what ought to count (hedonistic happiness, fulfillment of desires, or objective measures), and whether costs and benefits can be balanced on the same scale remain questions worthy of debate. But one rough-and-ready measure of human welfare is per capita world gross product—the sum of each nation's per capita gross domestic product. Increasing the world's GDP raises the number of people who can consume goods and services that improve their living conditions and happiness.[24] Nations at least should not shy away from wars where the benefits outweigh the costs.

Formal international rules prevent the common-sense weighing of costs and benefits or consideration of material human welfare. Nor would a balancing approach to war open the floodgates to conflict. Both the UN Charter rule and a human welfare approach, for example, would prohibit aggressive wars fought for territory. Death and destruction to redraw a territorial border will waste lives and resources without any compensating rise in benefits. If a nation could exploit another country's resources more effectively, it could simply negotiate for economic rights without the need for conflict. But the UN Charter, borrowing from the criminal law, treats all intervention as wasteful wars of conquest. This overinclusive approach mistakenly prohibits wars that improve global welfare. An appropriate early use of force might preempt a dangerous regime that seeks war against its neighbors, thwart a human rights catastrophe, or stop the spread of terrorist groups or weapons of mass destruction. Domestic criminal law can seek to minimize or eliminate violence between citizens because the police and courts exist to stop one person from harming another. Because no supranational government capable of maintaining international peace and security exists, the use of national force is inevitable if greater harms are ever to be stopped.

Rather than a criminal law model, the international system should adopt a regulatory approach. It should follow rules encouraging the use of force where the benefits outweigh the costs. From a consequentialist or utilitarian perspective, the current law enforcement approach to conflict is utterly dysfunctional. It produces the exact opposite effect from the one the world needs. This is because peace and security are public goods. A public good is defined as a good from which others cannot be excluded and is not depleted by their use. In economic terms, public goods are nonrivalrous and nonexclusive.[25] At the domestic level, national security or domestic law and order are classic public goods. If the United States is secure, citizens can conduct business and their private affairs without the threat of external or internal harm. One citizen's consumption of the benefits of national defense does not reduce the benefits for the next citizen, nor can the market prevent some from enjoying the benefits without preventing it for everyone.

Public goods also exist at the international level. Peace and security are classic examples of a public good at the international level. If the world is at peace, people everywhere can better raise their families, create businesses, and produce and consume goods and services with less fear of violence.[26] Nations can devote resources to raising living standards and improving citizens' welfare, rather than on soldiers and arms. Consumption of peace by one nation does not deplete its benefits for other nations. Another example might be free navigation of the world's oceans. Because of the seas' vast size, ships can generally make passage without interfering with the ships of other nations (aside from some heavily congested points like the Straits of Hormuz in the Persian Gulf). All nations benefit from the ability to move freely people and goods on the seas, a point recognized as early as 1609 by international law scholar Hugo Grotius.[27]

Standard economic theory predicts that no one will provide enough of a public good. Producers cannot exclude anyone from enjoying a public good, so they cannot charge enough to recover the costs. There will be free-riders: those who benefit from the good but do not pay for it. All citizens benefit from national defense, for example, but some will choose not to pay unless compelled, no matter the level of security provided. Public goods will exist at a suboptimal level unless a government can tax all who benefit and thereby enable producers to recover their costs. In the United States, for example, the federal government secures the national defense because it is the only government able to tax properly all American citizens.

At the global level, the provision of public goods is even more unlikely, because no truly effective supranational government exists that can tax all nations to share the burdens. No individual nation will provide the optimal amount of global peace and security because it cannot compel contributions from every other benefiting nation. Free-riding will be rampant. Even in the 1991 Persian Gulf War, the United Nations did not levy a tax on all nations to pay for the ouster of Iraqi forces from Kuwait. Instead, the United States and its allies took up the UN Security Council's request to come to Kuwait's aid and then sought voluntary contributions from wealthy nations, such as Japan.

A related economic concept at work here is externalities. Externalities are activities where an actor does not fully realize the costs or benefits imposed on others from his conduct. A factory that pollutes a river creates a negative externality, unless it is required to pay for the damages caused to landowners downstream. Without that liability, the factory overpollutes because it is not accountable for the full costs of production. A domestic government, however, can create a liability or property rule to hold the factory responsible for costs it is forcing others to bear and give the factory proper incentives to balance costs and benefits.

Internationally, the lack of a supranational government exacerbates the problem of externalities. A factory in one nation, for example, may emit air pollution that travels into a neighboring country. But territorial sovereignty prevents the neighbor from regulating the activity within another state's borders. No world government can establish legal rules to force one nation to compensate the other. So again, the factory will overproduce because it is not held accountable for the costs of the pollution abroad.[28]

Think of the Balkans or sub-Saharan Africa. Ethnic fighting in one nation may spread to similar groups in neighboring countries or stoke rivalries among regional or even great powers. The 1914 assassination of Archduke Franz Ferdinand, heir to the Austro-Hungarian throne, in Sarajevo provided the spark for the conflagration of World War I. Civil war may produce streams of refugees that burden neighboring countries. And ultimately there are innocent civilians killed, resources destroyed, and cultural, religious, and historical assets lost—damaging the inheritance of mankind. For all its costs, intervention may forestall this heavier pain. Sending troops to prevent civil war and facilitate a peace agreement could save the lives of thousands (if not more) and prevent the spread of war, disease, and terrorism. The use of force can reduce these externalities by increasing the costs to those who cause them or by taking away their expected benefits. An international system that effectively bars all wars, except those of self-defense, condemns the world to suffer a litany of harms that hover beneath the surface of the nation-state.

III. Toward a New International System

Approaching war in this way helps resolve some of the most difficult challenges for global security, but also poses its own problems. If the international system were to permit war when the benefits outweigh its costs, then conflict becomes a spectrum rather than a black-and-white, either-or proposition. Many questions about war will fall in a gray area beyond clear-cut cases of self-defense. But weighing benefits against costs, properly comparing the short-term with the long-term, and remaining aware of competing trade-offs will help us escape artificial distinctions between preemption and prevention, human rights versus realism, and freedom versus stability. And these differences, drawn by thinkers over the years, are actually arguments over questions of timing, expectations of benefits and costs, and the perils of uncertainty.

Self-defense, preemption, and prevention are all different labels for the same balancing of costs and benefits over war. They only vary in the certainty of the expected gains or harms from the conflict. Take a war of self-defense against a cross-border invasion. The probability of the enemy attack in such a case is 100 percent—by definition, the attack is already underway, so the expected costs of war can be predicted with a high level of certainty. Now consider preemptive war. As currently interpreted by many international lawyers, officials, and scholars, international law allows a first strike as self-defense only if the defending nation has a level of certainty that an attack is coming. In the famous nineteenth-century *Caroline* case, for example, Canadian rebels based on U.S. territory launched targets on British targets across the border. When British troops crossed the U.S. border in pursuit, the United States lodged a protest. Secretary of State Daniel Webster argued that British intervention was justified only if the necessity of force was "instant, overwhelming, leaving no choice of means, and no moment for deliberation."[29] The *Caroline* example made an appearance as an important definition of aggression in the Nuremburg trials at the end of World War II, and it later influenced the International Court of Justice when it held illegal the United States' alleged mining of Nicaragua's harbors in the 1980s. In the decades since, scholars have widely hailed the *Caroline* case as a strict limit on the preemptive use of force in anticipatory self-defense.

But the *Caroline* rule simply elevates certainty, as well as a healthy respect for territorial sovereignty, over other values, such as limiting the greater destruction of future war, advancing democracy, or reducing systematic government oppression. Some of these may not prove as valuable to the international system, over the long-term, as territorial sovereignty; yet sovereignty can shield looming problems from an international solution. There may be times when territorial sovereignty must give way before anticipatory measures to preempt an aggressive attack or head off a human rights disaster, but that does not mean that our analysis does away with the principle of sovereignty itself. Instead, territorial control by a government representing a people, capable of upholding its international obligations, remains the enduring organizing rule of the international system. But this book argues that, like any legal rule, sovereignty must give way to defined exceptions—just as private property owners generally have an absolute right to use their land as they wish, but still must give way to limitations, such as environmental restrictions, that bring greater gains for public welfare in the aggregate.

A more realistic and nuanced view should assess the probability and magnitude of harm in light of the degree and timing of force that could stop it. Preemption calls for force in anticipation of an attack, when an enemy is mobilizing its forces or moving them into offensive positions. Prevention applies pressure even earlier, when a shift in the relative balance of power makes an enemy more dangerous in the future. When the expected harm of attack is low because the probability of war is similarly low, we are speaking of prevention. As the likelihood of an enemy attack increases, we begin to think of preemption. As the possible harms of war increase, the amount of force a nation may use should increase at a similar rate. Chapters 4 and 5 will more deeply analyze the various theories of preemption and preventive war and how they can be better understood through a cost-benefit lens.

Understanding prevention and preemption as facets of the same problem sheds light on the controversy over the "Bush Doctrine." In 2002, the United States declared it would use force to stop terrorist attacks before they occurred and suggested it might even intervene to prevent rogue nations from obtaining WMD. "The greater the threat, the greater is the risk of inaction—and the more compelling the case for taking anticipatory action to defend ourselves," the Bush National Security Strategy declared, "even if uncertainty remains as to the time and place of the enemy's attack."[30] Because WMD may cause massive civilian casualties, nations must use force prior to attack in order to forestall the threat. Acting earlier in anticipation of events that have not yet occurred, however, also makes it incumbent on nations to act with narrower, more surgical uses of force.

Reordering international law to expressly allow military force to improve global welfare raises challenging questions of institutional design. Part of the last century's failures derives from dysfunctional international organizations. As the primary governing document in international law, the UN Charter stands badly in need of reform. This is not to say that the Charter has been a failure. It has made many valuable contributions in the areas of international health and education, humanitarian relief and a permanent forum for international diplomacy. At its best, it can act as a neutral arbiter that helps warring nations reach settlements and helps monitor peace agreements. And as a negotiated treaty, the Charter may well be fulfilling the intentions of its founders, who may not have wanted a more active international government.

But the UN Charter's rules, as generally understood today, have codified paralysis in the use of force because of their ban on all nondefensive wars and the design of the Security Council. Our modern reading, however, may ignore a more realist perspective on the part of the UN's designers. The original drafters may have established an unforgiving rule prohibiting war except for self-defense, but they also included an exception for wars that preserve international peace and security. And, as the United States argued at the time of the signing of the treaty, Article 2(4) of the Charter expressly declared that force would not be used in any manner "inconsistent with the Purposes of the United Nations." As historian Marc Trachtenberg has observed, the evidence "shows...that the US drafters did not believe that they were giving away very much by accepting the Charter." American drafters believed that in Article 2(4), the United States reserved the right to use force, even in the absence of Security Council action, to prevent aggression and preserve international peace and security.[31]

But in the years after, a bevy of scholars, international lawyers and officials, and foreign governments have sought to limit member states by creating a bottleneck in the Security Council. According to later interpreters, only the Security Council could authorize the use of force by member nations for purposes other than self-defense, and the Charter itself limited those instances to cases of international peace and security. The Security Council, however, suffers from a crippling, perhaps fatal, defect. It allows its permanent members (the United States, Russia, China, Great Britain, and France) to veto any action, which means these countries with competing, often conflicting, interests must agree before the use of force is authorized. The requirement of unanimity paralyzes the international community. During the Cold War, for example, the Security Council only authorized the use of force twice: the 1950 Korean War at the dawn of the postwar world (when the Soviet Union boycotted UN meetings) and the Persian Gulf War, when the decline of superpower competition jumbled the usual alignments.

New rules for war demand a revolution in institutions. Little will change if the Security Council retains its vetoes for permanent members, who can be expected to use their power to secure their individual interests. Even if the Charter were understood to permit force beyond just self-defense, the paralysis of the Cold War will continue. Legitimizing humanitarian intervention by recognizing a "responsibility to protect" is a sound goal, but it will be doomed to failure by the requirement of unanimity among the Permanent Five (P5) of the Security Council. Adding Germany, Japan, India, or Brazil to the P5 may bring the UN's structure into closer alignment with the contemporary balance of power. But without a change to the permanent veto, greater numbers will only increase the transaction costs of deliberation, making any decision harder to reach. Deadlock will only become worse.

Changing the rules of war will not be enough to tackle the twenty-first century's security challenges. We also need an international body with real authority. Armed conflict has not disappeared during the UN's paralysis; instead, nations go to war regardless of any rules. When it comes to war, states have divorced their international institutions. Critics may argue, however, that any change toward more flexible rules will only increase pretextual uses of force—Germany claiming self-defense when it invaded Poland at the start of World War II, for example. To make sure new rules do not provide cover for pure territorial aggression, some international institution must help police the use of force. Contrary to the beliefs of many scholars, however, it should be less, rather than more, formal. A looser coalition may work better than a highly formalized body like the UN with its cumbersome bureaucracy and high costs of maintaining a permanent body—something less like the European Union and more like the Concert of Europe. What is important is not where the headquarters is located, how large the staff is, or how many clauses are in the treaty, but whether nations will actually cooperate to use diplomatic pressure or force to prevent harms and looming threats to global welfare.

This presents a challenge to current U.S. policy. The Obama administration recognizes the fundamental issues of public goods and externalities that underlie today's global problems. In his April 2010 speech before a Washington, D.C., nuclear summit, President Obama observed: "whether we like it or not, we remain a dominant military superpower, and when conflicts break out, one way or another we get pulled into them." Unfortunately, responsibility and costs may not come into balance.

President Obama continued: "And that ends up costing us significantly in terms of both blood and treasure."[32] President Obama sees that the costs of guarding international peace and security bear too heavily on the United States. In a 2010 commencement address to the graduating cadets at West Point, he declared: "The burdens of this century cannot fall on our soldiers alone. It also cannot fall on American shoulders alone. Our adversaries would like to see America sap its strength by overextending our power." In other words, the United States' role as a supplier of an international public good—stability—forces it to bear greater costs than benefits because the world's free-riders do not contribute.

In contrast to its predecessor, the Obama administration believes the United States should reinforce, rather than reform, the institutional status quo. In its 2010 *National Security Strategy*, the Obama White House declared: "we must focus American engagement on strengthening international institutions and galvanizing the collective action that can serve collective interests."[33] The Obama administration wants to give a "broader voice—and greater responsibilities—for emerging powers," and to modernize international institutions "to more effectively generate results on issues of global interests." Facing the challenge of failed and rogue states, international terrorism, and WMD proliferation will come in expanding—not reducing—the nations with a say over security decisions. In his Nobel Peace Prize acceptance speech, President Obama called for more states, through the United Nations, to become involved in peacekeeping, rather than leave "the task to a few countries."[34] To manage this expansion of states with a voice, the administration seeks to reinvigorate the existing structure of international governance. "As influence extends to more countries and capitals, we also have to build new partnerships, and shape stronger international standards and institutions," President Obama said in his 2010 West Point Commencement Address.[35] More cooperation bounded by international rules and less unilateral action will provide the means to solve global challenges. "America has not succeeded by stepping out of the currents of cooperation—we have succeeded by steering those currents in the direction of liberty and justice, so nations thrive by meeting their responsibilities and face consequences when they don't."

Obama had the right diagnosis but the wrong treatment. Failed states, terrorism, WMD proliferation, and rogue nations have grown in the underbrush of the very political decentralization, economic globalization, and security umbrella promoted by the United States and its allies. Obama's answer is to seek a cure for the dysfunctions by reinforcing the status quo, which will only concentrate the burdens of treasure and blood on the few nations with military ability and determination, while spreading the benefits on all nations—discouraging the United States or any nation from undertaking action in the first place. Perhaps more partnerships will help reduce the costs of maintaining international peace, though public choice theory predicts that emerging powers will continue to free-ride on the efforts of the great powers. In other words, many nations may want to have a broader voice, but few will want to take on greater responsibilities—so long as they can rely on larger powers to continue to maintain global order.

This book will argue that the international system should facilitate, not burden, intervention. Fewer nations should have a veto over war, rather than more. Cooperation should take the form of informal networks and partnerships, not ever more formal and legalistic institutions. The rules on the use of force should gain flexibility, balance between costs and benefits, and adaptability to the challenges of the twenty-first century. An improved system should build from the foundations of long state practice, while displaying the flexibility to confront new security challenges.

Chapter 2 sets the context for this new framework for force by describing the evolution of the international system from the Peace of Westphalia in 1648 to today. The remarkable change, I argue, is the sharp reduction in great power war since the end of the Cold War and the corresponding increase in civil wars and humanitarian harms. Chapter 2 will show that the rules of the twentieth century, designed to prevent great power conflict, have become ill suited for the problems of disintegration emerging in the twenty-first century. Chapter 3 will trace the development of the international legal and political rules on force that have grown alongside the international system. Here, I argue that just war theory—today's meta-framework for thinking about war—jumped without good reason from the ancient and medieval political thought into the collective security schemes that made their appearance at the end of World War I. As developed by ancient and medieval scholars, just war thinking could provide an approach for addressing modern problems of rogue states and humanitarian crises. But when pulled from its moral and religious context, just war theory today only finds purchase in the undue prohibitions on force in the UN Charter.

The middle of the book will identify the faults of the existing rules and, from a rational choice perspective, propose a more effective approach. Chapter 4 examines the existing rules on force and, while finding them wanting, proposes reforms that work within the UN Charter system. Specifically, it argues that anticipatory self-defense should not depend solely on the imminence of an expected attack, but also should take into account the magnitude of expected harm. Nations might have leeway, under the UN framework, to act earlier against threats that go beyond border incursions to include large human rights deprivations or large-scale threats of attack. Chapter 5, however, proposes a more fundamental change in our understandings. It rejects the UN Charter's prohibition of nondefensive wars and instead argues that the great powers should have the legal authority to use force when the expected benefits to global welfare outweigh the expected costs of conflict.

The last third of the book will apply this new way to the wars of the twenty-first century and focus on related security threats, primarily those posed by failed states. Chapter 6 responds to criticism that departing from the UN Charter system could lead to international anarchy. It criticizes the Security Council's institutional arrangements and instead proposes a less formalized alliance of democracies, akin to the Concert of Europe that prevailed between the end of the Napoleonic Wars and the unification of Germany. Chapter 7 applies the book's analysis to the difficult challenge of failed states, where many of the twenty-first century's problems seem to meet. I argue that certain states have failed because they grew too large, beyond the needs of security and free trade. Breaking up some states will lead to fewer civil wars and civilian deaths, but only if the great powers have the legal authority to intervene to maintain bargains between competing groups and successor states. The final chapter will begin the challenge of applying the global welfare approach developed here to difficult contemporary cases, such as Iran's nuclear program, North Korea's totalitarian regime, and the uprisings in Syria and the Arab world.

Before beginning, it bears emphasis that this book's effort to bring public choice tools to bear on international legal rules is not an effort to disregard international law. Instead, it seeks to develop a new international legal regime that maximizes global welfare consistent with the realities of great power politics. Even though militarily dominant, powerful nations such as the United States and the United Kingdom desire legal legitimacy when they use force. But when the formal legal rules diverge so sharply from the actual incentives that influence nations, they will breed disrespect and dismissal because the great powers will simply violate the law to preserve their security and pursue their interests. During the Cold War, for example, the United States and its allies consistently sidestepped the UN Security Council, due to the veto threat from the Soviet Union and China, when they intervened in other lands.

Yet, at the same time, the great powers did not simply act without any effort at justification. Instead, they fought through proxies, as the United States did in the Vietnam War in asserting its allies' right to self-defense,[36] or—flipping sides—through rebel groups seeking a right of self-determination. Or they battled through regional coalitions, as the United States did with the Organization of American States during the Cuban Missile Crisis. Since 1991, when the gates to the Security Council temporarily opened, the United States and its allies acted abroad with UN permission where possible. Most notably, President George H.W. Bush sought and won Security Council approval for the Persian Gulf War. Interventions in the former Yugoslavia, Somalia, Haiti, and, more recently, Libya received the UN's blessing. These examples suggest that the democratic great powers, such as the United

States and the U.K., wish to act with legal legitimacy when they use force, even though they may ultimately forgo it when national interest demands.

Therefore, one way to understand this book's goal is to reconstruct the international rules on using force so that they more realistically regulate the conduct of nations. Too sharp of a divide between law and practice will place nations in a bind: they will either violate international law when it unduly restrains their national interests, or they will fail to act when they should, even when force would enhance global welfare, out of regard for an obsolete and inefficient rule. This book's task is to bring international rules and great power practice closer together so that nations will have greater respect for laws that encourage them to act in the best interests of the world's peoples.

2 Imperial Versus Humanitarian Wars

THE END OF the Cold War brought no end to war. In just the last twenty-five years, the United States has sent troops to Libya, Afghanistan, Iraq, Somalia, Panama, the Philippines, and the Balkans. It has conducted covert operations in South America, the Middle East, and Africa. But while war has continued, its purposes have changed—from a competition for territory, power, and influence to curing threats to international peace and stability.

The modern international system began with the Peace of Westphalia, which ended the Thirty Years' War in 1648. The treaty marked the rise of the nation-state as the superior territorial unit for a people's economic, political, and social organization.[1] France, Prussia, and the Netherlands used the conflict to free themselves of the claims of the Holy Roman Empire. These nations drew on greater resources than the Italian city-states that dominated the Renaissance or the princely fiefdoms of Germany and Eastern Europe. They forged loyalties under a single territorial banner, besting the polyglot empires that grew out of dynastic inheritances (like the Hapsburgs). First led by princes, then kings, then bureaucracies, these states have evolved into today's modern nation-state.[2] Philip Bobbitt claims provocatively that the nation-state itself will become obsolete in the approaching competition for capital and high-value labor rather than land. Whether his prediction comes true or not, the nation-state today continues to dominate international politics just as it has for the last four centuries. It has yet to meet its match.

The Peace of Westphalia validated a second principle: no higher authority prevailed above the nation-state. In a process that had begun as early as the Protestant Reformation, France in 1648 shrugged off the claims of the Holy Roman Emperor and the Church to temporal power in Europe. Nation-states pursued their own interests as equals and were masters of their internal affairs. Independence and equality, however, produced what realist scholars like Kenneth Waltz describe as global "anarchy": no supranational government can force nation-states to obey any law, keep any promises, or respect any peace. Because no higher authority can guarantee the peace, realists argue, nations will compete militarily out of fears for their own security or to expand their power. "The great powers seek to maximize their share of world power," writes John Mearsheimer, because "having dominant power is the best means to ensure one's own survival."[3]

Of course, the Thirty Years' War did not fully live up to its reputation. The Peace of Westphalia contained a freedom of religion clause providing that Catholics and Protestants could worship without interference from their state.[4] Freedom of religion normally falls within national internal affairs, so the treaty limited a sovereign's autonomy. Furthermore, the agreement did not validate the right of a state to use force at its discretion against others. Instead, the treaty pledged the signatories to a perpetual, Christian peace, though it would be a promise observed only in the breach.

In the decades to follow, nations resorted to war to expand their territory, seize trade routes, occupy resource-rich lands, unite ethnic groups, disrupt empires, and counter the expansive designs of competitors. The latter half of the seventeenth century witnessed the Anglo-Dutch Wars, the French-Dutch War, and the War of the Grand Alliance against France. The next century saw the flowering of great power conflicts between Britain, France, Prussia, Austria, Russia, and Spain. Nationalism reached a crescendo in the nineteenth century, with the German and Italian unifications and the emergence of the "classic" European balance of power.[5] States did not act out of desire for a Christian peace, but instead to pursue *ragione di stato*, in Machiavelli's words, or Cardinal Richelieu's *raison d'etat*.[6]

In the last century, nations pressed their drive for territory and security to new heights of destruction. World Wars I and II assembled broad multinational alliances, wielding giant industrial militaries, to conduct hostilities throughout the globe. Wilhelmine Germany attacked France to expand its territory and influence in Western Europe and to defend Austria's interests in the Balkans. Twenty-five years later, Nazi Germany pursued "lebensraum" and almost conquered the entire continent. In the realist view, the United States acted as an "offshore balancer" in 1917 and again in 1941 by preventing any single nation from dominating Europe—the same role played by Great Britain against Louis XIV and Napoleon's France.

The two World Wars also differed from the European conflicts of the past. New ideologies arose, their destructiveness accelerated by modern technologies. Nevertheless, nation-states pursued the same goals for three centuries: control of territory, population, and resources for power and influence.

While the Cold War magnified the power of the contestants and multiplied the stakes, it did not change war's purpose. The Soviet Union, whose influence was global, whose conventional forces were largest, and whose nuclear arsenal could have destroyed the United States in minutes, replaced Germany and Japan as the central security threat. It emerged from World War II in possession of Eastern Europe and half of Germany and soon gained allies in China and Africa, Asia, and Latin America. It had a large, well-educated population, ample natural resources, and an ideological alternative to democracy and capitalism. Competition with the Soviet Union and its allies presented the gravest external challenge to the United States in its history—by the end of the 1940s, Moscow had developed nuclear weapons; in the 1950s, its bombers and missiles could reach the United States; by the end of the 1960s, it achieved nuclear parity; in the 1970s, its conventional and nuclear forces arguably outmatched the West.

After earlier conflicts, the United States had demobilized its forces and drastically reduced defense spending. Not this time. The United States used force as part of a broad strategy to contain the spread of Soviet power.[7] President Harry Truman convinced Congress to place the United States in a permanent state of mobilization that was unprecedented in American history. American strategy focused on the defense of core industrial areas—Western Europe and Japan—valuable for their combination of strategic location, educated populations, and economic production. Truman's successors kept the United States committed to the strategy of containment over a period far longer—forty-five years—than any American "hot" war. The United States transformed itself from a passive arsenal of democracy to an active guardian of the free world.

While Nazi Germany's territorial ambitions focused on Europe, the Cold War struggle reached all continents, included the high seas, and even stretched to outer space. Conflict sometimes occurred through proxies, at points such as Korea, Vietnam, and Afghanistan, where the United States believed the Soviets sought to expand their sphere of influence. At other times, the United States resorted to force to stabilize its own sphere, as in Grenada and Panama at the periphery. Yet the main focus of American efforts remained the protection of Western Europe and East Asia with large conventional and nuclear forces. Throughout the Cold War, the United States and the Soviet Union competed to maintain and expand their influence over other nations—embracing goals broader in scope but not different in nature from those that nations had pursued since Westphalia.

America's Cold War victory changed the purpose of intervention. The wars of the last two decades focused on the maintenance of a stable, liberal world order, not territorial control or economic domination. American wars in Korea and Vietnam sought to keep these lands friendly to U.S. foreign and economic policy, at the periphery of a rising East Asian capitalist economic sphere. Following the tenets of the Monroe Doctrine, Kennedy's response in the Cuban Missile Crisis and Reagan's support of the Nicaraguan Contras aimed to keep the Western Hemisphere free from the influence of outside nations. The 1991 Persian Gulf War protected vital American allies—Kuwait and Saudi Arabia—in a region that supplies critical natural resources to the friendly economies of the United States, Western Europe, and Asia.

But the wars that followed had less to do with expanding American power or protecting Western economic interests, and more to do with ending ethnic strife and creating stable governments—often in areas of little strategic importance to the United States. Intervention in Somalia, Haiti, and Kosovo brought little advantage to the United States and arguably cost more than they brought in benefits. In Somalia and Haiti, for example, the United States intervened to stop mass suffering among the populations and to build states that could govern the country. These actions brought little value, from a purely realist perspective, to the United States. Somalia held little strategic importance, and the United States had virtually no economic interests in a land with few resources that was devastated by years of civil war. In fact, the United States tried as quickly as possible to rid itself of responsibility for Somalia, beating an ignominious retreat after the death of eighteen special operations soldiers in October 1993 (as dramatized in the movie *Blackhawk Down*). A poor country with few economic resources, Haiti had greater strategic significance. A more stable country in the Caribbean would reduce refugee flows to American shores. But neither intervention directly attacked a sovereign nation, but rather, used force to achieve humanitarian goals.

Unlike Somalia and more like Haiti, Kosovo involved some security interests—but those of America's NATO allies rather than those of the United States. In the wake of the Cold War, Yugoslavia disintegrated into its ethnic components: Serbia, Croatia, Slovenia, Macedonia, Montenegro, Bosnia and Herzegovina, and Kosovo. Balkan fractiousness had ignited World War I; European leaders reasonably feared that ethnic and religious conflict there could spread to Europe's southern flank, or drive refugees into Italy, Hungary, and Austria. The United States certainly faced no threat of attack from Serbia—the aggressor in the Kosovo War. Nor did it have any important strategic or economic interests in the Balkans at the time.

In the 1990s, therefore, war became more a tool to combat threats to world peace and stability, and less a means for conquest and influence. Nations have resorted to force to suppress civil wars, humanitarian disasters, rogue states, and international terrorism before they spread beyond a single nation's borders. At the same time, some domestic affairs—such as how a government treats its own citizens—that once fell primarily within a nation's sovereign authority are now understood to have broader impact. Our international political and legal system, however, continues to focus on the threat of large-scale conflicts between nation-states. As these great power wars recede into the past, the existing rules are proving increasingly inadequate for contemporary threats to international peace and security. Rules designed to deter major nation-state conflicts do not fit easily within the demands of international police work or humanitarian intervention. Such rules may deter the great powers from using force despite the clear benefits for global welfare, such as intervening to stop the genocide in Rwanda, stopping Serbia's aggression in the former Yugoslavia, or preventing the Assad regime's use of chemical weapons in Syria's civil war, because no UN Security Council authorization was forthcoming and no claim of self-defense could be made. It goes too far to claim that these international legal rules will completely prevent a nation from pursuing its core national interests—witness France's repeated interventions among the Francophone African nations over the last three decades, most without Security Council authorization. On the other hand, the lack of international legitimacy may add to other factors that already discourage intervention, such as the military costs and casualties, the lack of a clear gain for the great power's security, the difficulty of exit, and the political blowback caused by the asymmetric warfare often waged by insurgents.

Take the 2011 intervention in Libya, in which the United Nations approved a NATO no-fly zone over Libya. Clearing the skies required not just the grounding of Libyan aircraft but also the destruction of air defenses on the ground: anti-aircraft missile sites, command-and-control networks, and air force bases. But Libya posed no serious threat to the security of its neighbors, though in the 1980s it supported deadly international terrorist attacks. Libya posed little challenge to the United States or its forces abroad. Libyan dictator Moammar Gadhafi kept his military deliberately small, limited to about 50,000 troops despite Libya's large oil revenues, to avoid a military coup. In fact, after the invasion of Iraq by the United States in 2003, Libya had voluntarily given up its nuclear weapons program, compensated past victims of its international terrorism, and normalized relations with the West.

The West resorted to force not because Libya posed any imminent threat to its neighbors, but because of a civil war against Gadhafi's rule. In January 2011, a popular uprising in neighboring Tunisia overthrew the authoritarian regime of President Zine El Abidine Ben Ali, who had ruled since 1987. Later that month, sympathetic pro-democracy protests spread to Egypt and forced President Hosni Mubarak to step down after three decades in power. In February, the pro-democracy movement reached Libya, but Gadhafi had no intention to abdicate. He ordered the Libyan military and security services to fire on demonstrators, sparking a civil war. Rebels quickly freed the eastern half of the country and established their headquarters in Benghazi, but suffered a turnabout in their fortunes. After several weeks of indecision, the United States and its allies intervened when Gadhafi's forces threatened to snuff out the rebellion.

The West had no desire to seize Libya's oil or territory. Libya had already reopened its oil fields to Western investment. Libya posed no direct security threat to either the United States or its NATO allies. Instead, as President Obama said in March 2010, "Gadhafi must go" for wantonly killing Libyan civilians. In Resolution 1973, the UN Security Council authorized force strictly "to protect civilians and civilian populated areas under threat of attack." It called for a ceasefire enforced by an arms embargo and a no-fly zone, but not the regime change sought by the United States and its allies. Resolution 1973 specifically prohibited any "foreign occupation force," in other words, no long-term ground presence.[8] In a pretense of neutrality, its language also required NATO to stop the rebels if they targeted civilians too. It was a recipe for a prolonged civil war: the UN did not authorize any force for the purpose of removing Gadhafi or resolving the conflict itself.

The Libyan intervention certainly involves realpolitik. Were it not for Libya's large oil reserves, what NATO ally would care? Before the conflict broke out, Libya pumped 1.6 million barrels of oil per day—2 percent of global consumption—making it the seventeenth largest oil producer in the world.[9] Libya exports 85 percent of its daily production to Europe. After the rebellion won control of oil-rich regions in the East, Libyan oil production fell to 500,000 barrels per day. Western oil companies, such as ENI, Total, and Marathon, held a share of about 460,000 barrels per day of the prewar total.[10] Notably, NATO did not send its troops to other conflicts, such as those raging in Africa where the loss of life is as high or higher than in Libya but there is little oil.

However, if securing Libya's oil were the only goal, the United States and its allies intervened at precisely the wrong time. If political instability poses the greatest threat to oil production, pure self-interest would counsel maintaining the current regime in power. If a rebellion arises, oil-consuming countries should favor a quick resolution by one side or the other so that production can resume. With Libya, the United States and its allies intervened just as Gadhafi had reversed rebel gains and was preparing a final push into Benghazi. If oil were their only concern, NATO members should have decided to attack months earlier, when Gadhafi's regime was teetering on the edge after the defection of several army units and easy rebel gains. The worst moment was the one chosen, when Gadhafi had restored control over much of Libya and his victory looked likely. Intervention at that point prolonged the civil war and guaranteed that oil production would continue to suffer. This was not the optimal strategy for nations interested only in economic imperialism.

Instead, the Libyan war bears similarities in motive to earlier postwar interventions. Haiti, Somalia, Afghanistan, Iraq, and even the former Yugoslavia did not raise the prospect of nation-state war of the kind that characterized the nineteenth and twentieth centuries. Aside from Iraq in 1991, which posed a threat to Kuwait, Saudi Arabia, and perhaps Israel, these countries did not menace their neighbors with aggression. Instead, they threatened the international system because of the internal conduct of their regimes.

The international system has failed to grapple with the rise of these new threats because it is still focused on interstate war. In the postwar years, however, the death and destruction from large international armed conflict has declined just as the costs of civil wars and failed states have risen. Compared to earlier historical periods, classical interstate wars seem to have increased since World War II. The relevant figures are:

Years	Wars
1715–1814	36
1815–1914	29
1918–1941	25
1945–1995	38

From 1945 to 1995, there were thirty-eight interstate wars—which would increase to forty-two if Kosovo, Afghanistan, Iraq, and Georgia are included.[11] In the aggregate, the period since the end of World War II has witnessed a frequency of war equal to, or greater than, earlier epochs following the Peace of Westphalia.

Once we take into account the explosion in nation-states over the last half-century, however, we find that interstate war wanes. At the end of World War II, there were 74 independent nations in the world. Today there are 195.[12] We should measure the incidence of war per nation per year, just as we want to know whether the number of murders per capita has changed, not just the absolute number of murders. The relevant figures are:

Years	Wars/State/Year
1715–1814	.019
1815–1914	.014
1918–1941	.036
1945–1995	.005[13]

According to these statistics, the number of interstate conflicts changed little in the two centuries after the Peace of Westphalia. The World Wars upset this rate. Not only did the postwar period benefit from a reversal of the 1914–1945 jump, but it also saw a steep decline. Because of the near tripling of actors in the international system, the rate of wars per nation-state has declined in the second half of this century by a whole order of magnitude—a drop never before seen in the modern age.[14]

As the number of interstate conflicts has fallen, the horrors of war have not vanished. Instead, war has moved inside states, rather than between them. From 1946 to 2001, 225 wars broke out, 163 internal and 53 international.[15] One study estimates that close to 75–80 percent of all conflicts since World War II have been internal.[16] Nations are fighting their neighbors less, and themselves more.

As civil wars have risen, casualties have jumped. The twentieth century was probably the bloodiest in human history. Historian Eric Hobsbawm estimates that deaths "by human decision" reached 187 million from 1914 to 1991, while former Carter National Security Adviser Zbigniew Brzezinski estimates such deaths at between 167 and 175 million.[17] Both authors, however, include deaths from internal repression, such as the failed Chinese economic collectivization programs of the 1950s and 1960s and the forced Soviet transfers of populations of the 1930s. Other scholars put twentieth-century war-related deaths at between 136 and 148 million.[18] Of this total, World War I accounted for 13 million to 15 million and World War II for another 65 million to 75 million.[19]

As conflicts have moved inside states, so have the casualties. Conflicts in the postwar period have killed an estimated 40 million people, including both combatant deaths and civilian deaths from disease and starvation.[20] One study finds that the deaths from civil wars account for 80 percent of all those lost in wartime since World War II, while another suggests that 90 percent of the death toll in internal armed conflicts are civilians.[21] In other words, civil wars killed approximately 32 million people between 1945 and 2000. In a separate study, James D. Fearon and David D. Laitin report that, between 1945 and 1999, 25 interstate wars caused about 3.33 million battle deaths. Those wars involved 25 states and lasted three months on average. This same period witnessed 122 intrastate wars involving 73 states with a median duration of six years.[22] To provide some examples, the civil war in Cambodia has killed 1.77 million, Congo 1.75 million, Sudan 2 million, and Rwanda 800,000.[23] Conventional international wars, such as the German invasions of France, killed 8 million in the same period.

The post-1945 period witnessed a third transformation in the nature of war. War today is less global and more local. In World Wars I and II, multiple nations organized into broad alliances and fought in several theaters at once. Conflict since 1945 has remained rooted within individual countries and regions. The Korean and Vietnam

Wars, for example, did not spread beyond Asia, while the conflict in Kosovo never reached Europe. Interventions in Afghanistan and Iraq did not expand beyond Central Asia and the Middle East. War has even disappeared from regions where it had been all too familiar. In the first half of the century, Western Europe suffered the brunt of the two most destructive wars in human history. Since 1945, however, neither Europe nor North America has witnessed an international armed conflict. In the same period, nations have fought only one interstate war in South America—the Falklands conflict between Great Britain and Argentina. Africa has become the primary stage for the most wars, both international and internal.

Great powers have not gone to war with each other for almost seven decades, an unmatched record of peace in the modern world. Even the period between the end of the Napoleonic Wars and World War I witnessed the Crimean War, Prussia's unification of Germany, and the 1870 Franco-Prussian War. But is this due to a narrow definition of a great power? Scholars continue to debate the mix of military size, economic strength, and population that goes into making a great power, but most at least define it as military capability and likelihood of success on the battlefield.[24] "To qualify as a great power," writes Mearsheimer, "a state must have sufficient military assets to put up a serious fight in an all-out conventional war against the most powerful state in the world."[25] With the advent of nuclear weapons, a great power must also have a nuclear deterrent. Under this definition, European nations dominated great power politics from Westphalia until the 1890s, when the first non-European Great powers (the United States and Japan) emerged. After 1945, Great Britain, France, Germany, and Japan lost their status, and the only great powers left were the United States and the Soviet Union. China arguably joined them in the 1990s.

Whether one defines a great power narrowly or broadly, however, does not much alter the pattern of peace. From 1945 to the present, none of the European nations, the United States, the Soviet Union, or Japan went to war with each other. Only the U.S.-Chinese conflict in the Korean War might qualify, but in 1951, China arguably was not a great power, and it had no nuclear deterrent. Great powers have certainly launched smaller wars since 1945–such as the Falklands, the 1991 Gulf War, or the wars in Afghanistan and Iraq—but they have not been at war with each other. Interstate warfare was once dominated by the struggles of powerful European nations for supremacy. Not anymore.

Some international lawyers and officials might credit the decline in classical great power warfare to international rules. But they cannot claim that the UN Charter ban on war has had anything to do with the disappearance of nation-state conflict. What is the effect of international law on decisions to go to war? Nations seem to continue to use force to pursue their interests regardless of the UN. In the Cuban Missile Crisis, for example, the United States blockaded Cuba without UN Security

Council authorization to prevent the deployment of Soviet nuclear weapons. President John F. Kennedy's public statement during the confrontation exemplifies the United States' attitude toward the strict reading of international law. When asked by a reporter if the United States could invade Cuba without UN authorization, JFK replied:

> Obviously, the United States—let's use a hypothetical case, which is always better—the United States has the means as a sovereign power to defend itself. And of course it exercises that power, has in the past, and would in the future. We would hope to exercise it in a way consistent with our treaty obligations, including the United Nations Charter. But we, of course, keep to ourselves and hold to ourselves under the United States Constitution and under the laws of international law, the right to defend our security. On our own, if necessary— though we, as I say, hope to always move in concert with our allies, but on our own if that situation was necessary to protect our survival or integrity or other vital interests.[26]

President Kennedy simply sidestepped international law by referring to the blockade as a "quarantine."[27] Some leading international legal scholars, such as Michael Glennon and the late Thomas Franck, despair over the inability of legal rules to constrain war-making by states.[28] Franck, for example, argued as early as 1970 that powerful nations had "killed" the UN Charter's prohibitions on the use of force. In the wake of the 2003 Iraq War, he bleakly observed that the Charter's ban on war "has died again, and this time, perhaps for good."[29] However, it should be noted that this is likely not the view of the majority of international law scholars, such as the late Louis Henkin, who often argue that "almost all nations observe almost all principles of international law and almost all of their obligations almost all of the time."[30]

Scholars have identified several reasons for the "Long Peace" of the postwar period.[31] While popular culture criticizes the development of nuclear weapons for raising the chances and destructiveness of war (such as the movie *Dr. Strangelove*), the truth seems to have been far different. Instead of bringing Armageddon, the massive destructiveness of nuclear weapons has deterred war between the great powers. A retaliatory nuclear strike will inflict harm far beyond any gain from an attack. The United States and the Soviet Union sometimes waged war through proxies, but they studiously avoided direct conflicts that might escalate into a nuclear exchange. "The probability of major war among states having nuclear weapons approaches zero," political scientist Kenneth Waltz has argued.[32]

Some have even argued that the spread of nuclear weapons is responsible for the long postwar peace. "Never since the Treaty of Westphalia in 1648, which conventionally marks the beginning of modern history, have great powers enjoyed a longer period of peace than we have known since the Second World War," Waltz observed in 1990. "One can scarcely believe that the presence of nuclear weapons does not greatly help to explain this happy condition."[33] If war becomes unlikely between great powers with nuclear weapons, the logic of deterrence suggests that the more nations that have them, the better. Nuclear powers—the United States, Russia, Great Britain, France, China, India, Pakistan, and, according to reports, Israel and North Korea—have never so far gone to war with each other. Critics, however, respond that more is not better, that less stable nations will not have adequate operational safeguards, and that more nuclear states will raise the chances of a nuclear accident.[34]

Cold War fears of a nuclear conflagration obscured a second source of enduring international stability. The "bipolar" postwar world featured the unprecedented concentration of power in two great nations, the United States and the Soviet Union, which may have produced less war.[35] A "multipolar" system featuring several great powers may well have stimulated the wars that plagued the pre-World War I period by creating more potential sources of friction, greater imbalances of power, and more opportunities for miscalculation.[36] One power's expansion may go unchecked because the others expect someone else to deal with it (known by scholars as "buck passing"), minimize the threat, or encounter difficulties organizing a united opposition.[37] The more players involved, the higher the "transaction costs" (the difficulty in negotiating, reaching, and enforcing agreement) for collective action; although, as the Condorcet Theorem teaches, the more nations involved in a decision, the less likely it is that they will make an error because they can pool more information and bring better decision processes to the table. There are also more chances for wars between smaller powers, which might pull in the great powers. A fight is more likely to break out when there are more people trying to divide up a pie.

A bipolar world can alleviate these tensions. Politics becomes simpler with only one relationship and two great powers that might go to war. When two superpowers compete, they may order the minor powers into broad alliances, which may reduce conflict between actors throughout the system. The two great powers will avoid war between their coalitions for the same reasons they avoid it between themselves— because of the unimaginable costs of escalation. Thus, the Cold War reduced the chances of war between not only the United States and the Soviet Union but also the Soviet Union and Great Britain, and Poland and West Germany. Bipolarity also recognizes a balance between the great powers in material and human resources, which gives them the ability to deter each other and to restrain their allies from ruinous engagements. A superpower will detect and respond to its competitor's destabilizing moves with reasonable accuracy. With five or ten nations rather than just one in play, the focus blurs. Superpower competition proved not more dangerous but more stable, suppressing the destructive great power wars of the previous century.

Changes in the world economy may also have contributed to the decline in great power war. Globalization and the changing nature of economic power may have eased the competition for territory and natural resources between nations. Great power conflict itself has not disappeared. Nations still seek economic resources that enhance their military position and security. But economic strength no longer depends solely on possession of natural resources, population size, or industrial production—though these factors continue to be dominant in war. Nations compete more broadly for the global capital and well-educated labor force that brings economic growth, which makes possible the surplus for high-tech weapons systems and highly trained specialized armed forces.

War's costs may have risen, while its benefits have fallen. Territorial expansion—the aim of earlier wars—may undermine efforts to attract global capital and labor. As the United States found in Iraq, controlling territory is expensive, especially if the occupier intends to remake a nation. There may be fewer benefits of holding conquered territory if its educated workforce flees with their capital to other lands. The conqueror itself may experience capital flight to avoid the high taxation needed to finance war. Conquest may provoke higher internal costs, especially if ethnic or religious divisions increase with larger size, or if economic growth cannot accommodate new population. China, for example, has pursued a one-child policy to shrink its population, while Pakistan seems mired with a large population without the economic growth to support it.

War's decline may also be due not to the external policies of states but to their internal politics. Great political philosophers have rarely addressed international law and relations. David Hume wrote an essay on the balance of power; Jean-Jacques Rousseau wrote two on peace; John Stuart Mill wrote on treaties and intervention.[38] But these minor works were not central to their thought. John Rawls extended his liberal theory of the welfare state to international politics, but to my mind with mixed results.[39] Immanuel Kant, however, is one philosopher who did blend his thinking on domestic and international affairs to seek an end to war. He first proposed the idea of "world federalism," a global governance structure that would solve the problem of great power conflict. Its "cosmopolitan constitution" would make the legal and political arrangements to preserve the peace among and within states by extending world citizenship and human rights to all.

As recently expanded by Jurgen Habermas, Kant's cosmopolitan constitution would establish an association among states that would prove more sturdy and binding than traditional defensive alliances and trade pacts. Complete submersion of states in a larger political union, unitary world state, or global empire would be unnecessary. For Kant, the then new federal system of the United States provided one model, on a local scale.

Kant proposed what modern observers call the "democratic peace thesis," which has both empirical and theoretical elements. At least since the mid-nineteenth century, if not back to the ancient world of Greek city-states, no democracy has ever waged war against another. While this seems surprising, the statistical evidence is quite robust, and extensive testing shows a strong relationship between democracies and peace.[40] This is not to say that democracies are less warlike. Democracies often fight autocracies. They are more likely to initiate those wars than vice versa and are more likely to win than chance would predict. After they start a conflict, democracies fight shorter wars with lower costs. Transitional democracies are more warlike than older ones, and larger democracies are less likely to go to war than smaller ones.[41] As Michael Doyle writes, "[e]ven though liberal states have become involved in numerous wars with nonliberal states, constitutionally secure liberal states have yet to engage in war with one another."[42] This view has its critics, and some say the stability of the Cold War or nuclear weapons are the true explanations.[43] But so far, the democratic peace is the closest thing to a scientific law in international politics.

So Kant predicted that the emergence of a league of republics would bring an end to great power war. The moral imperative to achieve a permanent peace could only be satisfied, Kant argued, by "a universal union of states (analogous to the union through which a nation becomes a state)."[44] He did not recommend a single suprastate that dissolved the identities of nations. Instead, Kant suggested "a permanent congress of states," like the assembly of European powers that had met periodically at The Hague in the late 1700s and early 1800s. In *Perpetual Peace*, his most widely read work on international affairs, Kant sketched out a solution that proposes neither a unitary world-state like the Chinese or Roman Empires, nor a loose alliance like the Hague Congresses, nor a global government modeled on American federalism. Here, in place of the "positive idea of a world republic," Kant offered the "negative substitute of an enduring and gradually expanding federation likely to prevent war."[45] While this "negative substitute" falls short of a "world republic" or unitary global government, it provides the basis for a feasible program of action that can, over time, foster the conditions for a lasting global peace.

Despite its pretensions to world government, the United Nations could not fulfill Kant's vision even if it had more resources at its disposal. Rather, the United States and its NATO, Asian, and Latin American allies might perform the role of Kant's league of republics—an international alternative to the strengthened UN also proposed by Robert Kagan in *The Return of History and the End of Dreams*. Since the end of World War II, the sphere of nations, organized along democratic and capitalist lines, has slowly but steadily expanded, whether by self-conscious design or to build sound alliances to contain the Soviet Union. Taiwan, South Korea, the Philippines, and several Latin America nations transitioned from authoritarianism to democracy during the 1970s and 1980s. The U.S.-led alliance system may have served as a way to resolve disputes peacefully without resort to war. Although it lacks any federal or league structure, and Kant did not identify why a republican alliance would produce peace, the American web of postwar alliances may well have produced the reduction in war that Kant predicted.

Democracy's spread itself, not world constitutionalism or the United States' security alliance, may account for the reduction in great power war. More countries have become democracies since World War II. Defeat in World War II transformed fascist Germany, Italy, and Japan into democracies, decolonization made India one, and the former Soviet states have begun a transition—albeit a slow, fitful one in the case of Russia—away from totalitarianism. Of the great powers, only China remains authoritarian, although there, even broader economic freedoms have spread that might lay the groundwork for democracy. The democratic peace thesis predicts that war should disappear among the democratic great powers, as it has, but that it might increase between China and the rest.

Kant may have predicted the disappearance of great power war with the spread of democracy, but he never explained the mechanism. While democratic nations themselves are not inherently peaceful, for decades, U.S. policy has sought to protect human rights and promote democracy in hopes that global peace would ensue.[46] Undoubtedly, the United States has been encouraged in that effort by its remarkable successes after the Second World War in transforming former enemies into stable, peaceful, democratic allies and trading partners.[47] Democracy promotion was a significant motive for several recent American military interventions abroad, including those in Panama, Haiti, and Iraq. Under President George W. Bush, the United States explicitly linked the spread of democracy to peace and the reduction of threats to the United States:

America's vital interests and our deepest beliefs are now one. From the day of our Founding, we have proclaimed that every man and woman on this earth has rights, and dignity, and matchless value, because they bear the image of the Maker of Heaven and earth. Across the generations we have proclaimed the imperative of self-government, because no one is fit to be a master, and no one deserves to be a slave. Advancing these ideals is the mission that created our Nation. It is the honorable achievement of our fathers. Now it is the urgent requirement of our nation's security, and the calling of our time. So it is the policy of the United States to seek and support the growth of democratic movements and institutions in every nation and culture, with the ultimate goal of ending tyranny in our world.[48]

While spreading democracy may be a higher good, to be achieved when possible, President Bush's second inaugural address recognized it as a central protection for American national security. By 2005, Kant's democratic peace thesis had become an underlying principle of U.S. foreign policy under the Bush administration.

Hegemonic stability, nuclear weapons, economic globalization, and the spread of democracy have all led to the decline in great power war. But this does not mean that peace will continue indefinitely. China is rising, and a revanchist Russia is rattling its saber. Smaller powers, such Iran and Venezuela, seek dominance in their regions, while others, such as Pakistan and North Korea, foment instability. Nevertheless, the most pressing threats to international peace and security today come from within states, due to the harmful effects beyond their borders. In the last decade, democracies waged war in Libya, Iraq, and Afghanistan not to conquer territory but to intervene in the internal affairs of these nations for reasons both altruistic and self-interested: to eliminate the negative externalities inflicted on the international system by these troubled nations.

Many have long predicted the loss of U.S. military, economic, and political primacy and suggest reliance instead on the UN Charter system. Fears of American decline have periodically erupted from Vietnam to the Iraq and Afghanistan wars—fears that America's postwar hegemony is an anomalous consequence of the destruction of the industrial bases of Europe and Japan in World War II and that a normal multipolar balance of power will reassert itself. As the United States' relative power declines, some predict, it will no longer dictate world events as a hegemonic power. International law and institutions will fill the gap. In *After Hegemony*, for example, political scientist Robert Keohane argues that international cooperation in a multipolar world could prevent the disorder produced by American decline.[49] Absolute bans on the use of force would benefit the United States by limiting the ability of rising competitors, such as China or even the European Union, to leverage their growing militaries into political and economic influence.

The United States surely faces challenges. A deep recession has prompted the Obama administration and its congressional allies to embark on a massive Keynesian stimulus. The national deficit has ballooned as a result. Entitlement spending for a retiring baby boom generation threatens even worse financial problems in the future. The United States has emerged from the deepest economic downturn since the Great Depression with high unemployment, a battered banking system, and stiff overseas competition. Wars in Iraq and Afghanistan have cost billions in dollars and thousands in American military casualties. Future economic constraints may force the United States to reduce its military spending and pull back from its role as global policeman.

But these concerns overstate American decline and ignore the challenges facing potential competitors. Although China's spectacular economic growth echoes Germany's emergence as a continental power in Europe at the turn of the twentieth century, the parallels end there. Germany was a rising power, but it confronted nations, such as Austria-Hungary, France, and Russia, in economic and military decline. China faces a democratic counterweight in India that is enjoying an economic boom itself. A constellation of vigorous economies in Japan, Korea, Vietnam, Australia, and the Philippines share an interest in containing Beijing. China's demographics, moreover, might prevent its economic growth from translating into lasting military predominance. Although China's economy is the second largest in the world by gross size, it is among the smallest in the world per capita. China may surpass the United States in a few decades in absolute GDP, but it will not come close to the U.S. in average per capita. Today, its population is the world's largest, but its one-child policy means that its population will start shrinking during this century, with smaller numbers of the working age supporting an expanding army of the elderly. China has brought 500 million people out of poverty, but it still has another 500 million waiting. While China has recently boosted military spending and reasserted itself in the region, its slowing economic growth may cause internal challenges to the regime and a reduction in military spending.

Other power centers in the world pose less threat to American global leadership. Foreign policy analysts once found it fashionable to portray the European Union as a superpower competitor to the United States. However, declining populations and sluggish economies have prevented the EU from fulfilling those optimistic predictions. The domestic overspending of southern EU members Greece, Spain, and Italy has raised the question of whether the Union will even survive in its current form. European militaries will shrink, not grow—Great Britain has even decided to demobilize its lone aircraft carrier. Meanwhile, the United States spends more on its armed forces than all of the European and Asian powers combined. In both Kosovo and Libya, NATO nations could not intervene without the indispensable leadership, command-and-control, and smart weaponry of the U.S. armed forces. Even though it possesses a dangerous nuclear deterrent, Russia suffers from similar problems—its shrinking population and sluggish economy prevent it from fielding a conventional military capable of challenging the United States.

Regional powers may have revisionist hopes, but they do not possess the strength to oust the United States and its status quo allies. Armed with a revolutionary Islamist ideology and oil revenues, Iran seeks a new balance of power in the Middle East. Nonetheless, it cannot field a serious conventional military and instead spreads its influence through the asymmetric means of funding terrorists, guerrillas, and authoritarian regimes such as Syria. Iran's challenge has sparked a counterbalancing coalition of Sunni states, such as Saudi Arabia and Jordan, that have drawn themselves even closer to the United States. Even the overthrow of dictatorships in Tunisia, Libya, and Egypt during the so-called Arab Spring has not led to a united front of fundamentalist Islamic republics. Venezuela seeks a similar anti-American alliance in South America, but it too has gained little ground. The region's most dynamic economies, such as Chile, Peru, and Brazil, remain firmly rooted in the Western capitalist system, while strategic nations such as Mexico and Colombia continue to follow foreign policies aligned with American interests.

After long wars in Iraq and Afghanistan, the United States may well have to retrench. But any reduction in the American military does not produce an inevitable reduction in U.S. hegemony. Nations that have long benefited from the U.S. security umbrella have not improved their capabilities to keep pace and show little sign of straying far from American leadership. Potential revisionist powers suffer from their own economic and demographic problems and have provoked opposing coalitions that depend on U.S. security guarantees. As a result, the United States should have little interest in a multipolar world—and an international system that helps to keep it frozen in place—because of fear of a diminished future. Instead, it should seek to change the current international rules that raise the costs on efforts to use political and economic pressure, and ultimately force, to maintain the postwar liberal order that has so advanced global welfare.

The decline in interstate war and the rise in the destructiveness of internal conflicts should produce a corresponding change in the rules of war. Today's system, embodied in the United Nations Charter, seeks to prevent the wars of the last century. But their understandable fear of the destructiveness of the world wars led the creators of the UN system to draw their rules too strictly. They suppressed not just wars of aggression but also wars that advanced global welfare. This chapter has shown that the threat of the former has dissipated, while the theoretical need for the latter has become only more acute. Of course, any new framework will have to grapple with the precise measures, and balance, of the costs and benefits of intervention case by case, and only by testing these theories in the crucible of real crises can we see whether they are workable. But as the deaths and destruction from internal wars and disorder overshadow those from international conflict, the international system needs to change to allow nations to solve the problems before us, not those behind us.

3   From Just War to False Peace

THOSE WHO SEEK to outlaw war sometimes claim an ancient lineage, much like English aristocrats tracing their origins to a warrior who crossed the Channel with William the Conqueror. Modern political philosophers, who describe their work as falling within just war theory, invoke examples harkening back to Cicero's view on killing barbarians and medieval jurists' opinions on the Crusades.[1] Contemporary regimes to prohibit armed conflict, first introduced by the League of Nations and reinvigorated by the UN Charter, have called upon this history to claim that international law bans war as an unjustified interruption of peace. In this narrative, the great powers' unrestrained pursuit of *raison d'état* from the seventeenth to nineteenth centuries presents a sharp break from the history of international law. As Stephen Neff writes, the League of Nations and the period after 1919 "sought to reinstate the fundamental principle that underpins just-war strategies," that is, "the notion that the normal state of international relations is one of peace, with war permitted only as an exceptional act requiring affirmative justification."[2]

As utopian visions often are, this attractive account is often repeated. It may even describe what the drafters of the League of Nations or the UN Charter believed they were accomplishing. But it is fundamentally mistaken. The twentieth century's leagues and charters—and not the era of great power politics—attempted a radical change in the course of history. From ancient times on, international rules on *jus ad bellum* (the law governing the start of war), in contrast to *jus in bello* (the law governing conduct during war), remained fundamentally separate from political philosophy or religion. Ancient thinkers and medieval scholastics may have argued over just war, but their claims remained rooted in the abstract world of philosophy and morality, not the real world of diplomacy and conflict. One, of course, might influence the other, but a war that might violate Christian morals did not automatically run counter to international law, and vice versa.

Confusing justice with the rules of international politics is not only a mistake of intellectual history. It has also led to the dysfunctional UN Charter system that formally governs war today. It prohibits military conflict when everyone—the great powers, the states where civil war is occurring, and innocent bystanders—would benefit. At the same time, it creates the illusion that the current rules themselves promote justice, when instead they protect a status quo that can do little to restrain the rivalry of the great powers while discouraging interventions that would improve global welfare. Once we understand that the current system marks a sharp anomaly from the traditional rules of international politics, we can begin to rebuild a system that better reflects the world as it is and gives nations the proper incentives to heal its worst problems.

I. From Ancient to Early Modern Times

A. War and Ancient Greece

War, of course, did not emerge in the world along with the nation-state and modern militaries. Armed conflict has beset humanity throughout its history, and even before its history. And from those earliest times, mankind has sought to reach agreement on its limits. An example can be seen in ancient Greek city-states that followed certain rules restraining the worst excesses of war. In his *Peloponnesian War*, Thucydides describes a number of customs that had prevailed among the city-states, such as giving immunity to emissaries, sparing women and children, and protecting religious places. Sophocles's play, *Antigone*, centers on the general Greek practice of allowing opponents time after a battle to bury the dead. In the play, King Kreon of Thebes proclaims a mandatory exception to this practice for traitors. But in contrast to the force of the customs described by Thucydides, Antigone is sentenced to death for attempting to uphold religious practice and burying the body of her treasonous brother, Polynices.[3] As we will see, the laws of war bear these same characteristics from the days of the city-states in Greece to the city-states of Italy almost two millennia later. Nations today do not regulate the rules of *jus in bello* with written agreements; instead, they follow custom and tradition.[4] Nations today generally do not restrict *jus ad bellum* with extensive written codes; they regulate *jus in bello* far more extensively. To the extent that they limit the start of war, religious, moral, or policy considerations still seem to enjoy primacy over legal ones.

Thucydides's account of the Peloponnesian War (431–04 BCE) most famously illustrates these principles. The war pitted the two great superpowers of the Greek world, Athens and Sparta, against each other in a contest for supremacy. Athens remained dependent on control of the seas and trade, while Sparta fielded the dominant land forces of the time. Both cities sought to build alliances with dozens of other city-states to support a struggle that spanned decades. The many interactions between these states, both peaceful and hostile, provide a great deal of information about the practices of the ancient Greeks in international affairs. As Thucydides is often considered the first modern historian and first "realist" scholar—he discounts religious or supernatural explanations for events, focuses on the intentions and incentives of different states, and sees their struggle as one for power—his account is more reliable than other Greek sources of the time, which often attributed events to the will of the Gods.[5]

In the Melian dialogue, as recounted by Thucydides, the Athenians present the inhabitants of the island of Melos with the choice of either joining their Delian League or being destroyed. The Athenians say that they will put aside "specious pretense," such as claims that the Melians harmed them first or that their leadership of Greece in the Persian Wars justifies their empire. The Athenian envoys plainly declare: "[Y]ou know as well as we do that right, as the world goes, is only in question between equals in power, while the strong do what they can and the weak suffer what they must."[6] The Melians complain that the Athenians only speak of "interest" and not of "right," and that this destroys "our common protection, namely, the privilege of being allowed in danger to invoke what is fair and right."[7] Pleading to remain neutral in Athens's struggle with Sparta, the Melians appeal to "justice," while they accuse the Athenians of speaking only of "expediency." The Athenians are unimpressed by appeals to the gods. "Of the gods we believe, and of men we know, that by a necessary law of their nature they rule wherever they can."[8] When the Melians remain unconvinced to join the empire, the Athenians lay siege to the city and eventually conquer it. They put to death all the men of military age and send the women and children into slavery.

In Thucydides's retelling, we see the main elements of the international rules on war. Melos does not rely on any written treaty to claim that Athens should refrain from an attack. Instead, its people appeal to a shared understanding of justice among the Greeks. The Melians' claim takes the form of an appeal to the gods rather than any notion of "law." To them, it is religion, rather than the idea of positive law, that limits the freedom of states to go to war. In the end, invocation of religious ideals fails Melos, and the contest is resolved in favor of "interest," as Thucydides puts it. This is analogous to Antigone's appeals to the gods (and religion) to justify her actions; when Antigone's sister Ismene refuses to go along with the burial of Polynices,

Antigone states, "If you believe you must, cast out these principles which the gods themselves honor."[9] In the end, for Antigone, like Melos, invocation of religious ideals fails her, and the contest is resolved in favor of power and might. The Athenians presented the right of the strong to rule the weak as a principle of natural law, but not as a standard of international law. Some scholars, such as Coleman Phillipson, have asserted that the Greeks would always find some legal justification for armed conflict, but the Peloponnesian War shows this to be untrue, at least with regard to any concept of secular law.[10] The Athenians, and the Spartans in turn, might cite self-interest, religion, or undefined notions of justice as reasons for going to war, but not international law as such. When the term "just war" appears in the Greek sources, it is used first by Aristotle to describe wars by Greeks against barbarians, where only moral principles and not law prevailed.[11]

Religion's importance becomes more prominent with regards to the rules for the conduct of war once war has begun. Much of the Greek restraint in war—for example, permitting religious ceremonies to continue—promoted respect for sacred objects and places.[12] Greeks generally gave religious sites and personnel, such as temples and priests, immunity in combat. During the Peloponnesian War, for example, Athens committed the rare act of fortifying a religious site during the fighting in Boeotia. Athens did not argue that it had violated custom, but instead claimed that military necessity had forced its troops to retreat to the redoubt.[13] Contending nations also paused the fighting to allow religious ceremonies: the Olympic Games continued during the Peloponnesian War, and states would refrain from attacking on holy days. Even the principle of respecting the dead stemmed from religion. Warring Greeks returned dead bodies to the enemy and provided a time for their burial. This was not done for humanitarian reasons, but to respect religious funeral rites.[14] In *Antigone*, the tragic heroine does not invoke international law to support her violation of her city's decree. Instead, she appeals to religion to justify her effort to bury the dead body of her brother.[15]

We can see the religious point in clearer relief against the contrast of the conduct of war itself. Ancient Greeks did not understand humanitarian considerations to limit the methods of warfare. No external norm restrained the Greeks in their choice of weapons or tactics. No international law of war prohibited, for example, killing prisoners in battle. Greek historians—including Herodotus, Thucydides, Xenophon, Polybius, and Diodorus—tell of numerous examples where Greek forces massacred enemy fighters or enslaved survivors, even those who had surrendered.[16] As in the Melian dialogue, the lack of legal rules applied even to civilians captured during a siege. After one siege, Thucydides reports, the Athenians debated at length whether to massacre the male population of Mytilene, but only on the grounds of policy. The debate did not include a discussion of whether custom or law barred the choice.[17] Earlier in the war, Sparta decided to put to death the entire garrison at Plataea, an ally of Athens, after it had surrendered.[18] Religious observance did not protect noncombatants from death in war.

Ancient Greek states also seemed to settle on a related point. War between Greeks differed from war with foreigners. Conflict within a city-state was *stasis*, while war between Greeks and foreigners was known as *polemos*. Although city-states divided the Greek world, they remained united in language, culture, and heritage—even conflict between the Greeks became more a form of civil strife than war.[19] Greeks remained fiercely loyal to their city, but they also shared a common ethnic and cultural identity that shaped their view of war.[20] At the same time, the city-states carefully guarded their sovereignty and independence, which meant that conflict would often break out among them. Greek competitiveness meant that they were in conflict all the time; as one of Plato's speakers observes in *The Laws*, "in reality every city is in a natural state of war with every other, not indeed proclaimed by heralds, but everlasting."[21] In the Greek universe, there was no permanent state of peace from which war erupted unnaturally.

We should not obscure the debate among classicists over whether any legal rules restrained war among the Greeks. Military historian Victor Davis Hanson argues that some rules did exist among the ancient Greeks, such as those restricting hoplite warfare to certain seasons and limiting the pursuit and killing of civilians and the defeated.[22] Hanson argues that these standards gave way before the higher stakes of the Persian and Peloponnesian Wars in the fifth century BCE. Others, such as Adriaan Lanni, argue that the earliest signs of restraint grew out of the limits of hoplite warfare, which depended on slow, heavily armed farmers, rather than out of any norms—once the technology of Greek warfare changed, war could and did become more destructive.[23]

Regardless of the outcome of this debate, it should remain clear that the Greeks did not believe that any limits applied to the choice of when to go to war—only how to wage it. Self-restraint may have arisen from religious obligation, self-interest, or concern over reciprocal treatment, but the Greeks did not understand any legal rules to bind their decisions on whether to go to war.

B. The Roman Empire and Just War

Roman understandings of war more closely resembled our own. Scholars conventionally point to the writings of Marcus Tullius Cicero (106–43 BCE) as the starting point of a just war tradition that has been passed down to us through the ages.[24] Though Roman practice and thought was changing and diverse over a thousand-year history, Cicero is a central figure. He first introduced the idea that war should advance some good beyond merely a national self-interest in expansion. For Cicero, the natural state of mankind was of peace; war, therefore, was an unnatural interruption that required declaration and justification.[25] "Wars, then, are to be waged in order to render it possible to live in peace without injury," wrote Cicero in *De Officiis*.[26] A Roman leader should have a just cause, a *iusta causa*, to go to war. "No war can be undertaken by a just and wise state, unless for faith or self-defense," Cicero wrote.[27] If not for self-defense, war should come only in response to an earlier wrong, such as an attack on allies or ambassadors, a breach of treaties, or support for an enemy. Cicero acknowledged that just causes might also include punishment of the enemy, but the unifying idea remained that Roman war occurred in response to an earlier wrong.

Rome observed its just war tradition with religious ceremony. A just war could not begin without the approval of a special college of priests, the *fetiales*. The *fetiales* existed to "take care that the Romans do not enter upon an unjust war against any city in alliance with them," and to perform the ceremony of demanding justice of the enemy before hostilities could begin.[28] Ceremonies included dispatching a priest to the enemy territory to demand satisfaction (*repetitio rerum*), declaring war if no response was forthcoming after thirty-three days, and throwing a spear into enemy territory to symbolize the beginning of hostilities.[29] While there is some argument over the precise nature and order of the procedure, the central point remains that, in Cicero's words, "in the public administration, also, the rights of war are to be held sacred."[30] War was not just a tool of state policy; it was governed by religious principles translated through human interpretation. According to Alan Watson, the Roman gods served as more than mere witnesses to the observance of religious forms. They were the arbiters in contests between peoples, much in the way judges resolved private disputes between individuals.[31]

Cicero, however, discusses just war theory at length without reference to religious sanction. For him, just war was an element of natural law. "In a republic the laws of war are to be maintained to the highest degree. For there are two ways of deciding an issue, one through discussion, the other through force," Cicero wrote in a well-known passage. "The former [is] appropriate for human beings, the latter for beasts."[32] Peace was the normal state of human relations in nature, and war therefore was an unnatural interruption. It follows for Cicero that Rome must fight a just war honorably and must show mercy to the conquered, though Roman war permitted the seizure of property and the enslavement of the population. For Rome, a war must be *iustum piumque*: just and pious.

In practice, however, just war thinking did not impose any meaningful restrictions on the reasons for war. Romans focused more on observing the forms of the law of hostilities than its substance. We can see just war doctrine's weakness—in contrast to the restraints imposed by religious consequences—during the expansion of the Roman Republic. While there were instances where Rome obeyed just war principles, there were many, if not more, examples where Roman leaders manufactured events to satisfy the form, but not the spirit, of just war. Rome would enter into an alliance with an ally that was threatened or already engaged in hostilities with another city, deliberately to produce grounds for war, violations of neutrality, mistreatment of ambassadors, and breaches of treaties. As Polybius observed, Rome always sought a pretext for war so as not to be the public aggressor. While the Senate honored the forms required by legal and religious ceremony, Rome did not need to defend herself by expanding across Italy and the entire Mediterranean world.[33]

We find situations where no just war restraints seem to be present. The First and Third Punic Wars provide clear examples. At the time of the First Punic War in 264 BCE, Carthage rivaled Rome in the Mediterranean, but she carefully avoided giving any cause for hostilities—Roman intervention in a war between Syracuse and Messina in Sicily sparked the conflict. While the Second Punic War might have been inevitable, by the time of the Third Punic War, Carthage no longer posed a threat. Rome destroyed her old enemy anyway.[34] Another well-known example of Roman war without attention to ideals of justice was Julius Caesar's conquest of the Gauls. In his *Gallic Wars*, Caesar did not produce an arguable case of harm done to Rome by Gaul—the war was motivated by conquest, a fact that did not go unnoticed among Caesar's critics. By the end of the Republic, Roman wars seemed to honor the just war ideal only in its breach. Cicero even speculated that the Roman Republic deserved its end because of the lack of *causus belli* in the many conflicts it pursued in the first and second centuries BCE. "So long as the sway of the Roman people was maintained by the bestowal of benefits, not by injustice," Cicero wrote, "our sovereignty might then have been termed the patronage, rather than the government, of the world." But once this policy of just war was "abandoned" in the years after Sulla's dictatorship, "we are being justly punished" with civil wars and "the republic we have completely lost."[35] Just war theory might have been just that: a theory. Romans may have liked to claim that they had fulfilled their religious or legal duties, but in reality, the doctrine crumbled before republican and, later, imperial demands.

Rome rarely, if ever, followed just war doctrine in its long conquest of the Mediterranean world. Other scholars, such as Phillipson and David Bederman, accept Cicero's view and suggest that the Roman law of war had become secular. "It is hard to discern a legal institution from these aspects of Roman religion and (almost) magical belief," Bederman writes of the *fetiales* ceremony, "[b]ut there was one."[36] These principles of just war, however, were not part of the *jus gentium*, the law that applied to all people. The Romans, for example, could not expect a foreign nation to follow the procedures of the *ius fetiale*, though they might wish an enemy to declare war only for certain circumscribed reasons.[37] As Cicero writes, the *fetiales* were part of the "human laws," but "under all guarantees of religion."[38] It was the particular genius of the Romans to transform a religious practice into a legal concept. A just war would have secular reasons but still needed the approval of a college of priests. A *bellum justum* must still be a *bellum pium*. Whether the Romans followed the ceremonies or not, they did not allow justice to stand in the way of conquest.

C. Just War and Christianity

With the end of the Republic came the end of concepts of just war and religious oversight. The emperor retained the sole power to declare hostilities, the college of *fetiales* faded away, and wars to unify the empire or attack its enemies needed no justification. Constantine's conversion and the establishment of Christianity as Rome's state religion, however, produced a return to just war thinking. Christianity's injunction to "love thy neighbor" created deep tensions with the secular demands to defend the empire from barbarian invasions.[39] Christian theologians began their long struggle over whether military service and killing in war were sins. After Constantine's conversion, thinkers such as St. Ambrose began to view the empire as the protector of Christianity and military service and war as the necessary shield for civilization and peace.[40] A Christian could fight to keep the barbarians at bay to protect the state and church, but the reasons for doing so remained less than clear.

St. Augustine began the intellectual work of resolving the conflict between Christianity and war by resurrecting just war theory. It is important to understand that the work of medieval thinkers did not train their sights primarily on state policy and notions of international law. Rather, the question remained whether individuals could serve in the military and fight in combat without violating their Christian ideals—early Christian thought had urged against serving in the imperial armies.[41] As with Roman and Greek understandings, the Christian approach turned on the religious duty owed by the individual, not the secular law that governed states. In his *Contra Faustum*, for example, St. Augustine described the dilemma thus: "[I]s it sinful for a Christian to wage war?"[42] The Christian theologian answered "no." A Christian could wage war when he did so not out of malice or hatred, but because of love of his enemy. War punished the wrongdoer and prevented him from sinning again, rather than serving any desire for glory or revenge.[43]

St. Augustine's understanding of individual religious duty led him to a similar view of just war. War served the purpose of avenging injuries, either those inflicted by another state or by its citizens.[44] In *City of God*, he compared both capital punishment and war that advanced divine instructions as examples of killing that did not violate the Ten Commandments.[45] In its goal, however, St. Augustine's approach justified a broader scope for war than under Cicero. Cicero's just war was either defensive or sought compensation for a past injury. Christian just war pursued a broader, punitive dimension that sought not only to make the state whole but also to punish the wrongdoer for violating moral principle.[46] Because it is punitive in nature, war relied on more than a simple plea for compensation. Instead, it demanded reference to a broader set of moral rules. For St. Augustine, war arose to enforce the *ius*, an *ius* not limited to commonly accepted legal rules, but an *ius* that included righteousness and *iustitia*—justice. St. Augustine's innovation linked earlier Roman legal and religious notions of just war to Christian principles. While clearly borrowing Ciceronian concepts, St. Augustine infused war with the divine purpose of advancing the will of God and biblical principles.[47] As Arthur Nussbaum observed, Augustine's rules on just war were "religio-philosophical. . . . In no way did they lay down legal rules."[48]

In the disorder that followed the collapse of the Roman Empire, early medieval thinking returned just war to its religious origins, but this time in the service of Christ rather than Olympus. Popes and clerics encouraged European kings and nobles to defend Western Christendom from external competitors and internal disorder. Popes blessed wars to convert barbarians, heretics, and nonbelievers, and to defend the boundaries of the Holy Roman Empire from Muslim incursions.[49] At the same time, they opposed secular wars among the European nobility. The Crusades became the highest expression of papally inspired war—the liberation of the Holy Land. Just war changed its purpose from secular conflicts over compensation and punishment to missions to defend and spread the faith. Sanctions for unjust wars came from the religious threat of eternal damnation, not the law.

Roman lawyers in this period continued to link an individual right to resort to violence with the greater right of a state to go to war. Commentators on Justinian's *Corpus Iuris Civilis*, known as the post-Glossators, established just war upon the individual's right of self-defense. Private individuals could kill to forestall their own murder or robbery, but not to seek gain or vengeance. Similarly, a public war would become a *bellum licitum*—a "permissible" war—under the *ius gentium* and natural law if it prevented injury to the self or another. Permissible war aggregated the right of self-defense of all of a state's people and preserved the peace.[50] Gratian's great compilation of canon law in 1140, the *Decretum*, declared a war against heretics to be just because it punished sinners and prevented them from sinning again. Gratian stated that a war was just if a state seeks compensation for stolen property, responds to an enemy attack, or punishes past injuries.

It is important to see the difference between a *bellum licitum* and a *bellum justum*. Descending from the thought of Cicero and St. Augustine, the latter occupied the universe of religion and morality. The former, however, arose from natural law and therefore conceptualized the rights of nations in a way similar to the rights of individuals. Law and justice were separate and distinct, with the doctrine of just war acquiring its force from religion and philosophy.[51]

An important, perhaps overriding, issue for these scholars, known as "Decretists," was the source of authority for declaring war. In the disorder after the fall of the empire, these thinkers prohibited war from being declared by private individuals. War had to be declared by some public authority, but, with no single Roman emperor, the right devolved to kings and princes. This diverted attention from analysis of the just causes that could support war and instead focused on the political or—in the case of the Crusades—religious authorities who could declare hostilities. By the end of the twelfth century, lawyers and philosophers had done little to advance just war theory beyond the frameworks of Cicero and St. Augustine, and instead used law to regulate the process of declaring war. "The just war was the province of princes, popes and prelates," medieval historian Frederick H. Russell summarizes. "[I]ts use was justified when it was necessary to defend the *patria* against hostile force and to protect the Church from its many enemies."[52]

In the following century, canon lawyers known as the "Decretalists" sought to give more precise legal form to these ideas. They developed a number of criteria for a just war: *persona* (role or character), *res* (object or thing), *causa* (cause or reason), *animus* (spirit or mind), and *auctoritas* (authority). First, war had to be fought by laymen, not members of the priesthood. Second, the purpose of war had to be to recover stolen property or to defend the country or the Church. Third, a just cause required that war be necessary. Fourth, Christians should not go to war to punish, but to make whole. Fifth, a prince, king, or emperor of proper authority had to declare war. Rather than focus on the substantive causes for war, just war theology concentrated on the jurisdiction of princes, kings, popes, or emperors to legally start war. A war's justice became the proper consideration of soldiers and vassals, who could suffer spiritually for following a superior's orders in an unjust conflict.[53] Due to the personal spiritual responsibility of the individual, war became an aggregation of many conflicts between soldiers as well as states. For them, a legal war narrowed down to an analysis of the legitimate political authority to declare public hostilities rather than whether the causes of war were just.[54]

Even as these writers narrowed the scope of a legal war, they conceived of self-defense differently. Repelling attack became understood as part of the natural law, which did not need to meet any of the five requirements for just war.[55] John of Legnano, a fourteenth-century professor at the University of Bologna, viewed self-defense as a "particular war" waged by a single individual, as opposed to a "universal war" by a whole community, which derived from the individual right of self-preservation.[56] Without self-defense as a possible *causa*, just war resembled dispute resolution or law enforcement. A just cause for war sought compensation for a previous harm or to enforce rights. The Crusades assumed the status of a war of self-defense because popes considered the Holy Lands to belong to Christendom.[57]

It was the task of St. Thomas Aquinas, in his *Summa Theologiae* of the latter half of the thirteenth century, to codify these different strands in Christian approaches to war. As others have observed, Aquinas sought to harmonize canonical teachings with the views of Aristotle and natural law.[58] He accepted St. Augustine's view that war is not a sin when it is: (1) waged by a public authority; (2) for the purpose of punishing wrongdoers; and (3) with the intent of securing peace and helping the good or avoiding evil.[59] Aquinas referred to the second factor as just cause: "those against whom war is to be waged must deserve to have war waged against them because of some wrongdoing."[60] Quoting St. Augustine, he observed: "A just war is customarily defined as one which avenges injuries, as when a nation or state deserves to be punished because it has neglected either to punish the wrongs done by its people or to restore what it has unjustly seized."[61] Aquinas accepted the punitive character of war, but he also expanded upon the duty of kings and princes to maintain the public good by killing malefactors (just as a doctor could amputate a diseased limb), maintaining order and peace, and preserving the Christian faith.[62]

Some have agued that the Thomistic approach to war only restated conventional Christian understandings. It is also important to understand that Aquinas did not address temporal law, only religious and moral obligation. To Aquinas, the issue that drew the most attention from medieval lawyers—the *auctoritas principis* of secular leaders—merited little discussion. Instead, Aquinas provided a comprehensive moral restatement of the Christian approach to war, which provided the jumping-off point for later scholars. That thinking culminated in the work of two Spanish monks, Francisco de Vitoria and Francisco Suarez, as the West emerged into the modern world.

Spain's conquest of the New World prompted Vitoria to address just war. In two works, "On the Indians Lately Discovered" and "On the War Made by the Spaniards on the Barbarians," Vitoria outlined how the Spanish empire in the Americas could yet become just. But first, Vitoria disputed the asserted justifications for the Spanish conquest: the Holy Roman emperor or the pope possessed the whole world and could grant the Americas to Spain; a right of discovery applied to lands already peopled by the Indians; the Spanish had a right to conquer non-Christians and stop their violations of natural law; the Indians were already Spanish subjects.[63] Even accepting Augustine's and Aquinas's punitive purposes for just war, the Indians had not inflicted any harm upon Spain.[64] Instead, Vitoria concluded that Spain could resort to armed force because the Indians sought to exclude her citizens from travel, trade, settlement, and propagation of the faith in the Americas. The Indians, however, might reasonably use force to defend themselves from the strange, threatening Spanish. In a departure from the law-enforcement approach of earlier medieval thinkers, Vitoria raised the possibility that both sides of a conflict might have a just cause.[65]

Suarez rejected Vitoria's notion that a war could be just on both sides. Writing only a few years before the publication of Grotius's *De Jure Belli ac Pacis* (On the Law of War and Peace), Suarez stressed that war was the outcome of a judicial process between contending nations.[66] War amounts to a judgment against a wrongdoing nation, and therefore a just cause could only benefit the nation that had suffered harm. Although they disagreed on this point, Vitoria and Suarez still shared an important overall assumption. For Vitoria, a just war did not seek vindication through the law of nations. Its justice remained a matter for the *forum conscientiae*, the forum of conscience, not law.[67] Similarly, Suarez's just war did not rely on a legal system for existence. It remained the domain of popes and priests, who enforced the rules through excommunication, the threat of eternal damnation, or the release of subjects from their duty of loyalty.[68]

Just war theory from its ancient origins through the medieval period bears striking differences from the just war of today. Just war emerged from the obligations of individual morality or religion; it had little purchase as a legal rule that governed relations between states. Indeed, the idea that war must have a just cause demanded little attention in legal and political practice. Greeks held no concept that a legal war must have a just cause, while the Romans viewed the idea as a matter for religious ceremony, one that might be readily manipulated. While medieval thinkers refined and extended the theory, just war still primarily held sway over the individual conscience. The causes justifying a legal war went largely unexplored, in contrast to long debates over process and form—whether the proper public authorities had declared the start of hostilities. Contemporary appeals to just war restraints, as embodied in public international law or the UN Charter, invoke a doctrine ripped from its intellectual and historical moorings.

II. From the Early Modern Period to the Twentieth Century

The Protestant Reformation and the rise of the modern state led to fundamental changes in the European view of the relationship between justice and war. As the hold of claims of papal supremacy in theological and political matters weakened, and as national sovereigns concentrated control over the instruments of violence in their hands, the question of "justice" came to have less importance in the conduct of international relations. Indeed, by the early twentieth century, international law had come to hold that the decision of whether to wage war was a prerogative whose exercise lay within the discretion of every sovereign state.[69] This right was considered to be an essential element of sovereignty, if not indeed sovereignty's "ultimate expression and prerogative."[70] Although statesmen continued to justify their decisions to wage war in moral terms, no "cause" was considered necessary for war to be lawful. For the prominent English publicist John Westlake, attempts "to determine in the name of international law the conditions on which a recourse may be had to arms, as that an offer of arbitration shall have been made," merely represented "the counsel of morality," not "rules of law."[71]

At least three major interacting trends in thinking about international relations brought about this transformation. First, the rise of modern public international law, especially in the work of Hugo Grotius (1583–1645), rejected just war theory. Second, the shift in emphasis away from *jus ad bellum*, which can also be credited largely to Grotius, led to a growing preoccupation with *jus in bello*. Third, two approaches to international relations emerged: *raison d'état*, or reason of state, and balance of power theory. Both of these doctrines served, as just war theory had aimed to do, to limit the occasions of war.

A. Public International Law

Hugo Grotius was, and remains, a vastly influential presence in international law and political theory.[72] Yet he is difficult to interpret. Philosopher Michael Walzer and others claim that Grotius "incorporated just war theory into international law."[73] Other readings, however, suggest that Grotius did not spurn war. Philosopher Richard Tuck argues that Grotius's "*De Jure Belli ac Pacis* reminded his audience that he was still an enthusiast for war around the globe."[74] Grotius's law of nations arguably overturned traditional just war theory.[75] Yet, he did not openly display a revolutionary intent, which leads some today to include him in the tradition of Cicero, Augustine, Aquinas, and the Spanish theologians. But Grotius did not so much codify just war theory as weaken it by declaring that disputes between parties over the justness of a war were irresolvable.

At first, Grotius's *De Jure Belli ac Pacis* appears to follow earlier writers. Rejecting Christian claims against all war, Grotius writes:

> In the first principles of nature there is nothing which is opposed to war; rather, all points are in its favor. The end and aim of war being the preservation of life and limb, and the keeping or acquiring of things useful to life, war is in perfect accord with those principles of nature.[76]

Grotius relies on authorities, both ancient and biblical, to defend his argument that nations could use force for self-defense as well as for defending others and protecting ambassadorial missions. At the same time, however, Grotius limited the law of nature with "right reason" and "the nature of society," which "do not prohibit all use of force, but only that use of force which is in conflict with society, that is, which attempts to take away the rights of others."[77]

Grotius's invocation of natural law has led some scholars to place him comfortably in the natural law tradition on just war. "Grotius held that war is justifiable when, and only when, it serves right. Since the conditions for service to right are numerous and nonobvious, he must expend considerable effort identifying and explicating them."[78] Grotius's approach is not fundamentally different, but he went to greater lengths than any before him to lay out the various just causes for war.[79] He expanded the just causes for war not only to include self-defense from a current attack but also to prevent a future harm or to punish a past one, and even to enforce significant natural law rights.[80] Even under this interpretation, Grotius's theory of just war becomes thinner by enlarging the just causes for war, though it also forbids a state to defend itself if attacked by an aggressor who was "serviceable to many."[81] But contrary to traditional just war doctrine, Grotius would be understood to permit preemptive and preventive wars.[82]

Other statements have led some commentators to detect in Grotius a narrowing of just war doctrine that renders most wars illegal. Relying on the ancients such as Cicero and Aristotle, Grotius finds that wars of self-defense are legal. He even quotes the ancient philosopher and physician, Galen, for the proposition that "man is an animal born for peace and war." On the other hand, if Grotius believes that wars that violate the rights of others are not justified under international law, then he has narrowed just war doctrine to self-defense. Such comments have led some modern commentators to argue that Grotius indeed limited the scope for *jus ad bellum* well beyond where the Spanish commentators had left things. According to early twentieth-century international lawyer Hersch Lauterpacht, "there breathes from the pages of *De Jure Belli ac Pacis*, a disapproval amounting to hatred, of war."[83] Contemporary philosopher Larry May argues that Grotius is a "contingent pacifist" who does not object to war in principle, but finds most of them unjustified in practice.[84]

When we apply Grotius's views to the real world of international relations, however, we find that he did not limit just war so sharply. First, Grotius recognized that a just cause for war included not only self-defense but also "the obtaining of that which belongs to us or is our due, and the inflicting of punishment."[85] Here, Grotius drew his grounds for a just cause from the natural law right of an individual to defend his or her life and property. Nations could direct wars of "punishment" against those whom the laws of nature allow anyone to exact a sanction, against those who have harmed the nation in the past, and against those who injure mankind as a whole.[86] Grotius's version of just war theory did anything but narrow the grounds for war—it expanded them beyond only self-defense.

Second, and more important, Grotius's approach to just cause contains the seeds of just war's undoing. The key problem rests with Grotius's answer to the question of whether "[w]ar cannot be just on both sides, just as a legal claim cannot."[87] That assumption is crucial to any genuine theory of just war, because the very point is to identify which of two belligerents is acting rightly in deciding to wage war, and which has the obligation to surrender.[88] But for Grotius, the question does not generally yield an answer. Even though two sides of a case cannot both be right, he observes, "yet it may actually happen that neither of the warring parties does wrong." Instead, "no one acts unjustly without knowing that he is doing an unjust thing, but in this respect many are ignorant," Grotius concludes. "Thus either party may justly, that is in good faith, plead his case."[89] Typically, therefore, all belligerents will claim to be in the right, and neutral third parties will be reluctant to decide between them.[90] "When two States are engaged in War," he wrote, "it would be dangerous for any other to pronounce on the Justice of their Cause, for by that Means that State might quickly be involved in a War with other People."[91]

Sovereignty and the legality of war in general produce the situation where both sides might go to war with just cause. In the absence of any higher sovereign who has the power to evaluate the claims and control the actions of nation-states, the latter can lawfully do as they please; like kings, they are answerable to no one else.[92] Grotius implies that even if men could distinguish between the justness of two nations' claims, no earthly power can restrain them. The law of nations can help contending nations settle their disputes through negotiation, diplomatic conferences, arbitration, or even by lot or single combat.[93] But Grotius accepted that war itself might erupt when peaceful alternatives were exhausted. "The sources from which wars arise are as numerous as those from which lawsuits spring," Grotius observed, making the comparison between legal dispute resolution and international conflict explicit. "[F]or where judicial settlement fails, war begins."[94] Thus, just war theory cannot be invoked to decide which belligerent may lawfully wage war and which must concede once nations resort to force. For Grotius, just war theory is like pacifism: it is a doctrine that, whatever its attractions might be, is impracticable in conducting relations between sovereign states in the real world.[95] Furthermore, Grotius maintains that just war theory itself may contribute to the likelihood and ferocity of war, since men are more apt to wage war, and to fight with greater violence and tenacity, if they think their cause is just.[96] The bitter religious and ideological struggles of the Thirty Years' War, which Grotius himself witnessed, must have underscored that view.

For Grotius, the justice of war became a question of formalities. Although he fully recognized that war could in fact be waged without formalities, he believed that certain procedures were required to give war a lawful character. The main formal conditions were that the war be made on both sides by sovereign states and that it be duly declared. The existence of declarations by proper public authorities sufficed, for Grotius, to license warring states in harming each other; no reference to substantive "justice" on either side was needed. But because each side could appeal to a just cause, and Grotius had expanded the list of such causes, observation of the formalities meant that just war theory could not meaningfully restrain nations' decision to go to war. As Yoram Dinstein comments, Grotius and other natural law writers of this period "brought the just war doctrine in international law to a *cul de sac*."[97]

B. Jus in Bello

What now constitutes the corpus of international *jus in bello* began to take shape in early modern Europe between, roughly, 1550 and 1700. A new normative framework for the emerging European states system was necessary not only to "fill[] the void created by the collapse of the unity and authority provided by the Church of Rome" but also to accommodate the growing centralization of military power and domestic legitimacy in territorially based states.[98] The search for new rules to govern the conduct of hostilities, abundantly evident in Grotius's work, reflects the interests of such states both in limiting the pervasiveness of "private" violence, and in applying standards of instrumental rationality to their violence against each other.[99]

Any emerging European tradition of *jus in bello* firmly drew upon the past. British military historian Geoffrey Parker argues that "the laws in war in Europe have rested since the Middle Ages upon the same five foundations." First, prescriptive texts, including the Bible, Roman law, canon law, and the writings of St. Augustine and St. Thomas Aquinas set the foundations for the law of nature, the law of nations, and the laws of war. Second, the Catholic Church promoted two movements to limit war: the Peace of God taught that no harm should come to the weak who could cause no harm; and the Truce of God, which restricted war between Christians only to certain weekdays. Third, the armed forces of nations and empires issued military manuals and articles of war that set their own rules for war, including obeying superiors and God, vigilance, loyalty, and humanity to civilians. Fourth, nations developed customs arising from the Western practice of war. Fifth, combatants grew in their appreciation of the advantages of restraint in warfare, including honoring truces and surrenders and sparing captives and the wounded, which created a framework of expected behavior that reduced the chaos and danger of war.[100]

Contrary to those who trace a consistent lineage of just war theory from the ancients to the moderns, the Reformation and afterward saw a decided turn away from *jus ad bellum* and toward the development, and eventually the codification, of *jus in bello*. Legal scholars Stephen Neff and Yoram Dinstein, among others, observe that by the end of the eighteenth century, the natural law tradition no longer constrained states in their decisions to go to war.[101] Several reasons lay behind this turn. First, as we have just seen, there was a growing skepticism about the feasibility or even desirability of framing standards of substantive justice to govern international relations. Second, the very prevalence of *jus ad bellum* theory in Europe before the seventeenth century had inhibited the growth of *jus in bello*.[102] As Inis Claude argues, there is a conceptual, not merely a historical, connection between the rise of one and the waning of the other: war is more likely to be regulated when it is not forbidden.[103] Just war theory intrinsically tends to weaken the inhibitions of a belligerent, believing itself to be required or permitted to wage war, against using the most dreadful measures available. On the other hand, if an unjust war is forbidden, there is no need to regulate its violence. Finally, instrumental rationality combined with religious and humanitarian feelings to minimize suffering and loss of life in war. Why go to unnecessary extremes of atrocity and destructiveness when: military victory could be obtained without such harm; a more lenient policy could forestall retaliation; peace would be more durable if the defeated side had fewer memories of the victor's harshness; and the evil reputation that a belligerent would earn for exceptional cruelty in warfare could be avoided?[104] Economy in the use of force seemed to dictate the same methods as moral restraint.

This new spirit of moderation in warfare infused even Spain, which, by the seventeenth century, labored under the odium of being particularly cruel and ferocious in war.[105] Painfully aware of this reputation, Spanish rulers and generals consciously sought to overcome it. Thus, historian John Nef pointed to "the presence of a new chivalry—adjusted to novel and horrible weapons, hitherto unused" in Diego Velásquez's great painting from (perhaps) 1634–1635, *The Surrender at Breda* (*Las Lancas*). *Las Lancas* portrayed the surrender in 1625 of the defeated Dutch forces under Justin of Nassau to the Italian aristocrat and Spanish commander, the Marquis of Spinola.[106] General Spinola's terms for the garrison's surrender were magnanimous—reflecting, perhaps, seventeenth-century Spanish ideals for the treatment of defeated enemies. "In spite of the religious wars [of the seventeenth century]," Nef writes, "Europeans had at their disposal remnants of the medieval conception of universal Christian community. They also had remnants of the old chivalry and the pageantry that accompanied it."[107]

Others, while recognizing that a new humanitarian spirit was at work in Europe by the seventeenth century, attributed its origin to more secular causes. Notable among these was the great nineteenth-century Prussian strategist, Carl von Clausewitz. Clausewitz recognized that the seventeenth century had seen the beginning of a new rationality and humaneness in warfare. But he ascribed this less to a lingering tradition of Christian chivalry than to what he called "intelligence":[108]

> It had ceased to be in harmony with the spirit of the times to plunder and lay waste the enemy's land, which had played such an important role in antiquity, in Tartar days and indeed in medieval times. It was rightly held to be unnecessarily barbarous, an invitation to reprisals, and a practice that hurt the enemy's subjects rather than their government—one therefore that was ineffective and only served permanently to impede the advance of general civilization. Not only in its means, therefore, but also in its aims, war increasingly became limited to the fighting force itself. Armies, with their fortresses and prepared positions, came to form a state within a state, in which violence gradually faded away.[109]

Clausewitz was aware that, even if eighteenth-century intra-European war was "limited," the advent of the French Revolution and of Napoleon had changed all of that. For the first time in centuries (or perhaps ever), European war had become "total," in that one state pitted the entirety of its people and its resources against another.[110] Indeed, the very scale and intensity with which the French nation and people fought those wars may be due, in part, to their perception that they were engaging in a new species of "just war."[111]

Yet even the Revolutionary and Napoleonic Wars did not permanently arrest the trend toward a more developed humanitarian legal regime for war. Gradually but insistently, throughout the latter half of the nineteenth century, military manuals and, thereafter, multilateral treaties began to codify *jus in bello*.[112] Thus appeared such landmark instruments as the 1863 Lieber Code—used by the Union Army in the American Civil War,[113] which is regarded as the origin of "Hague Law;" the 1864 Geneva Convention for the Amelioration of the Condition of the Wounded in Armies in the Field,[114] from which later "Geneva Law" derives; and the 1868 Declaration of St. Petersburg,[115] which introduced restrictions on the use of certain types of weaponry in war. The Hague Conferences of 1899 and 1907 issued important conventions that regulate the conduct of warfare and the use of weaponry, including the 1907 Convention (IV) with Respect to the Laws and Customs of War on Land.[116] The codification of *jus in bello* thus attained new heights even as the doctrine of just war theory approached its nadir.

C. Reason of State

Reason of state, or *raison d'état*, can be described as the doctrine of the primacy of the state over all competing interests or considerations. Or, in Kenneth Waltz's formulation, "the conditions of international politics [do not] permit statesmen to think and act in terms of the moral and legal principles that may be both serviceable and acceptable in domestic politics."[117] Like medieval just war theory, the doctrine was addressed to rulers and their advisers. It instructed them to pursue the interests of the state (France, for example) above the interests of other claimants to their loyalty, such as the papacy, as well as dynastic or personal interests. Moreover, it dictated a policy driven by rationality rather than by passion or whim.

Although sometimes understood as a description of how states do or even must behave, it is better seen, and in its origins it was seen, as normative guidance for how states should behave.[118] One normative justification offered for the reason of state doctrine was, therefore, that the rational pursuit of a state's goals in international relations tends toward the limitation of war and the mitigation of its horrors. Another justification was that the doctrine admonished statesmen "to carry out a foreign policy in the interest of the whole nation and not just in the selfish interests of the ruling elite."[119]

Reason of state originated in the post-Reformation period while the modern European state was still forming. Other powerful actors in European affairs, including the papacy and the Holy Roman Empire, were pressing competing claims to universal loyalty and obedience over the heads of local rulers. Likewise, political actors at the substate level, such as local lords and magnates, sought to command the population's allegiance and to extract its resources. The reason of state doctrine legitimized the priority of the king's claims over the competing claims of the Church, the Empire, and the aristocracy. In return for the subject's undivided loyalty, a king promised that he and his forces would provide the population with security within the borders of his realm. Reason of state enabled the ruler to make good on that promise.

It is also important to see that the doctrine (again, like just war theory) "represented an attempt to order policy to cope with a universal predisposition to conflict."[120] Conflict was understood to arise from "passion," which could most effectively be checked by the sober, farsighted, and "interest"-based calculations of "reason."[121] For example, "reason of state" counseled kings to observe the treaties that they had made: the long-term reputational advantages of treaty compliance were seen generally to outweigh the benefits of breaking a treaty in order to exploit another state's momentary weakness, despite the opportunity for making conquests that such vulnerability might seem to afford.[122]

Finally, "reason of state" represented an attempt to solve, or at least to mitigate, a problem inherent in the theory and practice of an emerging royal absolutism. If the Church, feudal custom, and the law could no longer check the power of the monarch (as in the premodern period), how could monarchy be distinguished from tyranny?[123] Reason of state doctrine, which purported to identify an objective and rational standard that the monarch could grasp and follow, was one of three overlapping solutions; the other two were "princely virtue," which attempted to instill the habits of self-restraint in the monarch, and "enlightened despotism," which sought to direct absolute power to the pursuit of the common good.[124] Reason of state bore strong affinities with the rise of other secular developments in thinking on war, such as an international law based on national sovereignty, the turn toward *jus in bello* rules, and Clausewitz's application of rational instrumentalism to war. Like these other changes, reason of state sought to render the rules of *jus ad bellum* more rational and to distance them from their religious roots.

Although reason of state doctrine has long been condemned as immoral, its most thoughtful defenders have seen it as a necessary, indeed virtuous, response to a tragic situation. Discussing Machiavelli, Waltz posed the question: "Why should the success of the prince in establishing internal order and contriving a defense against external enemies be taken as the criterion by which any act [of statecraft] can be justified? Why define success in terms of princely or state interest instead of, say, in terms of living a moral life?"[125] Machiavelli's answer, said Waltz, appealed to the desperate straits of Italy of the fifteenth and sixteenth centuries. Italy was, Machiavelli said, "a country without dykes or banks of any kind" to be used against foreign foes; had she been "protected by proper measures, like Germany, Spain, and France, this inundation...would not have happened at all."[126] In conditions in which a state is unable to defend its people from devastating and repeated foreign invasion, there is no possibility for its citizens to live with a measure of independence, decency and virtue. To secure the state against the ruthless foreign enemies, Machiavelli argued, Italy's rulers must prove to be no less unscrupulous than their opponents. As Waltz put it, "[i]f by cruelty the dykes and banks are built and kept in good repair, then cruelty is the greatest mercy. If by practicing virtue they are torn down again, then virtue is the greatest vice."[127]

Paradoxically, the "immoral" reason of state doctrine offered a plausible and attractive alternative to just war theory. Its exponents could argue that it was at least as well suited as the more traditional doctrine to limit war and preserve peace. By forcing rulers to meet the exacting standards of rationality, it discouraged dynastic wars and forced them to consider the best interests of their peoples. Its regular practice instilled virtues that tended to promote peaceable habits, including fidelity to treaties and a willingness to negotiate. It served to protect the state and its people from foreign aggression. And it enabled kings building nation-states to justify their claims to rule instead of the pope, the emperor, or the aristocracy.

D. Balance of Power

Like the reason of state doctrine (to which it was both historically and conceptually linked), balance of power theory emphasized the security of individual states against the encroachments of other states or empires seeking to aggrandize themselves. And like reason of state, it counseled rationality and long-term calculation in the pursuit of self-interest. An individual state survived by maintaining the existence of the system against the domination of any single member. Although balance of power thinking accepted the inevitability of war, including preventive war, it kept the peace by offering a permanent check on individual states' drive for self-aggrandizement.[128]

Balance of power doctrine has been in the making for centuries. Waltz finds Thucydides expounding the doctrine in the fifth century BCE and Polybius in the second century BCE.[129] As early as the fifteenth century, European statesmen began to think of international relations in terms of a "balance of power" as a means to maintain peace and prevent one state from dominating others. In his 1612 *De Jure Belli Libri Tres* (Three Books on the Law of War), renowned international lawyer Alberico Gentili argued that the European states were justified in resisting the claims to universal domination by Spain on the one side and the Ottoman Empire on the other. Balance of power theory reached new heights in the eighteenth century, and the policy of maintaining the balance "appeared to many observers as something with moral justification of its own, almost independent of any practical value it might have."[130] In other eighteenth-century formulations, however, the balance of power was more mechanical and automatic than moral and voluntary. It was compared to gravitational forces in the planetary system or to the "invisible hand" that transformed selfish market choices into socially beneficent outcomes.[131] As Jean-Jacques Rousseau put it, "[t]he balance existing between the power of these diverse members of the European society is much more a work of nature than of art. It maintains itself without effort, in such a manner that if it sinks on one side, it reestablishes itself very soon on the other."[132] Balance of power posited a natural process of alliance diplomacy that ensured that no single power would remain unchecked if it sought to take excessive advantage of its superior position and capabilities.

Even in its eighteenth-century heyday, however, balance of power theory had severe critics. Immanuel Kant rejected the idea that "a so-called European balance of power" could bring permanent, universal peace. That notion, he said, was "a pure illusion."[133] Kant was appalled by the partitions of Poland by Prussia, Russia, and Austria, which led to the utter annihilation of Poland as a state—the very sort of outcome that the balance of power was supposed to prevent.[134] Some studies also suggest that the balance of power system that prevailed in Europe for most of the eighteenth century was in fact far more violent and war-prone than the Concert of Europe system that superseded it after the defeat of Napoleon and the great peace settlement at the Congress of Vienna in 1815.[135] As one scholar has written, "[b]alance-of-power politics—the politics of confrontation—generated intolerable international tensions, produced increasingly serious armed conflicts, and inspired progressively extravagant plans of aggression. It neither maintained peace nor preserved the independence of sovereign states; by the time of the French Revolution, the international system had broken down altogether."[136]

Scholars disagree over whether the nineteenth-century Concert of Europe differed from the eighteenth-century balance of power. One possible understanding is that the Congress of Vienna consciously sought to create a rough equality of power among the leading states, thus institutionalizing a mechanism that made it easier for blocking coalitions to be formed against a potential hegemon.[137] This view encounters the problem, however, that the settlement at Vienna left two of the great powers—Britain and Russia—stronger than any of the others.[138] In any event, whether conceived of as a balance of power system or as a distinctive kind of international order, the Concert brought Europe a "long peace" of almost a century (1815–1914) without a major war involving all of the great European powers. Of course, Europe was not free from conflict even during this period. Several smaller wars broke out, such as the Crimean War (1853–1856) and the Franco-Prussian War (1870–1871), and the system could not prevent the seeds of conflict that would explode in 1914. The Concert might have required some level of limited armed conflict as nations adjusted their coalitions against each other and measured each other's resources and political will. Nevertheless, it prevented any major great power war of the kind that had afflicted Europe for centuries and would destroy the continent in the next.

Like just war theory, balance of power doctrine offered a compelling normative goal: the maintenance of European-wide peace, together with the preservation of the liberty and independence of states great and small. Yet it could seem more practical than just war theory because it prescribed state conduct not on the basis of disputable moral judgments but by reference to the measurable phenomena of relative state power. Finally, although balance of power doctrine, unlike traditional just war theory, should permit preventive wars to maintain or restore balance, it should also limit such wars because they ought to stop when the balance was reestablished, rather than putting the enemy state's existence at risk.[139] Together, Grotian international law, the rise of *jus in bello*, reason of state, and balance of power thinking overshadowed traditional just war theory from the early modern period onward.

In the period from the Protestant Reformation to the early twentieth century, like the period from antiquity to the late middle ages, the moral and religious underpinnings of just war theory had little discernible influence on the actual conduct of states. The rise of the modern state and the decline of the Catholic Church as an arbiter of international affairs further robbed just war doctrine of practical import. European states went to war against each other regularly from the sixteenth century to the twentieth with little to no heed to the requirements of just war teaching. Eighteenth-century European wars, such as those of Louis XIV of France, were fought for purposes of dynastic glory, the acquisition of territory and populations, or the maintenance of the balance of power. Nineteenth-century European wars, such as the Napoleonic Wars, were fought to prevent one power from dominating the continent or to forge modern nation-states like Germany and Italy. Preventive wars that would surely have been condemned by classical just war theorists were not merely common, but an accepted and legitimate method of statecraft. When asked for his views on Polish nationalism, the German Chancellor Otto von Bismarck replied that while he had no particular hostility toward it, if the state of Poland were reconstituted, he would strangle it in its cradle.[140] Furthermore, European states in this period waged almost-incessant wars of conquest and annexation outside Europe with little to no consideration to the demands of elementary humanity. They overran the Americas, conquered the Indian subcontinent, partitioned Africa, and divided much of China and the Ottoman Empire into "spheres of influence." Although the doctrines of *jus in bello*, reason of state, and balance of power probably exerted some restraining effects on these actions (particularly within Europe itself), just war doctrine seems to have had a negligible impact.

III. Just War Doctrine and Collective Security

The picture begins to change with the First World War. The final collapse of the Concert discredited the idea of maintaining peace through a balance of power. President Woodrow Wilson took the view that the war was largely due to the inherent instabilities of an international order based on shifting alliances and efforts to balance power. In his celebrated "Peace Without Victory" speech of January 22, 1917, Wilson said:

The question upon which the whole future peace and policy of the world depends is this: Is the present war a struggle for a just and secure peace, or only for a new balance of power? If it be only a struggle for a new balance of power, who will guarantee, who can guarantee the stable equilibrium of the new arrangement? Only a tranquil Europe can be a stable Europe. There must be, not a balance of power but a community power; not organized rivalries but an organized, common peace.[141]

Victory did not change Wilson's mind. In his speech presenting the Versailles Treaty to the Senate on July 10, 1919, Wilson singled out the balance of power as the War's cause:

> [The sacrifices of the War] had been exacted because one nation desired dominion and other nations had known no means of defense except armaments and alliances. War had lain at the heart of every arrangement of Europe,—of every arrangement of the world,—that preceded the war. Restive peoples had been told that fleets and armies, which they had toiled to sustain, meant peace; and they now knew that they had been lied to: that fleets and armies had been maintained to promote national ambitions and meant war. They knew that no old policy meant anything else but force, force,—always force. . . . A war in which they had been bled white to beat the terror that lay concealed in every Balance of Power must not end in mere victory of arms and a new balance.[142]

Wilson was not alone in his conclusion.[143]

But Wilson's objections to the prewar international system ran even deeper than hostility to the balance of power. His conception of the postwar settlement called for more than merely an end to balance of power politics, "cabinet" diplomacy, and the pursuit of national interest. Wilson sought a revival of just war theory. In a manner reminiscent of the medieval philosophers, Wilson viewed aggressive war as a criminal activity. Defensive war represented prosecution and punishment of aggression. When America entered the war, Wilson held the view that the "military masters" of Germany were responsible for the conflict, but that the German people, as their mere "pawns and tools," could not be held to blame. As the war progressed, however, he concluded that the German people were behind their rulers' militarism. Consistent with his view of Germany as a criminal nation, Wilson considered himself and his Allied colleagues to be "sitting as judges" at the Versailles Conference. He was immovable "precisely on those questions that the Germans objected to most vigorously—questions that had a punitive character and involved national honor and prestige, such as exclusion from the League of Nations, the trial of the emperor, the delivery of war criminals, and of course the war-guilt clause of Article 231 [of the Treaty of Versailles]."[144] At the end of the Versailles peace conference, Wilson declared that the terms were "very hard, it is true, but at the same time every one must realize that the Germans themselves had brought on this horrible war, and that they had violated all ethics of international law and international procedure, and had created a series of crimes that had amazed and shocked beyond belief all the people of the world."[145]

Wilsonianism inspired later twentieth-century attempts to create new forms of international security and to frame new doctrines of international law, including the Covenant of the League of Nations, the Kellogg-Briand Pact and, eventually, the UN Charter. Although more of a realist about the potential of international organizations than Wilson had been, President Franklin Roosevelt echoed Wilsonian themes. Reporting on the Yalta Conference to a joint session of Congress on March 1, 1945, FDR declared that the creation of the UN "spells—and it ought to spell—the end of the system of unilateral action, exclusive alliances, and spheres of influence, and Balances of power, and all the other expedients which have been tried for centuries and have always failed."[146]

Some believe that the League of Nations, and still more the UN, reflect a return to just war doctrine and represent its incorporation into international law. Certainly, there were those who, in the immediate aftermath of the First World War, advocated that just war doctrine should be embedded into the rules that govern nations.[147] Even now there are many who think that the UN Security Council has something of the moral and legal authority on war that once the medieval papacy and empire possessed. In a particularly clear statement of this view, the contemporary British scholar Oliver O'Donovan writes:

> Nowadays any power contemplating a resort to war has more than a hypothetical or informal judgment to think about. Just as in the Middle Ages there was a Pope and a Holy Roman Emperor, whose authorization in these matters counted for something, so today there is the United Nations Organisation and its Security Council. To the judgment of this body there belongs not merely moral but positive authority, grounded originally in treaty. Its Charter claims for it the sole right to authorize or use armed force against states other than that undertaken for self-defence against armed attack. A belligerent power, then, ought to be prepared to defer to it, even if it sometimes rules in a way that a truly impartial and well-informed judge would not have ruled.[148]

This view mistakes the UN Charter's prohibition on the use of force for traditional just war doctrine. The Security Council, as a political body, possesses nothing like the moral authority or sanction of a pope, emperor, or judge, nor does the council follow the prescriptions of just war teaching in its practices. It was never intended to enforce just war doctrine, nor is it legally required to do so. The UN Charter expresses an overriding commitment, not to the aim of ensuring that only just wars are waged, but rather to preserving the existing international order. Wars cannot pursue the nondefensive purposes of medieval just war, for example, such as protecting Christendom, punishing those who harm the innocent, or stopping great harm to populations. The UN Charter drains war of any moral content, the exact opposite of medieval just war doctrine. Rather than advance Christian values, war under the Charter elevates the international peace and security as the goal of the international system—even to the point where the Charter does not provide an exception to its protection of nation-state sovereignty for the prevention of genocide.

The international legal system does not regulate war to ensure that it serves as an instrument of justice. Instead, the UN Charter has become a legal mechanism for protecting state sovereignty against even the most compelling demands of human welfare. Instead of preventing or punishing atrocities, the Great Power politics that dominate Security Council deliberations serve only to conceal and shelter them. And the mistaken beliefs that the Charter is designed to regulate war-making in the name of justice, which itself is subject to competing interpretations, and that the council is generally successful in executing that task, serve only to obscure its radical defects. Even when the Security Council has authorized intervention to stop human rights abuses, such as in the former Yugoslavia, it has to characterize the action as restoring international peace and security.

A. Just War in the Twentieth Century

In order to truly understand the UN Charter, it is essential to recall its central purpose. This is stated in Chapter I:

> To maintain international peace and security, and to that end: to take effective collective measures for the prevention and removal of threats to the peace, and for the suppression of acts of aggression or other breaches of the peace....

In other words, the central purpose of the Charter is to prevent war, not to promote justice or correct injustice. The Charter, for example, does not provide exceptions to its protections for the territorial sovereignty and political independence to protect human rights or remove oppressive regimes, only for self-defense or to stop threats to international peace and security. During the San Francisco conference, the British and Soviet delegations successfully opposed U.S. proposals to allow intervention to stop human rights abuses because it would interfere with a sovereign's control over domestic affairs.[149] Recent scholarship even argues that the framers of the UN had other, perhaps unavowed, realpolitik purposes. International historian Mark Mazower argues that the UN owed its origin largely to the thought of British imperial internationalists who saw it as an organization that would protect the British Empire, cement its ties to the United States, and create a good working relationship with the world's other great power, the Soviet Union.[150] By the time of the 1956 crises in Hungary and Suez, Professor Julius Stone recognized "the persistent illegality and injustice which the extreme view [of the Charter] would require States to tolerate indefinitely."[151] If it could be argued that order and justice are sometimes at odds in the international system (but not always), the Charter makes a definite and unambiguous choice for the former.[152]

Assigning absolute priority to order over justice demonstrates just how far the UN Charter has ventured beyond traditional just war theory. Just war traditionally justified the use of force to serve the ends of corrective justice. Waging a just war is akin to prosecuting a crime and (if the war is successful) imposing a punishment on the offender that an impartial judge would find appropriate. Preserving peace is not the overriding priority. The established order may perpetuate the very injustice that a just war is intended to remedy; consequently, an offensive war may be as just as a defensive one.[153] The UN Charter scheme retains nothing of this conception of war.

Far from incorporating just war into international law, the Charter system obviates the need for the moral reasoning at the heart of the theory. "The just war thinker insists on the need for moral judgments, for figuring out who in fact in the situation at hand is behaving in a more or less unjust manner," writes Jean Bethke Elshtain; "[f]or the just war thinker, moral appeals are the heart of the matter."[154] The practical reasoning involved here must reflect the tension between a normative demand "to limit resort to arms" and a conflicting demand "to respond to the urgent requirements of justice."[155] But under the Charter scheme, there is no need for such moral deliberation and no occasion for weighing the harms of violence against the evils of injustice. The fact that a party has initiated a war is of itself sufficient to brand that party as the aggressor, though the system has difficulty in grappling with interventions short of war.[156] This is not to claim that the Charter has nothing to do with morality—the United Nations advances some important values in its health and educational activities—but only to show that it rejects such considerations with the use of force.

B. Just War Theory

Woodrow Wilson bears responsibility for just war doctrine's leapfrog into the twentieth century. Just as scholars are rediscovering Wilson's critical role in shaping the constitutional and political framework for the modern American state, so too should we appreciate Wilson's central position in the emergence of the post-World

War I international order.[157] The child of a Presbyterian minister who liberally sprinkled his addresses with references to the Old and New Testaments, Wilson is often portrayed as an inflexible moralist who launched the United States on a crusade "to make the world safe for democracy," as he put it when he announced U.S. entry into World War I. But Wilson was also a political scientist who had authored classic studies of American government. He had more than just morality in mind for his new world order. Wilson sought to reintroduce just war theory through the institution of the League of Nations to come to grips with a new world changed by industrialization, globalization, and imperialism. As Akira Iriye has argued, we should regard Wilson as an internationalist rather than an idealist—someone who believed that the new world that emerged from the ashes of World War I demanded more vigorous action from the world's most powerful nation.[158]

The conventional narrative maintains that America intervened in the Great War to protect neutral rights. Most assume that Wilson tried to keep the United States out of the fray and trade freely with both sides, but that Germany's campaign of unrestricted submarine warfare ultimately forced the United States to enter the war on the side of the Allies. But, as Walter MacDougall argues, Wilson's foreign policy is better understood as an effort to maximize American control over the peace.[159] Central to Wilson's vision was collective security. Just after the war started, Wilson wrote privately that he sought a peace settlement that included sovereign independence for all nations, no territorial conquest, and an "association of nations wherein all shall guarantee the territorial integrity of each."[160] In his January 1917 "Peace Without Victory" speech, Wilson rejected a peace that advanced the war aims of the combatants, and called for a doctrine of nonintervention in the affairs of other countries. He led the United States into war in April 1917 not because Germany's submarine warfare had suddenly become intolerable or because of a newfound desire to protect neutral rights, but because he came to the realization that the United States must fight to bring about the desired peace.[161] He made his object clear in his "Fourteen Points," which generally called for national self-determination in Europe, free trade and navigation, and a "general association of nations [that] must be formed under specific covenants for the purpose of affording mutual guarantees of political independence and territorial integrity to great and small states alike." On July 4, 1918, Wilson further explained that the postwar settlement would create a new international organization that would "make it certain that the combined power of free nations will check every invasion of right and serve to make peace and justice the more secure."[162]

Collective security became so central to Wilson's vision of the postwar order that it doomed the peace. Once Germany surrendered, the United States lost its leverage to dictate terms, while British Prime Minister Lloyd George and France's

Georges Clemenceau came to the conference after strong electoral showings at home. The Versailles Conference became the scene of another great power struggle over the fruits of victory, with even Britain and the United States competing for naval supremacy. Wilson, however, tolerated the harsh terms imposed on Germany in exchange for Allied acceptance of the League of Nations. He believed that the League, thus fortified, would be able to cure the ills of the Treaty of Versailles.[163] Not only did the League fail at the international level, but it also failed domestically. Republican senators rejected the treaty because of the collective security guarantee, even though they were not hostile to the tough terms on Germany or American membership in the League itself. They believed that Article X, which laid out collective security, should not replace the freedom of the United States to act on its own. As MacDougall argues, U.S. opponents believed the League required force to back up its terms, "in which case it was a league to make war, not peace," a futile goal because it attempted "to freeze the global status quo." It was poor policy because "it would involve the United States in conflicts where its interests were not at stake," and it violated congressional powers and conflicted with American exceptionalism and America's ability to act unilaterally, especially in the Western Hemisphere.[164]

Wilson refused to compromise over reservations to the League Treaty, which would have declared that the United States had the independent right to judge whether to go to war, to enforce the Monroe Doctrine, and to continue unilateral control over internal and economic matters. And so the League of Nations died in the United States. Why did Wilson gamble so much for the sake of collective security? While the conventional account blames his religious background, Wilson's political thought has much more to do with that background. Wilson, the former political scientist and Princeton president, was heavily influenced by the academy in his outlook. While a graduate student at Johns Hopkins, Wilson absorbed the theory that evolutionary forces governed political and social phenomena.[165] In *The State*, Wilson wrote: "Society, therefore, is compounded of the common habit and is an evolution of experience, an interlaced growth of tenacious relationships, a compact, living whole, structural, not mechanical."[166] Wilson also found inspiration in British thinkers, such as Burke and Gladstone, and that "natural law decreed a self-regulating world of free individuals, hence his devotion to free trade and hostility to big corporations, labor unions, and bureaucracy."[167] Merging Burkean thought with religious ideas, Wilson would come to the view that the "objective of international law" was to create "a moral and legal system" that led a "moral sense of community among states."[168] Wilson gave lectures on international law at Princeton from 1892 to 1894, which remained an important source of his worldview on international relations upon winning the presidency.

Scholars have identified additional influences on Wilson. Michael Desch posits that Immanuel Kant's essay "Perpetual Peace" and his idea of the "democratic peace"—that peace could be secured by promoting democracy throughout the world—heavily influenced Wilson's thinking on the League of Nations.[169] A peace movement, whose most famous member, William Jennings Bryan, was Wilson's first secretary of state, pressed for Anglo-American friendship, arbitration treaties, and a permanent court to settle disputes between nations, along with international treaties that would make wars difficult to start if not illegal.[170] Progressive internationalists (composed, in Knock's definition, of various groups of reformers, liberals, socialists, feminists, and pacifists) pushed for an international institution of some kind. When the Great War broke out, Theodore Roosevelt called for the establishment of "an efficient world league for the peace of righteousness" and criticized the balance of power system—though by November 1914, he had turned away from internationalism and demanded American entry on the side of the Allies.[171] Turn-of-the-century socialism, which advocated greater government control and ownership of big business and public promotion of labor rights, influenced Wilson's thought.[172] In his 1898 *The State*, Wilson advocated greater public intervention in the economy for the same reasons as socialists. "We ought to all regard ourselves as *socialists*," he wrote.[173] Leading figures of the Socialist Party of America had access to the Wilson White House, and even the President himself.[174] Intent on keeping a neutral America out of the war, Socialists anticipated much of Wilson's thinking. As early as 1914, the Socialist platform called for no change in territories without the consent of their peoples and the creation of an international organization to guarantee disarmament, democracy, and the political independence of nations.[175]

Republican internationalists, including leading Republican lawyers such as Elihu Root and former President William Howard Taft, agreed that international politics demanded a different set of rules and institutions. Some proposals modestly focused on an arbitral mechanism that would seek judicial resolution of disputes between nations, though a lack of meaningful enforcement measures would have made it an unlikely guardian against great power conflicts. Other ideas were more ambitious. Taft's followers, for example, founded the League to Enforce Peace, which called for an international assembly to pass legislation, the submission of disagreements between countries to a board for arbitration, and a commitment by members to prevent any military conflicts. Taft's vision called for a comprehensive international government of a kind that still has yet to exist, but it surely influenced Wilson to pursue a permanent postwar settlement that rejected balance of power or reason of state thinking. Wilson agreed that "we must begin with solemn covenants, covering mutual guarantees of political independence and territorial integrity," but without the constitution-like creation of legislatures, courts, and administrative procedures.[176] President Wilson may have shared the goals of America's internationalist lawyers, but he did not share their ambitious vision for world institutions that mimicked domestic government. Nonetheless, during this period, Wilson came to believe that an organization stronger than arbitral courts would become necessary to achieve the postwar revolution in international affairs.

While the idea of the League of Nations did not spring forth from his mind alone, Wilson was its most powerful adopter and he synthesized different elements to make it his own. He brought to the table a progressive's belief that government could cure a systemic social problem through rational planning and management. He started with the idea that the world had become a community of nations with certain shared principles and interests, prewar notions that had circulated among labor, peace, socialist, and progressive movements—often for different reasons and with different means in mind.[177] Because of the growing interconnection of the world (what we today might call globalization), Wilson believed that:

> [N]ever again would it be possible for the world at large to regard a quarrel between two nations as a particular and private quarrel, but that an attack in any quarter was an attack on the equilibrium of the world and that the safety of the world demanded such a combination of the force of the nations as would maintain peace throughout all the world.[178]

The only way to deter such conflicts in the future was through collective security.

It would be a mistake, however, to understand Wilsonianism as the product of the same legalistic mindset of Root or Taft.[179] American international lawyers during this period were coming to have a profound effect on U.S. foreign policy—every secretary of state between 1889 and 1945 was trained as a lawyer. They shared Wilson's suspicion of balance of power politics, with its dependence on force and coercion, and his solution in international law and institutions that would peacefully settle disputes. But Wilson's idea for a League that could conquer war flowed naturally from the Progressive Era's faith that man's technological conquest of nature would be matched by similar gains over society, economics, and politics.[180] Robert Wiebe's description of progressivism as a "search for order" took on an international as well as domestic dimension.[181] It blossomed not only in Wilson's management of World War I itself but also in his efforts to govern the peace.

As is well known, the League of Nations failed both in the United States and globally. In both cases, the collective security guarantee doomed the League. Under Article X signatories would "undertake to respect and preserve as against external aggression the territorial integrity and existing political independence" of all members. Republican senators refused to give their advice and consent to the treaty without a reservation that made clear that Article X did not obligate the United States to send troops abroad without congressional consent.[182] Some suggest that Wilson did not believe Article X could impose a legal obligation on the United States, which could block a League decision for war as a member of the League Council anyway. Nevertheless, Wilson would not compromise with Senator Henry Cabot Lodge of Massachusetts, who led the opposition (the two men despised each other). Wilson's inflexibility, on this issue and against all reservations, ensured the treaty's defeat.

Meanwhile, the League ultimately could not guard the peace. At first glance, the League seemed to create a new international order that still relied on the central foundations of the old. Five victorious powers—Britain, France, Italy, the United States, and Japan—drew up the agreement and each kept a seat on the nine-member council. Europe remained the center of the world, and the main players were still— aside from Japan—the European great powers.[183] While there was an assembly of all nations that would meet periodically, the powerful nations were to remain dominant. Great powers and the persistence of their politics emerged not just in the structure of the League's council but also in developments outside of it. Important military and political agreements continued to take place outside the League's framework, such as the Washington Naval Treaty of 1920 to limit fleet sizes, the Locarno Pact to guarantee European borders, and even the Kellogg-Briand Pact to outlaw war.

Most important, the League could not restrain war. Several of the great powers refused to follow League dictates, especially as authoritarian governments emerged in the 1930s with expansionist aims. Fascist Japan embarked on an effort to control East Asia by invading Manchuria in 1931 and then much of China. As a council member, Japan vetoed efforts to stop the aggression, and it soon left the League. Fascist Italy, one of the World War I Allies, invaded Ethiopia in 1935. Although the League attempted to impose economic sanctions against Italy, Germany and Japan refused to participate. Italy prevailed within a year and thereafter withdrew from the League. Upon Adolf Hitler's assumption of the chancellorship, Germany withdrew in 1933 after only gaining admission seven years earlier. It proceeded to seize Austria and Czechoslovakia before invading Poland and setting off World War II. Although the Soviet Union joined in 1934, it invaded Finland in 1940 and was thereupon expelled in one of the League's last, ineffectual, acts. The League Charter prevented it from compelling military action by member states to stop these invasions.

Despite its more open international nature, the League simply could not influence the great powers on these matters of state. Worst of all, the most powerful country in the world, the United States, never joined. Even if the absence of the United States had not crippled it, the League had no military forces at its disposal to cure the imbalance of power between a resurgent Germany and Britain and France. If anything might have halted the rise of the Axis powers, it might have been an American guarantee of British and French security. But the League could not draw in the two most powerful nations, the United States and the Soviet Union, to restore the balance of power in Europe.[184]

C. Collective Security and the United Nations

The League's record of failure, however, did not discourage the victorious WWII Allies from trying their hand at collective security again. After Pearl Harbor, historian Walter MacDougall observes, "the nation clambered back to Wilson's tent with the zeal of repentant sinners."[185] President Franklin Roosevelt made the creation of an international security organization a postwar priority. He followed the conventional wisdom that the American failure to join the League of Nations had allowed the rise of Germany and Japan, even though it is unclear whether American membership would have stopped the rise of Hitler. As early as the August 14, 1941, announcement of the Atlantic Charter, FDR agreed with British Prime Minister Winston Churchill to call for disarmament "pending the establishment of a wider and permanent system of general security."[186] Just two months before the Pearl Harbor attack, FDR approved the start of State Department planning for a postwar world order, and on January 1, 1942, the United States signed the United Nations Declaration, which committed two dozen nations to fighting the fascist powers to achieve the Atlantic Charter vision. Even while the fighting raged, FDR devoted considerable resources to developing an international structure that would keep the United States engaged in the world and prevent a repeat of the isolationism of the interwar years.

Over the next several years, American planners worked to improve upon, rather than reject, Wilson's basic plans for the League of Nations. In their minds, the League's decentralized structure and its lack of enforcement mechanisms had led to paralysis and the dodging of responsibility. They sought to remedy these defects by building a new body that might recognize the legal independence of all members, but that would prove less egalitarian on the matters that truly mattered.[187] Officials struggled over whether to make the future UN more universal or whether to rely on regional representation that would recognize spheres of influence and a balance of power among the great powers. As Mark Mazower has revealed, some leading British and Commonwealth officials hoped the UN would even preserve the British Empire or establish an Anglo-American co-dominium.[188] Churchill not only wanted to preserve the empire but also believed that regional organizations and alliance could provide the foundation for a balance of power.

As plans for the United Nations developed during the war, FDR remained convinced that the great powers would guarantee international security. A main theme of American thinking on the postwar world was that the new international organization should avoid utopianism in favor of realism. Roosevelt believed that the "Four Policemen"—the United States, USSR, Britain, and China—should maintain order and stability in the world. While he pursued Wilson's goals of collective security, national self-determination, disarmament, and freedom of commerce, FDR's acceptance of great power politics "turned Wilsonianism on its head."[189] He did not believe open diplomacy, the spread of democracy, and popular opinion would rule. Rather, the world would be governed by the four great powers with the threat of force behind them. In his Fireside Chat after the 1943 Tehran Conference, FDR told the American people that the Allies must remain "in complete agreement that we must be prepared to keep the peace by force." He specifically addressed the Four Policemen:

> Britain, Russia, China and the United States and their Allies represent more than three-quarters of the total population of the earth. As long as these four nations with great military power stick together in determination to keep the peace there will be no possibility of an aggressor nation arising to start another world war.[190]

While he rejected the idea that "the strong shall dominate the weak" in international affairs, he turned right around and made power the glue that would hold the world order together: "if force is necessary to keep international peace, international force will be applied—for as long as it may be necessary.[190]

FDR's realpolitik vision of the future found its expression in the basic structure of the UN. Thus, the General Assembly could make recommendations, but only the Security Council could require nations to act. World War II's victorious allies, responsible for maintaining the peace, would sit on the council with the authority to veto any of its decisions. FDR may have hoped that the Security Council would allow the great powers to jointly manage international security, but the veto could also render the UN paralyzed, which would allow the great powers to divide up the world into individual spheres of influence.[191] Historians continue to argue to this day over whether FDR was a naïve idealist when it came to the postwar settlement, and hence believed in a functioning UN, or whether he was a tough realist who understood that the latter outcome was the more likely. When it came time to negotiate the shape of the world organization in Dumbarton Oaks, the other Allies did not take as strong an interest as the United States delegation—the American draft became the foundation for the Charter.[192]

FDR also agreed with the common view that without a commitment to a postwar order, the United States would return to the same isolationism that had guaranteed the return of world war. The United Nations would keep the United States engaged in international affairs in Europe and Asia even after the guns fell silent. To prevent a repeat of history, FDR unknowingly repeated history. He again accommodated territorial demands in exchange for commitment to a new international organization. Even during the war, British and American officials drew the lesson from the League of Nations that postwar peace would fail without the participation of the United States and the Soviet Union. So at Yalta, FDR accepted Stalin's sphere of influence in Eastern Europe to win Soviet cooperation in the UN.[193] British officials were concerned more with keeping the United States enmeshed in an international institution than with the exact shape of its design. They would not be left, as they were after Wilson's failure, solely responsible for the balance of power in Europe.

Despite these changes in structure, the United Nations did not fundamentally alter the main goals of a world organization. The United Nations Charter maintained the League's guarantee of political independence and self-determination. It banned war, except in cases of self-defense. Force would remain the province of the Security Council, as would coercive measures short of war, such as economic sanctions. Article 42 declares that the Security Council "may take such action by air, sea, or land forces as may be necessary to maintain or restore international peace and security. Such action may include demonstrations, blockade, and other operations by air, sea, or land forces of Members of the United Nations."[194] Article 51, however, contained the great exception for self-defense: "Nothing in the present Charter shall impair the inherent right of individual or collective self-defence if an armed attack occurs against a Member of the United Nations, until the Security Council has taken measures necessary to maintain international peace and security."[195]

The Charter itself does not define self-defense. Does it apply only to cross-border attacks by conventional armed forces? Or does it include anticipatory or preemptive uses of force by a nation threatened with attack? It is not even clear from the Charter's text whether it rules out preventive force—a preemptive attack against a longer-term, rising threat. Self-defense could depend on the eye of the beholder. Although, as we will see, American delegates to the San Francisco conference believed the Charter did not restrict the United States' freedom to use force, but it is difficult to square this view with the Charter text.

Perhaps even more remarkable than the UN's provisions for collective security and self-defense, which make no quantum leap beyond the League of Nations, are its efforts at enforcement, which do. Instead of the League's feeble enforcement powers, the Charter envisioned a UN military—composed of units contributed by member states—that could intervene to end conflicts. Article 43 requires nations to "make available to the Security Council, on its call…armed forces, assistance, and facilities, including rights of passage, necessary for the purpose of maintaining international peace and security." Impressed with the influence of air power during the recent war, the Charter even requires that states "shall hold immediately available national air-force contingents for combined international enforcement action." It establishes a Military Staff Committee to plan and coordinate UN military action, but—underlining again the control of the great powers over questions of war and peace—only the chiefs of staff of the Big Five are eligible for membership. Nevertheless, these putative UN military forces fell victim to the Cold War, depriving the world organization of any military resources of its own. Instead, it would have to call upon member states to intervene independently to prevent a threat to international peace and security—as it did in Korea in 1950 and Kuwait in 1991. The UN provided a political forum for discussion of war and peace, but it could not contribute to the military execution of its mandates. Enforcement measures remained in the hands of the great powers.

Postwar international history highlighted the gap between the UN's goals and means. It pursued the vision of ending war between nations, which borrowed the language of just war theory but ripped it from its moral and legal foundations. In a system dominated by international anarchy, the great powers might use their own resources to enforce morality among nations. But under the Charter, no war can be just. Article 51 banished the ancient principle that nations could use war to punish nations that violated certain moral norms. Self-defense took the place of justice. Even when the Security Council authorizes force, it can only seek to restore international peace and stability—even though the existing order may perpetuate greater harms.

Under this world view, the UN pursues a more ambitious aim than the just war, which relies on nations engaging in self-help. It seeks to replace international anarchy with the same kind of peace and stability that exists in domestic society. Nations, like individuals, can no longer resort to violence against each other because the UN, like a domestic government, would maintain the peace. The UN's institutional structure, however, introduces a fatal flaw into the scheme: the UN does not have the resources to play the role of international peacekeeper on the same scale as a government of domestic society. While the Security Council's design recognizes the central place of the great powers in fulfilling this role, the veto reserved for the United States, Russia, China, France, and the UK biases the international system against taking any action at all. Between 1950 and 1991, the years of the Cold War, the Security Council did not issue a single authorization to use force. In the years since, it has proved unable to act—in places such as Yugoslavia, Iraq, Georgia, and now Syria and Iran—where any of the permanent five have interests or just wish to balance the power of one of their fellow members. Collective security may be a worthy ideal, but one that has become increasingly divorced from the reality of great power competition and new international challenges.

It is important to recognize that the United Nations Charter did not have to produce this outcome. International lawyers and officials today have developed an interpretation of the agreement that bans all uses of force other than self-defense. It is one that arose soon after the UN's establishment and has assumed almost canonical status today, thanks in part to the forceful arguments of Thomas Franck in the United States and Ian Brownlie in Great Britain.[196] That reading came to the fore during the 2002–2003 debates over the Iraq War, where European leaders accused the United States of destroying the international legal system to force regime change in Iraq. "In the twenty-first century," German Foreign Minister Joschka Fischer said, "You can't use war to force disarmament." French President Jacques Chirac said, "War is always the worst of solutions." The United States, both countries argued, could not use force in Iraq without Security Council authorization. America's war in Iraq, Fischer said, raised the "question of a new world order after the end of the Cold War."[197] The Bush administration defended the war based on Iraqi violation of earlier Security Council resolutions from the 1991 Gulf War, but it also claimed the right to use force in the absence of UN approval. In January 2003, for example, Secretary of State Colin Powell announced that the United States had "a sovereign right to take military action against Iraq alone."[198]

But this reading of the UN Charter mistakes current hopes for the international system for the original understanding of the treaty's drafters. The United States' delegation to the Dumbarton Oaks conference, as historian Marc Trachtenberg has shown, did not understand the Charter to limit future American uses of force. One question that arose from the delegation, for example, was whether the United States would require Security Council authorization to continue enforcing the Monroe Doctrine in the Western Hemisphere. In a May 1945 meeting of the U.S. delegation, Senator Arthur Vandenberg warned that limiting the use of force to self-defense might prevent the United States from preventing conflict within Latin America without the approval of Russia and China. John Foster Dulles, a fellow delegation member, responded: "at no point would the member states give up their right to use force in all circumstances." [199] Under Dulles's logic, states agreed to refrain from war consistent with the principles of the United Nations. "Since the prevention of aggression was a purpose of the organization, action to prevent aggression in the absence of action by the Security Council would be consistent with the purposes of the organization." Therefore, "if a European nation vetoed action to prevent action in the Western Hemisphere," Dulles concluded, "we would be entirely free to use force." Leo Pasvolsky, the key State Department official on the Charter negotiations, confirmed that "there was certainly no statement in the text under which we would give up our right of independent action."[200]

American understanding of the preservation of the United States' freedom of action continued during the negotiation of the Charter. American delegates understood that other nations might disagree. Senator Vandenberg himself had thought that the Charter called for a "general renunciation of the right to use force," but Dulles and Harold Stassen immediately informed him "that this was not the case." Vandenberg declared that "the people would be disillusioned beyond words when they realized the plan."[201] In a later meeting, Pasvolsky explained to the delegation that "if the Security Council fails to agree on an act, then the member state reserves the right to act for the maintenance of peace, justice, etc." Therefore, the United States could safely reject a French amendment that Security Council inaction did not preclude further measures by member states. Pasvolsky informed his colleagues, however, that their British allies "were shocked by the American concept of self-defense." "It was to them a new thought," he said, "that self-defense can operate outside of a nation's territorial limits."[202] The British now understood that the Charter would not constrain the United States' freedom of action. "The successful working of the United Nations depends on the preservation of the Great Powers," the British Foreign Office's observed in its published commentary on the Charter. "If this unanimity is seriously undermined no provision of the Charter is likely to be of much avail." "In such a case, the Members will resume their liberty of action."[203]

While international lawyers are more reluctant than their American counterparts to consult such materials, the understanding of the signatories at the time must bear on the question of the meaning of a treaty. And those materials show, as Trachtenberg makes clear, that the governments that signed the UN Charter "did not think that the use of force without Security Council sanction and for purposes other than defense against actual armed attack would be legally impermissible no matter how divided the great powers were—no matter how poorly, that is, the Security Council regime functioned."[204] This is not to say that the UN Charter's text does not contain the seeds of the current international legal system that we have today: a collective security regime that prohibits war except for self-defense or by permission of world government. But this history shows that the dominance of those rules is due far more to the subsequent interpretation of international lawyers and foreign governments than the intentions and actions of the great powers in 1945 and the years thereafter.[205]

IV. Conclusion

Neither the UN Charter system nor the classic just war theory provides an adequate *jus ad bellum* for the twenty-first century. As currently interpreted, the Charter forbids humanitarian intervention except in the unusual cases where the interests and views of the permanent members of the Security Council coincide. Moreover, it is wholly unrealistic to hope that the Charter system can furnish the basis for a durable peace. The "Long Peace" in Europe after the Second World War was maintained by the balance of power between the United States and the Soviet Union, not the UN. If the peace in Asia is to be kept in the twenty-first century, it will arise from an understanding between the United States, China, and the other Pacific and South Asian powers, not the UN.[206] The classic just war doctrine is also unsuited to our present needs. Although it permits humanitarian interventions, it forbids preventive war: war is only "just" when, like the criminal law, it serves corrective justice. The injuries that war can properly redress, according to classic just war theory, are *past* ones; the threat of *future* injury, no matter how grave, cannot justify war except when the injury is actually impending. In an age when rogue states can credibly threaten millions of innocent civilians with instantaneous destruction, that consequence is simply not acceptable. Both international justice and the promotion of peace would be far better served by a more flexible approach that is the subject of the next chapters.

4   Force Rules

IN AN EFFORT to abolish war, the victorious World War II nations adopted a law enforcement approach to war. They founded the United Nations as an instrument to enforce a new ban on war, with an exception only for self-defense. But their effort contained a fatal flaw: it disconnected the legal rules from political reality and the cost-benefit trade-offs that face states. This chapter will develop a new framework to govern the use of force between nations, one that permits wars that improve global welfare but rejects those that cause more harm than good.

A sweeping change and replacement of international rules could be unduly disruptive. But if the great powers established the original rules under conditions that became outdated long ago, the benefits of a more effective order moving forward can surpass the costs of transitional instability. This chapter will describe an evolutionary approach that reinterprets rather than replaces the UN Charter. It will show that we can revise current doctrine to help include international security and global welfare within the calculus of war today.

I. Incorporating Expected Harm

Under the UN Charter, a state may use force in self-defense from an attack without Security Council approval. International legal scholars from a variety of perspectives recognize that states need not wait until an attack begins and can use force to forestall an imminent attack.[1] Imminence, as famously described in the *Caroline* incident, suggests a temporal meaning. In 1837, Canadian troops crossed the border in pursuit of rebels who had escaped to American territory, destroying their ship, the *Caroline*, in the process. In an exchange of notes over the sinking, Secretary of State Daniel Webster accepted anticipatory self-defense when an attack is "instant, overwhelming, and leaving no choice of means, and no moment for deliberation."[2] This suggests a high bar: that nations must wait until the likelihood of attack approaches 100 percent. But self-defense should not only be about timing. By waiting until an enemy is about to cross the border, a nation has assured itself that an attack is almost certain—but also more damaging. The imminence standard puts states at a severe disadvantage because modern weapons have amplified the potential death and destruction of an attack.

Time should not be the only way to determine the probability of an attack. Suppose that an enemy sets in motion a train of events that will lead to an attack several days later. Once a nation moves toward war, standing down becomes prohibitively expensive or opens up its territory to attack. The World War I mobilization schedules of Austria, Russia, Germany, and France are a good example. As Barbara Tuchman vividly showed, once one nation mobilized for war, the others had to match that schedule to have a chance to defend themselves.[3] Though war would not come for several days, its probability became much more certain once Europe's leaders made the decision to mobilize. Standard imminence doctrine also has yet to adapt to advancements in military technology, such as cyberattacks or supersonic missiles, which reduce the warning time before an attack and increase its destructive power.

Game theorists even point out that taking an irreversible, costly step toward war may send a credible signal of resolve. Economist Thomas Schelling introduced the idea that a nation could gain a bargaining advantage during an international crisis by irrevocably binding itself to a course of events.[4] A nation attempting to reach a settlement in a crisis can threaten to trigger events that will automatically escalate into war should negotiations fail. Fixating on timing to the exclusion of other—at times more important—factors simply avoids difficult questions that must be faced in a crisis or a war.

Considering self-defense only through the lens of imminence also ignores the realities of modern weapons and warfare. Under current international rules, best expressed by the *Caroline* affair, a nation has the same limited right to stop a potential temporary border incursion as it does to stop a possible WMD attack. With the border incursion involved in the *Caroline* itself, a few dozen lives were at stake, and there was no significant threat to U.S. security. In their 1842 correspondence, which gave rise to the *Caroline* rule, Secretary of State Daniel Webster and British Lord Ashburton argued over the timing of an anticipatory use of force but ignored the magnitude of destruction. Meanwhile, a WMD attack might cause thousands if not millions of deaths and severely disrupt if not cripple the American economy. Yet in both cases, current international law dictates that a threatened nation cannot use force in self-defense until the very last moment before an attack.

The imminence rule ignores the magnitude of death and destruction wrought by modern weapons. It overlooks the windows of opportunity that may open to reduce the harm of an attack through limited preemptive action. It does not account for an enemy who comes into clear view at a time when his attack is not temporally imminent, but who can easily disappear into the civilian population. It does not accommodate a nonkinetic cyberattack, which could lay dormant for a time before it is triggered. In these cases, the earlier, discrete use of force might reduce overall damage and casualties on both sides. It is unrealistic to subject dissimilar threats involving vastly different levels of destruction, which can be prevented at different times and through different means, to the same rule of time.[5] Use of force should take into account timing, but international law should relax the proximity to an attack when other factors come into play.

Self-defense should broaden its reach to include the probability of an attack and its potential magnitude, which social scientists measure as expected harm. It should also take into account measures available at an earlier moment to prevent the attack. This more sensible approach would allow states more flexibility to use force as the expected harm of an attack increases. Modern weapon technologies that increase the magnitude of destruction, and reduce the time for warning, should allow states to use force earlier than before. The threat of unconventional terrorist groups should also give more leeway for preemptive measures. A nation may locate hostile terrorist operatives at a moment in time when the terrorist's plans are not sufficiently developed to qualify as temporally "imminent." Nonetheless, it may be impossible for a nation to be certain that it will be able to detect these terrorists later, when the attack looms.

While we should resist the temptation to anthropomorphize nations and their relations, an analogy can be made to the doctrine of self-defense in criminal law. A person may use force to defend himself if his life is threatened, the police are not at hand, escape is not possible, and the use of force is reasonable (and sometimes for far lower standards). While temporal imminence may be a factor when someone defends himself from attack, it is not the only one. If the harm cannot be avoided by waiting for the last moment, force may be used as early as possible to effectively defend oneself. Some scholars use the example of a person who is chained to a wall and told by his captor that he will be killed in a week. The use of force in self-defense at any time during that week (not just at the end of it) is justified.[6]

Similar logic underlies the "battered woman" defense, where women who have suffered severe and repeated physical abuse at the hands of their spouses resort to force in self-defense. For such a woman, going to the police may have little effect, and past abuse may lead her to reasonably believe that her life is at risk.[7] Debate over the battered woman defense focuses on the "objective" or "subjective" definition of the "reasonable person standard." But the battered woman's defense hinges on more than just imminence. Rather than timing alone, the battered woman's defense seeks to use past conduct—particularly escalating violence—to assess the probability that future harm is likely to occur. It seeks to defend a use of force that may be temporally disconnected from any individual, immediate harm, such as when a spouse who has suffered vicious, long-term physical abuse uses force when not under imminent threat. While the appropriate scope of a battered woman's defense is a complex and difficult issue, it demonstrates at a minimum that even domestic criminal law is considering transforming the imminence requirement from pure temporality toward expected harm.[8]

Another analogy comes from freedom of speech doctrine. While the First Amendment commands government to "make no law…abridging the freedom of speech," the Supreme Court has long understood that certain circumstances can justify narrower restrictions on expression. One such circumstance is the regulation of speech that poses a threat of imminent harm. In the classic words of Justice Oliver Wendell Holmes, the government may limit speech that presents "a clear and present danger" or threatens to incite violence or harm, such as crying out "fire" in a crowded theater.[9] As Judge Richard Posner has observed, these cases analyze imminence according to a cost-benefit approach: "Holmes's 'clear and present danger' test requires that the probability be high (though not necessarily as high as in the fire case) and the harm imminent; stated differently, the *danger* of harm must be great."[10] In other words, "discount (multiply) the harm if it occurs by the probability of its occurrence. The greater that probability, the greater is the expected harm and therefore the greater the justification for preventing or punishing the speech that creates the danger."[11]

Academics and judges have not broadly accepted a cost-benefit approach to free speech. This reluctance may stem from difficulties in measuring the long-term benefits and costs of restrictions on freedom of expression. Indeed, the government rarely can estimate the harm or benefits of censorship on robust political discussions, open market transactions, or vigorous intellectual debate. How can we determine the costs of restricting antimilitary protests at the funerals of soldiers killed in Afghanistan and Iraq, or barring Nazi parades in the communities of Holocaust survivors? But the challenge of estimating costs and benefits may not arise so acutely with the use of force in self-defense, nor does it undermine the argument in favor of using probability instead of only imminence.

In these other areas of law, judges and scholars are relaxing the strict idea of temporal imminence. The international arena should follow suit by at least taking the magnitude of threatened harm into account when allowing the use of force in self-defense. The advent of weapons of mass destruction (WMDs) and covert, sophisticated delivery systems has dramatically increased the degree of potential harm from a surprise attack. Advances in miniaturization have made smaller nuclear weapons possible, and even Third World nations now can develop ballistic missiles. At the same time, the broad dissemination of scientific knowledge and easy availability of equipment permits those with extensive scientific training to manufacture chemical or biological weapons. WMDs threaten devastating and indiscriminate long-term damage to the civilian population and environment. As the World Court recognized in a 1996 advisory opinion, nuclear weapons possess unique characteristics, "in particular their destructive capacity, their capacity to cause untold human suffering, and their ability to cause damage to generations to come."[12]

Globalization and technological development only compound the threats from new methods of warfare. Western nations have knitted together a smooth system for the transportation of goods, people, and capital that makes it easy to move money instantaneously between nations and to ship products just in time for manufacturing needs. But this same network makes possible unsophisticated delivery systems for WMDs. A suicide bomber can explode a dirty bomb by driving a large truck into a building or spread a biological or chemical agent with a crop duster. The same transportation and financial network that allows for the newest iPod or iPhone can also allow terrorists to transport operatives, move money, and deploy weapons.[13] Similarly, the newest forms of economic progress, such as computerization and miniaturization, Internet communication and exchange, and biotechnology, give rise to both new forms of commerce and new methods of warfare. These developments may allow financial markets to operate across national borders at breathtaking speeds, but they also allow nations to use electronic warfare to attack an opponent's economy. The Internet may reduce the costs of monitoring and controlling everything from utilities to transportation networks to grocery inventories, but it also creates vulnerabilities that an enemy can exploit to silently cripple water and electrical systems or bring air and rail transport to a halt.

The calculus of war must evolve to meet these technological and economic developments; the use of force should come earlier, depending on the nature of the threatened attack. The magnitude of harm threatened by modern weapons has grown, their detection has become more difficult, and the time necessary for their launch has decreased. Temporal limits on self-defense should diminish in a corresponding manner. If applied literally to the world of modern weapons, the *Caroline* test would be a suicide pact. In the wake of the 1963 Cuban Missile Crisis, Professor

Myres McDougal argued: "the understanding is now widespread that a test formu-
lated in the previous century for a controversy between two friendly states is hardly
relevant to contemporary controversies, involving high expectations of violence,
between nuclear-armed protagonists."[14] Contemporary American military lawyers
have similarly observed that Webster's requirement of immediacy is "too restrictive today, particularly given the nature and lethality of modern weapons systems
which may be employed with little, if any, warning."[15] Modern technology has pres-
sured imminence, because by the time a nation knows that an enemy is about to
launch an attack, the attack's speed and destructiveness may not permit an effective
counterattack.

Nor does the imminence test take into account the realities of unconventional
warfare, such as terrorism. Terrorist organizations, for example, do not deploy large
military forces. American intelligence cannot effectively use satellite reconnaissance to measure the deployment of terrorist units days, nor weeks, in advance.
Terrorists do not cross national borders and use force to seize territory or to coerce
foreign governments. Rather, they seek to covertly infiltrate a country, disguise
themselves by blending into peaceful domestic society, and then launch surprise
attacks—often on civilian targets. A temporal imminence test loses its value if a
nation cannot detect the preparations for an attack. By the time the nation detects
an imminent attack, it may well be too late to resort to force because the attack
will already have occurred. As WMD technology becomes cheaper and more available, the difficulties posed by terrorism will only increase. Groups such as al Qaeda
and its regional offshoots, Hezbollah, and Hamas have the financial resources to
acquire chemical, biological, and perhaps even nuclear weapons capable of killing
tens of thousands indiscriminately. Imminence as a limiting rule on the use of force
suffers both because nonstate enemies can launch attacks with greater speed and
surprise than ever before and because they have far more destructive weapons at
their disposal than in the past.

A more realistic approach to modern warfare would transform imminence into
a function of what economists call "expected value." Expected value is the real gain
or harm of an event that may or may not happen in the future. Suppose a person
buys a lottery ticket with 1 chance in 100,000 of winning the jackpot. If the jackpot increases to $1 million, the expected value of the lottery ticket would be $10
(the probability of winning times the value of winning). Our buyer should purchase
the ticket for any price below $10. Similarly, the use of force should depend on the
expected harm of an attack—the probability of an attack times the magnitude of
destruction. Courts have adopted a similar formula to decide when a defendant is
responsible for damages from an accident. According to the Learned Hand formula,
named after the famous federal judge, Billings Learned Hand, a defendant should be

liable if it could have taken safety measures that amounted to less than the probability of the accident multiplied by the cost of the potential injury.[16] In other words, the defendant should take precautionary measures when they cost less than the expected harm of an accident.

Although the Hand formula does not draw the exact line between war and peace, it clarifies how the rules on the use of force can evolve beyond imminence. Under the *Caroline*, temporal immediacy serves as a proxy for a high level of certainty of an attack. We can estimate that probability with other methods, however, including historical behavior, reliable intelligence, military capabilities, and signals of intentions. And, unlike the *Caroline*, international rules should also include the destructiveness and the probability of a potential attack to determine the use of force. In the *Caroline* case itself, the United States could demand a high level of certainty because the threatened harm—a cross-border raid by barely a dozen rebels—remained low. But if the magnitude of threatened destruction increases considerably, nations should have the right to intervene at earlier times, even if the probability of the threatened harm remains low. If a nation threatens an attack using nuclear weapons, the defending state need not wait until it sees the missiles fueling on the launch pads before acting in self-defense.

Understanding the use of force as a question of expected harm can clear up a difficulty that has beset the study of war for some time—the issue of proportionality. Just war theory, for example, has long claimed that nations should only begin a war where the ends bear some proportionality to the harm of the war itself. Nations, however, have launched wars whose objectives bear little relationship to the original grounds for conflict. Consider the Mexican-American War of 1848. After a small border conflict on the Rio Grande River, the United States launched an amphibious invasion of Mexico, captured its capital and deposed its leaders, and annexed one-third of its territory. Nations have had far more success in determining proportionality *during* the war—when the destruction caused must be related to the tactical objective—than when *starting* the war.[17]

With our new approach, however, proportionality can draw substance from the idea of avoiding an expected harm. Under the Hand formula, a person should spend money to take safety measures that cost less than the harm of an accident times its likelihood. Both the individual and society come out ahead, because the expenditure on avoiding the accident is less than the expected value of the harm. Similarly, a nation should intervene to preempt a threat when the costs of the war fall below the expected harm (magnitude times probability) from a potential attack. It may be the case that a nation can use less force and cause less harm by striking a terrorist group earlier before its operatives can infiltrate a civilian population. Acting earlier might allow a nation at risk of attack to use force more precisely and less destructively.

During the 1930s, for example, the Western allies might have forestalled much of World War II's destruction by intervening against Adolf Hitler, preventing Germany's rearmament, stopping her expansion into Austria and Czechoslovakia, or even crossing the western borders when the Wehrmacht invaded Poland. Going to war is proportional because the cost of the earlier intervention is less than the expected harm from the later, greater conflict.

American action during the Cuban Missile Crisis implicitly relied on this approach. Moscow's secret deployment of medium-range nuclear missiles only ninety miles from the United States posed a threat to American national security. For the first time in the Cold War, most of the United States would fall within the range of Soviet nuclear missiles. In response, President John F. Kennedy imposed a blockade on the shipment of military equipment to Cuba. A naval blockade constitutes an act of war because it requires military force to stop ships, search them, and prevent some from proceeding to their destinations.[18] The launch of the missiles, however, was not temporally imminent. The missiles were not fueled nor fully assembled. There was no indication that the Soviet Union was planning to use them immediately, or even in the near future. Their positioning in Cuba did not amount to the temporal threat of armed attack on the United States envisioned by the *Caroline* framework. Nevertheless, President Kennedy declared that the deployment "add[ed] to an already clear and present danger" and a "deliberately provocative and unjustified change in the status quo."[19]

President Kennedy justified the blockade, which his administration labeled a "quarantine," with a more flexible approach to the use of force. He told the American people in a nationally televised address on October 22, 1962:

> We no longer live in a world where only the actual firing of weapons represents a sufficient challenge to a nation's security to constitute maximum peril. Nuclear weapons are so destructive and ballistic missiles are so swift, that any substantially increased possibility of their use . . . may well be regarded as a definite threat to peace.[20]

Rather than imminence as the trigger for force, Kennedy argued that the greater magnitude of harm justified American intervention even though there was a lower probability of an attack. His choice of a blockade rather than an air strike or an invasion of Cuba meets our idea of proportionality. Acting before an immediate attack, JFK used a lower level of force that was more in line with the expected harm from the threat. The Soviet Union reversed its deployment in the face of the blockade, American threats to use even greater force against Cuba, and a deal to remove U.S. intermediate-range missiles from Turkey.[21]

The Cuban Missile Crisis is generally seen as a credit to Kennedy's presidency and the greatest moment of leadership in his administration. But substantial disagreement continues over the legitimacy of the Cuban blockade. At the time, the United States claimed the authorization of the Organization of American States, but under the UN Charter, a regional security organization does not have any greater authority to use force than its individual members.[22] While UN Ambassador Adlai Stevenson made a dramatic Security Council presentation revealing the Soviet deployment, the Council did not authorize a quarantine—not surprising in light of the Soviet Union's permanent veto. Within the U.S. government, the Justice Department opined that although "preventive action would not ordinarily be lawful to prevent the maintenance of a missile base, or other armaments in the absence of evidence that their actual use for an aggressive attack was imminent," the Monroe Doctrine of 1823 created a *lex specialis* for the Western Hemisphere that established "less restrictive conditions" for the United States' use of preventive force.[23] Later legal scholars have viewed the Cuban blockade as an act of anticipatory self-defense, although neither the Soviet Union nor Cuba had attacked the United States, was on the verge of attacking it, or had even publicly threatened to attack it.[24] Nonetheless, under the general understanding of the UN Charter and the *Caroline* framework, the blockade violated international law because the United States used force despite any evidence of an imminent attack originating from Cuba. Only under a more flexible approach to the rules of war, using a proportionality or expected harm framework, do Kennedy's decisions gain the respect that history has accorded them.

It will be difficult to reconstruct the rules on self-defense. Critics will say that dismissing a criminal law framework will allow nations to attack each other for any reason or for no reason at all. Or the great powers will use force against any competitor that might pose not just a current challenge but also a future one. Either criticism, however, would be hyperbolic because not every country that has a military would present a justified target. Probability requires us to measure the intentions as well as the capability of a potential enemy. Some nations, for example, already have the weapons to launch a devastating attack on the United States. Great Britain and France have long possessed nuclear weapons and the means to deliver them on targets abroad. Neither, however, has manifested any intent to threaten the security of the United States since the nineteenth century. Alternatively, there may be nations that hold a hostile intent but do not possess the capability to inflict serious harm. Iraq under Saddam Hussein might have had the desire to injure the United States, but it may not have had the ability to reach American territory or forces.

Taking into account estimated harm gives us a rough way to restrain the use of force against countries that pose threats somewhere in between these examples. Cuba, for example, bears some significant hostility toward, but does not have the military capability to launch a serious offensive attack against, the United States. Thus, American intervention against Cuba should rise no higher in destructiveness than the small estimated harm of a potential attack. This approach can also take into account changing circumstances that might call for a resort to more force. Since its 1979 Islamic Revolution, Iran has borne an open enmity toward the United States, which its leaders sometimes refer to as "the Great Satan." But until the U.S. invasion of Iraq in 2003, Iran did not have the ability to reach American forces in any significant way. As Iran's capability to harm American troops in the Middle East has increased, the United States' right to use force will rise too. Or, consider North Korea, which has long had the ability to attack American troops stationed in South Korea. But North Korea's development of nuclear weapons, and its effort to field a ballistic missile system, increases the estimated harm of a potential attack. The level of American intervention in anticipatory self-defense should increase as North Korea's capabilities improve, a commonsense principle impossible under the *Caroline* framework.

A critic might argue that changing the pure imminence rule into an expected harm standard here would cause more mistaken wars. If nations can resort to military force based on the probability of an attack, they might end up triggering unwarranted conflicts. But there is always the chance of a mistake, and errors are, of course, endemic to any human enterprise. Even if errors are not present, there may well be disagreement among nations about the level of expected harm necessary to justify the use of force. So the question is not whether a set of rules will produce an error-free world—that is impossible—but which set of rules reduces errors to an acceptable cost.

Mimicking the criminal law, the current UN-centered framework seeks to reduce war in the world to zero because of the chances of mistake and pretextual invasions of aggression. Social scientists call this a Type I error—cases of commission, where going to war was a mistake. If we live in a world filled with Type I errors—nations are going to war even when the expected cost of the conflicts outweighs their expected benefits—then we should design our system to suppress armed conflict. Some believe that the wars in Iraq and Vietnam are good examples of Type I errors, though the jury is still out on the former, and historians are reevaluating the costs of the latter in light of the large human costs after North Vietnam's victory and the frustration of communist expansion in Asia.

Less often considered but equally dangerous are what social scientists call Type II errors. Type I errors are mistakes of action. Type II errors are mistakes of inaction. Past and recent history provides cases of omission where the United States, for example, should have gone to war but did not. Because Western nations refused to intervene in Rwanda, even though the troops required were minimal, about 1 million civilians were killed in a genocide. The use of force in Cambodia prior to 1978 might have removed the Khmer Rouge and stopped its mass killing spree. Earlier American entry on the side of the Allies in World War II, or an allied invasion of Germany in 1939, might have forestalled Hitler's rise to power and his conquest of Western Europe and saved the tens of millions lost in the war and the Holocaust. If the UN Charter system permits war only in self-defense, it will bar interventions that prevent massive killing or stop the rise of a terrible dictator. Today's rule, which limits war only to self-defense from an actual attack, may reduce Type I errors, but it also dramatically increases Type II errors.

II. Rules versus Standards

Another way to understand the redefinition of self-defense as expected harm is to consider the difference between "rules" and "standards." As law and economics scholars have shown, these two types of norms can make an important difference in the operation of a regulatory system.[25] A typical example of a rule is a strict speed limit, such as a ban on driving on the interstate highways faster than 55 miles per hour. Government could also regulate speed with a less precise standard, such as a law that prohibits unreasonably fast driving. Choosing between the two strikes different trade-offs between accuracy and economy and before and after the fact evaluation of the circumstances. Rules are clear and easy to apply—anyone driving 56 mph has violated the law regardless of the reason. These clear rules reduce the costs to the legal system of determining violations, create greater certainty and predictability for private citizens, and demand less information to implement.

Rules have their downsides too. Future decision-makers cannot carefully apply the legal norm to all relevant facts. A strict 55 mph rule does not allow judges to take into consideration the flow of traffic or an emergency, nor does the rule punish an elderly driver who should not be behind the wheel but drives 54 mph. With a rule, a court will only consider whether a radar gun accurately measured if a car exceeded 55 mph. Because of their absolute nature, rules either sweep in too many people or too few people: they are inevitably overinclusive or underinclusive.[26] As a result, rules will produce higher error rates because they cannot take into account the totality of the circumstances of each case.

Standards bear the opposite trade-off between economy and error. Acting reasonably under all of the circumstances—a classic example of a standard—allows future decision-makers to consider all of the facts when determining guilt. A reasonableness standard, for example, would allow a court to take into account that a speeder caught driving at 70 mph was driving all alone, in the countryside, during bright daylight hours, in dry conditions. A standard will reduce error costs and increase accuracy by allowing decision-makers to apply the norm to all of the facts. But it will also increase decision costs and require more information. A judge cannot simply read the printout of the radar gun to decide a case. Instead, he or she must hear from the driver, the police officer, and witnesses and determine the road and weather conditions. Then the judge performs a balancing act to decide whether the speeder's conduct was unreasonable. While speeders might welcome such an approach, a standard may increase costs for all drivers because "reasonableness" will create less predictability and more uncertainty over the line between legal and illegal conduct.

Standards differ from rules in another important respect: the discretion given to future officials. Rules give more authority to the original legislator and narrow the power of those who enforce the rule later. In our speeding example, the writers of the strict 55 mph limit rule have granted future judges little ability to narrow or broaden the application of the law—they must fine everyone who drivers faster than 55 mph, no matter the excuse. By contrast, standards delegate more authority from the original legislator to officials in the future. A judge applying a standard of reasonableness will exercise a great deal of discretion in applying the law to an individual case. Of course, every system of criminal justice will bear some amount of inherent human discretion at the time of law enforcement. A police officer can simply choose not to arrest those who are clearly in violation of the speed limit, or a judge who believes that the law convicts too many speeders may just acquit defendants without reason. But at the level of comparative institutional analysis, a system of clear rules will reduce the level of discretion—at the time of law enforcement—in comparison to a system built upon standards.

Choosing between a standard or a rule will depend, in part, on our judgment about the quality of future decision-making. If legislators, for example, believe that the officials who will implement policy are mediocre, they will want to use a rule. The rule will reduce errors by removing discretion from the second-rate officials and keep authority with the higher-quality legislators. Or, if the legislators have superior information relevant to the decision, they will want to keep authority for themselves and choose a rule. For example, legislators might know that emotional appeals by speeders for exceptions (e.g., "I was in a hurry because I was late for an important appointment") tend to persuade sympathetic, overworked judges and actually encourage speeding and increase accident rates. Legislators should use standards, by contrast, when the opposite conditions hold. If a future decision-maker will have access to superior information and has more experience and better technical qualifications, legislators should use a standard.

Neither rules nor standards are perfect for all situations. One will outperform the other depending on the facets of a particular problem. The conventional approach to the use of force and imminence conforms more to a rule than a standard. The UN Charter system prohibits the use of force until an attack is temporally imminent—without exception. A nation cannot use force until an enemy is about to launch its attack, regardless of the enemy's intentions or the amount of destruction. Decision costs are low because the circumstances of each case are irrelevant—only timing matters. A rule based on temporal imminence, however, increases error costs. A strict rule will prevent nations from acting earlier to prevent an attack. Waiting until the last moment may not give a defending nation enough time to identify the attack or to launch a preemptive response that fully extinguishes the threat. The rule will always be underinclusive because it will permit some uses of force that should be allowed, but it will not permit all appropriate uses of force. A temporal imminence rule leads to errors because it does not allow any exceptions to intervene for global welfare or to use force to prevent an attack.

The imminence rule also prevents current leaders from taking specific circumstances into account here and now. Instead, it favors the decisions of the original rule makers: the drafters of the UN Charter and their predecessors, like those behind the Kellogg-Briand Pact and the Treaty of Versailles. It assumes that nations in the future will make worse decisions or have less reliable information than those who adopted the imminence rule. It anticipates, perhaps correctly, that aggressive nations will manufacture pretextual excuses or that nations in the heat of a dispute may make irrational choices. A strict imminence rule ignores the unique factual circumstances of a looming war—such as the source, magnitude and type of attack, the history of the region, the lives at stake, or the nature of the regimes in conflict—for determining the right to use military force. For a framework built on a strict temporal imminence rule, there are no unique cases. All wars are equally bad, and the use of force is so prone to error that even self-defense must await an aggressor's actual attack.

It should be clear that *jus ad bellum* should be governed by a standard rather than a rule. A standard allows more information to be considered, such as the probability of attack and the magnitude of harm. A more flexible approach will increase decision costs. Nations will have to devote significant resources to obtain reliable intelligence to accurately judge the intentions and capabilities of potential enemies. Error costs, however, will fall. Nations can resort to preemptive force earlier, before an enemy attack becomes unstoppable or difficult to blunt. They will be able to use force based on all of the circumstances, such as whether they are stopping widespread human rights abuses, calming the regional or international instability produced by an aggressive nation, or ousting a terrible dictatorship. A standard fits best when the circumstances make each case unique, the stakes are high, and it is difficult to predict the consequences. There are few human endeavors less predictable and with more at stake than war. "Never, never, never believe any war will be smooth and easy, or that anyone who embarks on the strange voyage can measure the tides and hurricanes he will encounter," Winston Churchill warned. "The statesman who yields to war fever must realize that once the signal is given, he is no longer the master of policy but the slave of unforeseeable and uncontrollable events."[27]

A standard recognizes that the nations of today are in the best position to make judgments about the value of war. Redefining the UN Charter rule to include expected harm transfers decision-making authority from the first creators of the imminence rule to today's nations. This approach makes sense because the original designers could not have foreseen the unique circumstances that currently challenge the international system. A strict rule becomes increasingly dysfunctional as new enemies, technologies, and capabilities emerge. Just as military tactics and strategies must evolve to confront new weapons and rivals, so too must international law adapt to current challenges.

An expected-harm standard will shift enforcement of the law to *ex post* rather than *ex ante* mechanisms. The *Caroline* version, for example, seeks to make its prohibition on force so clear that nations will obey it *before* any dispute. An expected-harm analysis, in contrast, will rely more on nations to sanction violators *after* a war. There are too many variables——such as the size of an enemy's force, its likely intentions, the readiness of the defender's military, and the size of a window of opportunity—to make any prejudgment of the situation possible. Rather than a rule's writers from long ago, the decision-maker will be the nation that uses force first. Afterward, other nations will choose whether to accept or oppose the results.

The threats of the twenty-first century demand the flexibility of a standard instead of the strictness of a rule. In the past, the cost of a rule may not have been as great as today. In the twentieth century, nation-states in Europe and Asia could only conduct significant attacks on each other using large mechanized armies and navies. Fleets and divisions took time to organize, train, and deploy. Nations would have a good chance to learn that an opponent was mobilizing before an attack, and thus have time to prepare defenses. Covert attacks could not cause a great amount of damage compared to large, mechanized armed forces. Although the advance of air and space capabilities increased the destructiveness of long-range attack, it also enabled earlier detection through surveillance.

Today, the error costs of the UN Charter rule can be staggeringly high. WMD proliferation, the spread of missile technology, and the emergence of rogue nations and international terrorist organizations have made the detection of attacks more difficult. Terrorist groups might carry out unconventional attacks that come with little warning, such as al-Qaeda's use on September 11, 2001, of civilian airliners to destroy skyscrapers in New York City. Terrorists disguise the movement of their personnel and arms as normal civilian conduct to escape detection and achieve tactical surprise. A rogue nation with little regard for civilized warfare could adopt similar tactics to gain an advantage. Iran or North Korea, for example, could launch a short-range missile from a disguised civilian cargo vessel off American shores—violating the rule that combatants must clearly identify themselves. Reducing the chances of detection alone would not give terrorists or rogue nations the ability to inflict serious harm on a great power. But the proliferation of WMD technology, combined with these unconventional attack methods, can inflict a level of destruction from a surprise attack that goes far beyond anything possible at the time current limits on force were conceived.

Costs, of course, also run in the other direction. A more flexible approach will increase decision costs—as all standards do—beyond those of the temporal imminence rule. In order to reliably assess the expected harm of an enemy attack, governments will have to invest in intelligence gathering and analysis. They will need to develop both technical intelligence about the abilities and deployment of enemy forces and human intelligence about rivals' intentions. Gathering such information involves more than simple border reconnaissance to detect an imminent invasion. Evaluating whether a level of expected harm exists to justify preemptive action will consume a great deal of time and resources. Consider the United States' decision to invade Iraq in 2003. Intelligence collection on Iraq had gone on for years, and UN weapons inspectors were continuously searching for the regime's WMD programs. Saddam Hussein left little doubt about his hostility toward the United States, his nation remained subject to severe economic sanctions, and no-fly zones continued over the north and south of the country. Nevertheless, the United States spent months gathering and analyzing intelligence, and more months concentrating on political debate, before it could decide whether to go to war. A rule that required an imminent Iraqi attack before any use of force in self-defense would have consumed far less time and energy.

III. Imminence in the Age of Terror

Iraq also teaches that a more flexible standard, one that relies on probabilities rather than the certainty of temporal imminence, can result in mistakes. Under the imminence standard, a defending nation must wait longer to observe its opponent's moves and gain more knowledge about its resources. This would result in a higher level of certainty and a better estimate of the expected harm of an enemy attack. The trade-off is that the enemy attack is more likely to occur at a higher level of destruction. Under a more flexible standard, a defending nation could misjudge its rival's intentions or capabilities and miscalculate the expected harm involved, which increases costs of mistaken use of force. In Iraq, for example, Western intelligence agencies agreed that the Hussein regime bore hostile intentions. But with all of the technical and human resources available, they erred in concluding that Saddam's regime enjoyed a WMD capability. On the other hand, acting earlier rather than deferring a preemptive attack should result in a less destructive, more narrowly focused use of force. Thus, the costs of mistaken uses of force are reduced.

One test of the suitability of a norm is whether it can accurately explain previous state conduct. If a rule diverges sharply from state practice, it may be too impractical to govern international affairs, or it may identify aspirational, quixotic goals. Recent examples show that nations actually make war decisions following the standard explained here rather than the strict UN rule. Earlier, we discussed the Cuban Missile Crisis as an example of the use of force before an attack was imminent. It is difficult to argue today that the Kennedy administration imposed a quarantine to guard against any immediate threat of attack. Rather, Soviet deployment of medium-range, nuclear-armed missiles in Cuba would have seriously altered the balance of power, which, until that point, had heavily favored the United States. By 1963, the United States had accumulated a massive arsenal of nuclear weapons and enjoyed broad superiority in the strategic bombers and missiles to deliver them half a world away.[28] A "missile gap" in favor of the United States existed between the United States and the Soviet Union. So Khrushchev gambled that he could score an equalizer quickly and without a massive investment in intercontinental missiles and bombers. And the Soviet premier no doubt guessed that Kennedy, who had poorly handled the Bay of Pigs fiasco and accepted the Berlin Wall, would, at most, weakly protest the deployment. If the United States had followed the UN Charter rules on war, Khrushchev would have won his bet. But, as we have seen, President Kennedy did not wait for an imminent attack and instead resorted to a limited use of force to prevent the new threat from materializing into a concrete deployment.

The Cuban Missile Crisis demonstrated that nations will act earlier, at lower probabilities of threat, when WMDs are involved. This is underscored by the example of Israel's 1981 attack on Iraq's Osirak nuclear reactor. Israel launched an air attack because it believed that the nearly completed facility would produce components for nuclear weapons. Iraq had not recently attacked Israel, though it maintained its opposition to the existence of the Jewish state.[29] Israel acted before the reactor became operational to take advantage of a window of opportunity that would soon close. If Israel had waited, it could have exposed the inhabitants of Baghdad to potentially lethal fallout. Although an Iraq armed with nuclear weapons would have raised the expected harm of an attack to Israel, the imminence of any attack was still temporally distant and certainly farther off than any threat like the Cuban Missile Crisis.

These factors may have led to the furious response to the Israeli attack. Two weeks after the raid, the UN Security Council condemned the attack as a "clear violation of the Charter of the United Nations and the norms of international conduct."[30] Several Council members agreed that Israel had failed the *Caroline* test: the use of force was not yet necessary because no Iraq attack on Israel was imminent (as suggested by the months spent planning the strike). Even the United States, which has traditionally used its permanent veto to protect Israel from attack at the United Nations, concluded that the attack violated international law. Jeanne Kirkpatrick, the U.S. Ambassador to the UN at the time, voted against Israel because it had acted too soon. Israel "failed to exhaust peaceful means for the resolution of this dispute," she said.[31]

Despite this criticism, Israel had the better argument. Israel implicitly defended itself on the ground that the destructiveness of WMDs justified an earlier intervention than granted by the imminence rule. The Israeli ambassador to the United Nations responded that to "assert the applicability of the Caroline principles to a State confronted with the threat of nuclear destruction would be an emasculation of that State's inherent and natural right of self-defense."[32] In hindsight, the Israeli attack on the Osirak reactor did the world a great favor. Despite his pleas to the contrary, Saddam Hussein did pursue WMDs and did come close to developing a nuclear weapon. Hussein acquired biological and chemical weapons, which he used on his own people and on Iranians in the Iran-Iraq War. He had a hostile intent not just against Israel but also against his Arab neighbors. He followed the stalemate of the Iran-Iraq war with the 1990 invasion of Kuwait, which provoked the Persian Gulf War. Even if Iraq had developed nuclear weapons at Osirak over the rest of the 1980s, it still might not have needed to use them in the Iran-Iraq war to shift radically the balance of power in the region. And if Iraq had been armed with nuclear weapons, the U.S. armed forces could not have achieved their stunning 1991 success in freeing Kuwait. The nations that took part in that war and in the 2003 invasion of Iraq can give thanks to Israel for eliminating Saddam's first effort to build nuclear weapons and setting back the program's efforts.

Yet, the Osirak example also shows the challenges of evaluating expected harm once we have cast aside the *Caroline* framework. In 1981, Iraq appeared to be complying with its international obligations governing the civilian development of nuclear energy. It had not yet invaded its neighbors to the east or the south. Despite its hostility to Israel, it gave no indication that it planned any immediate hostilities against Tel Aviv. At that time, Israel's estimate of the expected harm posed by Iraq would have depended on two pieces of intelligence analysis, one more tentative than the other. The first was the technical judgment of Iraq's progress toward a nuclear weapon and its ability to deliver that weapon. The second was Hussein's intentions.

With the hindsight of two wars, we can see clearly now that Iraq threatened to desta-bilize the region through aggressive wars of conquest. In 1981, Israel made the correct prediction, and the great powers on the Security Council did not.

Libya provides another example. Even before the 2011 armed revolution in Libya, events in Tripoli provided another testing ground for a different approach to war. In 1986, the United States launched air strikes against the Gadhafi regime after Libyan agents bombed a Berlin disco frequented by American military personnel. Libya's attack killed two, including a U.S. serviceman, and wounded 200 others, 50 of them Americans. President Reagan presented evidence that the bombings followed in a long line of Libyan-supported terrorist attacks against U.S. property, personnel, and citizens. In addition, the United States claimed that it had "clear evidence that Libya was planning a multitude of future attacks."[33]

President Reagan defended the attacks as anticipatory self-defense. He argued that the primary objective of the strikes was to forestall future terrorist attacks, even though they were not imminent. "This necessary and appropriate action was a preemptive strike, directed against the Libyan terrorist infrastructure and designed to deter acts of terrorism by Libya," such as the Berlin bombing.[34] Deterrence, of course, does not fit into the UN Charter framework for the use of force. The United States also pointed to the exhaustion of peaceful avenues to resolve its differences and the proportionate, restrained use of force. Targets were "carefully chosen, both for their direct linkage to Libyan support of terrorist activities and for the purpose of minimizing collateral damage and injury to innocent civilians."[35] Although several nations supported a UN resolution condemning the strikes, Australia, Denmark, France, and Britain joined the United States in opposing it.

Action against Libya in response to the Berlin bombing would not satisfy the imminence rule. Libya's conduct, however, overtly displayed its hostile intent, which raised the probability of future terrorist attacks. Successful bombings also revealed Libyan capabilities to harm American personnel and citizens abroad. Intelligence on Libya's future plans became critical for deciding on the use of force. Libya neither targeted the U.S. homeland nor threatened mass casualties. To rise to a level worthy of intervention, the probability of an attack had to approach certainty before the U.S. could launch its air strikes. Even so, Washington limited its use of force to a small number of sorties against Libya's command-and-control and terrorist infra-structure. Preemptive assault required that the use of force remain low in proportion to the reduced certainty of a future Libyan attack.

American intervention in Panama in 1989 provides yet another example of force in response to expected harm rather than an imminent assault. At the time, Panama had displayed some hostility toward the United States. The legislature there had declared that a state of war existed with the United States, and this was accompanied by inflammatory anti-American speeches from military dictator Manuel Noriega. Panamanian forces killed a U.S. Marine, beat a U.S. Navy officer, and threatened the latter's wife. "General Noriega's reckless threats and attacks upon Americans in Panama created an imminent danger to the 35,000 American citizens in Panama," President George H.W. Bush announced. "The deployment of U.S. Forces is an exercise of the right of self-defense recognized in Article 51 of the United Nations Charter and was necessary to protect American lives in imminent danger."[36] The State Department claimed that the "right of self-defense entitles the United States to take necessary measures to defend U.S. military personnel, U.S. nationals, and U.S. installations," and that Noriega had rejected all efforts to settle the matter peacefully.[37] The United States assured the Security Council that the use of force was the only way to protect U.S. citizens in Panama. In the midst of the fighting, the Security Council considered a draft resolution that would have labeled the invasion "a flagrant violation of international law," but Great Britain and France joined the United States in a veto.

At the time of the Panama intervention, scholars were divided over the invasion's legitimacy under formal imminence rules.[38] Although Panama threatened to harm U.S. citizens in the Canal Zone, it did not threaten an attack on the United States itself. But the Panama intervention can be understood as the consideration of probability and magnitude of an assault. Panama's actions, particularly its murder of an American serviceman, signaled a hostile intention toward the large base of American troops and civilians in Panama. Noriega's hostile activities may have increased the probability of further attacks. On the other hand, the magnitude of any harm would not have been great because Panama did not have the military resources to carry out an effective assault on the U.S. armed forces in the Canal Zone. It is difficult to conclude that the Panama invasion was a legitimate exercise of self-defense, even under the reformulated approach to self-defense developed here. It may be better understood as a war intended to shore up the stability of the international system, which we will consider in the next chapter.

American involvement in the Persian Gulf region also demonstrates that self-defense has expanded beyond the limits of temporal imminence. In the aftermath of the 1991 Persian Gulf War, the United States continued to use force against the regime of Saddam Hussein. In 1993, President Bill Clinton ordered air strikes on the Iraqi intelligence headquarters in Baghdad after Iraqi agents attempted to assassinate President George H.W. Bush. "The evidence of the Government of Iraq's violence and terrorism demonstrates that Iraq poses a continuing threat to United States nationals and shows utter disregard for the will of the international community as expressed in Security Council Resolutions and the United Nations Charter," the administration declared.[39] While Iraq had attempted to kill a former

U.S. President, the bombing did not anticipate an imminent attack on the United States. Rather, the Baghdad strikes sought to diminish Iraq's ability to carry out violence against the United States and to deter the regime from "such outlaw behavior in the future." Similarly, when the United States launched strikes against a series of Iraqi targets in 1998, no grand Iraqi attack was in the offing. Rather, the attacks came in response to Iraqi refusal to cooperate with inspections by the International Atomic Energy Agency.

Even before the terrorist attacks of September 11, 2001, the United States had employed a broader approach to self-defense against the al-Qaeda terrorist network. On October 7, 1998, terrorists killed 250 people in bombings of the U.S. embassies in Kenya and Tanzania. Based on "convincing evidence from a variety of reliable sources" that al-Qaeda was responsible, President Bill Clinton ordered cruise missile attacks on training camps in Afghanistan and a suspected chemical weapons installation in Sudan.[40] He claimed that the strikes were "a necessary and proportionate response to the imminent threat of further terrorist attacks against U.S. personnel and facilities." They were "intended to prevent and deter additional attacks by a clearly identified terrorist threat." Self-defense, however, seemed to exist only under the more flexible approach presented here. Al-Qaeda would attack again, but not until the bombing of the U.S.S. Cole two years later. Attacking the Sudanese pharmaceutical plant, moreover, would not have been necessary to stop any immediate al-Qaeda attack. Nonetheless, Ruth Wedgwood argued that "[e]ven by the demanding test of the *Caroline*…the danger of renewed assault [by al Qaeda] justified immediate action."[41] In its report to the Security Council after the strikes, the United States emphasized that it retaliated only after repeated warnings to Afghanistan and Sudan that they must stop harboring and supporting terrorist groups. The response of the international community to the attacks was mixed, but the Security Council took no formal action.[42]

Terrorism only reinforces the pressures on the temporal dimension of imminence reflected in these earlier cases. It depends on unpredictable, sporadic, and quick strikes on civilians using unconventional methods. Advances in transportation and communication and the proliferation of WMD technology allow terrorists to wield a destructive power that once was available only to nations. Few nations, in fact, could have leveled the World Trade Center and come close to destroying the Pentagon on September 11, 2001. Terrorists render themselves hard to locate because they disguise themselves as civilians and conceal their preparations as normal private activity. The hijackers, for example, pretended to be unremarkable passengers on U.S. domestic air flights. If a state waits until a terrorist attack is on the verge of launch, it will likely be unable to protect the targeted civilians—especially when the enemy employs suicide bombing, which is difficult to deter. As an attack nears, terrorists may already have burrowed deep into society, which may further limit detection and defensive options. To exercise its right to anticipatory self-defense, a nation may need to act within a window of opportunity to prevent an attack and minimize civilian casualties.

American policymakers have consistently approached terrorism with a broader sense of imminence, but they have not explained why. Thus, the United States claimed self-defense when it attacked terrorist targets in 1986 (Libya), 1993 (Iraq), and 1998 (Sudan), even though it sought to prevent attacks that were still in the planning rather than implementation stage. "A nation attacked by terrorists is permitted to use force to prevent or preempt future attacks," Reagan administration Secretary of State George Shultz said in defense of the 1986 strikes on Libya. "The law requires that such actions be necessary and proportionate. But this nation has consistently affirmed the rights of states to use force in exercise of their right of individual or collective self-defense."[43] It would be difficult, however, to claim that targeting Gadhafi, the Iraqi intelligence headquarters, or a suspected Sudanese chemical weapons plant was necessary to stop an attack in progress. Rather, these locations presented opportunities to minimize future harm and disrupt state sponsorship of terrorism. To require that states wait until a terrorist attack is temporally imminent would almost ask them to suffer an attack even before the right to self-defense could be triggered. As Shultz wrote more vividly: "The UN Charter is not a suicide pact."[44]

Events after September 11, 2001, highlight the change in self-defense from a temporal imminence rule to a more flexible standard. The September 11 attacks on the World Trade Center and the Pentagon demonstrated the destruction that could be wrought by the al-Qaeda terrorist network. Before September 11, al-Qaeda had succeeded in bombing American embassies in Africa and damaging a U.S. warship in a foreign port, but had posed no threat to an attack within the continental United States. While no further attack may have been temporally imminent in September 2001, the probability that al-Qaeda would launch attacks in the future remained high, given its past history and the public *fatwa* against the United States. UN Charter limits on the use of force would have required the United States to wait until al-Qaeda was just about to launch another attack from Afghanistan before invading and forcing the terrorist organization from its bases there.

But groups such as the al-Qaeda terrorist organization have a demonstrated hostility toward the United States and have shown their ability to launch devastating attacks on American targets both at home and abroad. In the last decade, al-Qaeda has continued its efforts to infiltrate operatives into the United States to carry out surprise attacks designed to cause mass civilian casualties. Given the clear intention and the magnitude of potential harm, the United States went to war in Afghanistan in October 2001 to defend itself, even though at the time there was no public evidence of an imminent attack on the United States. In fact, the government of Afghanistan itself had not carried out the September 11 attack, but had only refused to hand over Osama bin Laden and other al-Qaeda leaders responsible.

Temporal imminence may not affect the right to use force, but it might influence the amount of force. If al-Qaeda's plots are in the early planning stages, less destructive force may be called for. If they are closer to completion, more force might be warranted. An American strike against a suspected al-Qaeda leader far from any plots might demand the use of a drone strike with a high level of distinction and proportionality—in other words, the use of a relatively low-yield munition with limited civilian collateral damage. If a terrorist cell is training for an attack on a target, the United States might resort to larger munitions that might inflict higher civilian casualties. A defending state could use force to target specific terrorist leaders who are planning attacks, even if the exact nature of those attacks is unknown, so long as the strikes are limited. This could come close to violating the presidential ban on assassination, but, as Abraham Sofaer and Hays Parks have explained, assassination prohibits only murder and not killings undertaken in legitimate self-defense from attack.[45]

Many may interpret the 2003 Iraq War as an example of the dangers of a more flexible approach to war. But it also demonstrates the limitations of the strict imminence rule. At the time of the U.S.-led invasion, Iraq posed a security threat to nations in its region and in the West, but the gravity of the threat remained unclear. In Security Council Resolution 1441, passed unanimously on November 8, 2002, the UN Security Council declared its belief that Iraq was continuing to develop, if not stockpile, WMDs.[46] The Council recognized, for example, "the threat Iraq's non-compliance with Council resolutions and proliferation of weapons of mass destruction and long-range missiles poses to international peace and security." Iraq maintained its efforts to conceal its WMD efforts by frustrating international inspectors, oppressing its own population, and pursuing a policy of hostility toward the United States, which it had harbored since the 1991 Gulf War. As the Security Council found, Iraq remained in material breach of the ceasefire that had suspended hostilities by refusing to comply with its obligations to destroy and account for its WMD and ballistic missile programs.

Under the temporal imminence standard, the United States could not have claimed a right to use force against Iraq. There was no evidence that Iraq was preparing to launch an attack on the United States or its Western allies. Instead, any self-defense claim must rest on the concept of expected harm. Iraq's continuing development of WMDs threatened a high magnitude of potential harm to the United States and its allies. The legitimacy of the Iraq invasion is close to the line, however, because the probability of an actual attack remained so uncertain. Iraq bore strong hostility toward the United States, but it had no ballistic missiles capable of reaching American territory. Instead, the United States could have estimated the probability of an attack based on the prospect that Iraq might produce WMD and transfer them to nations or terrorists groups willing to use them against the United States. Only an expected harm analysis could justify the United States' decision to rely on both UN Security Council Resolutions and self-defense as justifications for the 2003 invasion of Iraq.[47] An imminence standard would have allowed Iraq to continue its WMD work undisturbed.

Decisions on the use of force rely on information collected and available only to the intelligence agencies and their political leadership. We can only judge their decisions using official public studies after the war. One official investigation, the Silberman-Robb commission, found that other Western intelligence agencies agreed with the CIA that Saddam Hussein's regime possessed WMDs. But, the commission found, the United States and its allies were ultimately wrong. In the commission's words, it was "one of the most public—and most damaging—intelligence failures in recent American history."[48] Even though U.S. intelligence was mistaken, however, the commission also found that Iraq was poised to reconstitute its WMD capabilities once it could break through the UN sanctions regime. Iraq presented an opponent with some probability of attack—it had hostile intentions and it had the knowledge and infrastructure to produce WMDs—but it lacked deployable weapons and the conventional means to deliver them. Because of Iraq's limited abilities, the probability and hence the expected harm of attack become lower. In that case, the United States should then have employed less destructive means to address the threats—surgical strikes, perhaps, rather than armored invasion.

The Iraq War underscores, if Kosovo or Rwanda did not, that self-defense can provide only a partial grounding for modern war. Nations have intervened where no attack was imminent, and hence no right to self-defense was triggered. Yet they also went to war without the aims of past wars of aggression, such as conquering territory, resources, or population. Some had the goal of preempting growing threats to international peace and security or stopping human rights catastrophes. A strict temporal imminence rule will prevent nations from using force to enhance global welfare because their own security is not directly threatened. Reconceiving the temporal imminence standard may capture some of the changes in international politics, but it will still result in a less-than-optimal use of force. Only a more ambitious reinvention of the international rules of war can provide a framework that encourages these good uses of force while still prohibiting aggressive wars. The next chapter begins this work.

5   Wars of Global Welfare

MODERN WEAPONS TECHNOLOGY, rogue nations, and terrorism pressure the international system's rules on war. Responding to these pressures by subsuming them all in the concept of self-defense is shortsighted. Limiting war only to cases of self-defense will prevent the world from reaching the optimal use of force in international affairs. Just as global welfare will decline if there is too much war, it will also suffer if there is too little. This is not some romantic vision found in literature: some wars can prevent outcomes worse than war itself, such as genocide, massive attacks on civilians, or abusive dictatorships in destabilized regions. As John Stuart Mill said: "War is an ugly thing, but not the ugliest of things."[1]

To adapt to the new world of security threats, the international system should reject rules that mimic criminal law. Once freed of the misguided notion that nations must follow the same self-defense rules that apply to individuals, we can develop a new framework to control the use of force. New rules should focus on maintaining global stability rather than advancing policies mired in inapposite concepts of criminal responsibility. The latter creates a vacuum where nations have little reason to cure harms to the international system as a whole. This leads to the counterintuitive result that the world suffers from too few uses of force, rather than too many. A new framework must align the incentives of the great powers to address threats to global welfare, even when other nations are the main beneficiaries.

I. Laws That Rule Individuals Cannot Rule War

Difficulties with the current rules on the use of force stem from borrowing a criminal law-based approach to responsibility. Rules created to curb violence between individuals within the same domestic community should not apply to an international system characterized by a lack of supranational government. Many scholars, however, believe that the problem begins with international rules that are too distant, rather than too close, to domestic criminal law. George Fletcher, for example, one of America's leading legal philosophers, criticizes the War on Terror and the war in Iraq because they are not justified under domestic criminal law concepts of self-defense.[2] Because "international law is still too thin to provide a reliable framework for understanding even such basic concepts as aggression and defense," Fletcher argues, "the solution is to draw on the leading domestic legal systems."[3] It is reasonable to use domestic self-defense law to inform international rules on force because "both fields regulate the actions of morally free agents in some way."[4] Fletcher even calls war "murder among nations."

Parallels arise between the rules governing the use of force in criminal and international law. In criminal law, a claim of self-defense against a charge of murder or assault can result in an acquittal. Many scholars agree that self-defense, used in this way, serves as a justification rather than an excuse for killing. The difference is that a justification asserts that the use of force itself is not wrong, even though the elements of murder might be satisfied, while an excuse concedes that the action was wrong but that it was not attributable to the defendant.[5] Shooting an enemy soldier, for example, is not murder because it is a justified act in wartime, even though the shooter intended to kill the individual. The laws of war recognize this principle by extending combatant immunity to soldiers who kill the enemy in wartime. An individual who is experiencing a psychotic episode and kills someone does not commit murder because he has the excuse that he was not responsible for his actions. On an international scale, self-defense justifies a defending nation's use of force, even if the defending nation commits the same acts as an attacker. In cases of anticipatory self-defense, the defender may even strike first but still not engage in illegal aggression.

Self-defense in criminal law has three common elements: imminence, necessity, and proportionality. As we have seen, imminence is a temporal concept: force can be used only when a defender can wait no longer, and it is based on a physical manifestation of an attack that makes clear that the moment for self-defense is "neither too soon nor too late."[6] The Model Penal Code defines it slightly differently: whether the defender "believes that such force is immediately necessary for the purpose of protecting himself."[7] Then, necessity demands that force remain the only option left to prevent an attack. If a victim can undertake a less harmful action that would protect himself, then force is unnecessary. A defender, for example, should seek escape or police protection before resorting to violence. Finally, proportionality requires that a defender not use force excessively or out of proportion to the threatened harm, which calls for a balancing of interests between the defender and aggressor.[8]

International law attempts to limit self-defense in nearly identical terms. A nation can resort to force only to stop an imminent attack. A resort to force must be made necessary only after peaceful alternatives have failed. Furthermore, a nation's application of force must be proportional to the threat. Scholars today even mix international and domestic approaches to force by illustrating domestic self-defense rules with examples drawn from international politics.[9] David Rodin observes that "national-defense is conceived, within international law and in the just war tradition, in very much the way that self-defense is conceived in domestic law and morality."[10]

Although it is an easy analogy, criminal law and world affairs are too different. Nations are not individuals, though it is a commonly misused mental shortcut to think of them as such. Henry Kissinger's quip that "nations do not have friends, only interests" tries to dispel this illusion. Nations are *collections* of individuals, just as other institutions are, and thus are better regulated by a different set of rules. The mistaken analogy, however, is understandable. During the founding of the modern international system, thinkers on world affairs thought of individuals and nations in similar terms, probably because most European nations were governed by hereditary monarchies. In his 1625 work, *The Rights of War and Peace*, for example, Hugo Grotius discussed national and individual self-defense in the same chapter. He argued that the right to kill an aggressor "derives its origin from the principle of self-preservation, which nature has given to every living creature, and not from the injustice or misconduct of the aggressor."[11] Explicitly borrowing from domestic rules, Grotius explained that "[w]hat has already been said of the right of defending our persons and property, though regarded chiefly private war [between persons], may nevertheless be applied to public hostilities, allowing for the difference of circumstances."[12] Swiss philosopher Emmerich de Vattel agreed: "every nation, as well as every man, has, therefore, a right to prevent other nations from obstructing her preservation, her perfection, and happiness—that is, to preserve herself from all injuries."[13]

Because almost all nations have abandoned monarchy, this view no longer makes sense, if it ever did. Allowing the rights of states to "naturally" mimic the rights of individuals is a concept that should fall by the wayside. Legal systems can grant institutions the same rights and duties as individuals, but they need not. For example, the U.S. Supreme Court has long held that corporations enjoy some of the due process rights of "persons" under the Fourteenth Amendment.[14] But commercial speech does not receive the same protection as political speech under the First Amendment,[15] though the Court recently (and controversially) held in *Citizens United v. Federal Election Commission* that corporations have the same right to engage in political campaign-related speech as individuals.[16] Institutions can even have greater rights not available to private persons: governments sometimes enjoy immunity from lawsuits, both under international and domestic law.[17]

Some scholars, however, take this argument to its extreme and argue that modern nation-states have no right to self-defense. Instead, they posit that any such right draws from a collective summation of every citizen's right to self-defense. David Luban, for example, declares that "wars are not fought by states, but by men and women," while philosopher Thomas Nagel notes that "war, conflict, and aggression are relations between persons."[18] Under this view, only the right of individuals to protect themselves and the lives of others exists. If a soldier's right to use force is no different than the right of an individual, war becomes simply a contest between groups of hostile individuals.

Artificial entities like governments and corporations, however, have an existence beyond a mere collection of individual persons. One of the most important concepts in war—the difference between *jus in bello* and *jus ad bellum*—depends on that construct. Under the laws of war, a conflict's lawfulness remains distinct from the fighting within the war itself. The soldiers who fight on either side of a conflict, for example, receive combatant immunity (freedom from prosecution for murder) and may attack and kill members of the enemy, regardless of the reasons for the war's outbreak. During World War II, not all Axis soldiers were war criminals, even though Germany's invasion of Poland was illegal. Conversely, even a nation that uses force for just and legal reasons may still violate the rules of warfare in its conduct of hostilities. A just war does not provide a writ to commit any and all measures to prevail. Philosopher Michael Walzer, for example, argues: "It is perfectly possible for a just war to be fought unjustly and for an unjust war to be fought in strict accordance with the rules."[19]

If national defense derives solely from the individual rights of the soldiers to self-preservation, the distinction between *jus in bello* and *jus ad bellum* breaks down. Soldiers who fight on behalf of a nation that illegally started a conflict would have no right to use force against their opponents. Just as an individual who seeks to murder a victim has no legal right to violence, soldiers of an illegally invading army could not legally use force. Some well-known philosophers, such as John Rawls, have suggested the adoption of this rule.[20] Nagel, for example, argued against the morality of fighting in the Vietnam War: "if the participation of the United States in the Indo-Chinese war is entirely wrong to begin with, then that engagement is incapable of providing a justification for any measures taken in its pursuit."[21] Philosopher Jeff McMahan has recently resuscitated the point: "It is morally wrong to fight in a war that is unjust because it lacks a just cause."[22] Even Fletcher calls this position "shocking." It would transform every death in the Iraq war into a murder and turn every American soldier into a murderer.[23] The international system continues to maintain the distinction between *jus in bello* and *jus ad bellum* today for many reasons: the contested nature of what constitutes a just war, the ambiguity over the rules of *jus in bello*, the unfairness of holding soldiers liable, and the dangers of blurring moral lines on the battlefield.[24] War, as it is actually fought, does not dissolve into thousands of individual duels between two opponents who pose an imminent threat to each other.

Some specific rules of combat illustrate the value of this distinction. Under the laws of war, soldiers may attack beyond the frontline units on the battlefield. For example, an army may target supporting forces, supply units and reinforcements, and nonfighting members of the armed forces such as clerks or cooks. It may also destroy units and infrastructure well behind the frontlines, including bases, munitions factories, and command-and-control facilities. It may even pursue and kill members of a broken and retreating army that can continue to fight and have not surrendered. In the 1991 Gulf War, for example, the U.S. Air Force utterly destroyed an Iraqi column fleeing Kuwait City with stolen booty. In all of these cases, soldiers may attack enemy elements that pose no imminent threat of direct harm. In a related example of *jus ad bellum*, a nation can go to war to repel border incursions or seizures of territory, even if no lives are in danger or the land is uninhabited.

Only by distinguishing between the individual and the national rights to use force can the broader, legitimate purposes for war be justified. Criminal law, for example, requires continuing necessity throughout a confrontation in order to use force.[25] Once a defender disables an attacker, the defender's right to use deadly force ends. For example, a homeowner who shoots an intruder in the leg so the latter cannot give chase must generally attempt to escape rather than continue to use deadly force. In global affairs, however, a nation need not end hostilities once it has expelled an invader from its territory. Instead it can continue to wage war, invade the defeated attacker, and occupy the invader's lands. In World War II, the Allies did not stop combat operations once German forces withdrew to their 1939 borders. Nor did they have to stop once they had forced the Japanese out of the Philippines. The Allies could continue on to defeat the Axis armed forces, change their regimes, and occupy Axis territory. Unlike individuals, a nation can continue hostilities to destroy an enemy's capability to renew its threat of aggression in the future.

Vast differences between domestic and international systems provide an even more compelling reason to treat individuals and nations differently. With individuals, the state holds a monopoly on violence. We are enjoined from using force because police and courts can use force to protect us from attackers. Individuals can only resort to violence when a threat is imminent and deadly and the police are not available to prevent the attack. As long ago as Blackstone, the duty to retreat requires that "the private use of force is tolerated only because the state fails in its task of providing protection against aggression."[26] The government's effectiveness in preventing violence relieves us of the ability to use force.

The logic of applying individual self-defense notions to nations breaks down because physical escape is not possible, and there is no police to step in and protect against aggression. Criminal law seeks to achieve the "legal outlawry of the arena of self-help in the settlement of potentially fatal personal conflicts," in the words of the U.S. Court of Appeals for the D.C. Circuit.[27] In international affairs, however, anarchy reigns and self-help is the norm. There is no central world government that can effectively protect nations from attack. Although the UN Charter prohibits wars of aggression, it has no military forces to live up to its mandate. The Security Council can order nations to send forces to oust an aggressor, but it has no resources to enforce its dictates—and it has a woeful track record of persuading third parties to help. Between the Korean and Persian Gulf wars, the Security Council could not agree on a single war that justified a call on member states for a military response. Failure of the great powers on the Security Council to agree reduced the United Nations' military role to peacekeeping—a far different use of force than intervention or war. UN peacekeepers do not begin or end conflicts but maintain ceasefires and peace treaties, monitor borders, and, more recently, have attempted to stabilize conflict-torn societies—with mixed results. After the Cold War, the tempo of UN peacekeeping operations rose dramatically, but that resulted in some notable failures in Somalia, Rwanda, and the Balkans.[28] Despite the burst of smaller interventions after the Cold War, Security Council action remains the exception, rather than the rule.

II. War As "Not the Ugliest of Things"

Another significant difference between the domestic and international systems is the optimal level of conflict. Within a nation, a community wants to reduce the number of homicides to zero. The government draws self-defense rules strictly to prevent mistaken, ill-conceived, or pretextual murders. Restricting the use of force only to cases where a deadly attack is open and imminent, with no chance of escape, limits justifiable violence to those cases that will result in death or serious harm. Self-defense should not increase the overall level of violence by much. Leading scholars commonly make similar arguments about international politics. They argue that, without strict standards to govern the use of force, states will use self-defense as a pretext whenever they seek to advance their own self-interests. Professor Thomas Franck argues, for example, that "a general relaxation of Article 51's prohibitions on unilateral war-making to permit unilateral recourse to force whenever a state feels potentially threatened could lead to [a] reductio ad absurdum."[29] International law, according to Franck, must require more than threats before self-defense may be triggered: "The law cannot have intended to leave every state free to resort to military force whenever it perceived itself grievously endangered by actions of another, for that would negate any role for law."[30]

Franck and others assume that there is a correlation between the strictness of a legal rule and the ability of nations to use the rule as a pretext. Nations have often claimed self-defense to justify attacks, both before and after the UN Charter, and there is no indication that the rate of these claims has declined as a result of a more restrictive set of rules.[31] Germany, for example, claimed self-defense when it invaded Poland, while the Soviets argued that its invasions of Hungary in 1956 and Czechoslovakia in 1968 were justified under international law. Similarly, a more flexible rule may have little effect on whether states continue to claim pretextual justifications for war. In domestic law, using a formal rule may reduce the level of pretextual claims by police or judges. But there is little evidence that formality will have the same effect on the international rules on the use of force, in part because domestic police and judges are subject to thicker institutional constraints that do not restrain nations, such as appellate review and override by Congress.

The main point is that the desirable level of force in the international system is greater than zero. States have used force at various levels of intensity to achieve goals that have benefited all members of the international community. Great Britain, for example, used its unmatched naval dominance in the nineteenth century to destroy the slave trade at a high cost to itself in men, ships, and money.[32] It enforced a *Pax Brittanica* on the high seas that led to increased international commerce and free navigation. In 1917, the United States intervened in World War I to maintain a balance of power on the Continent and prevent the victory of the autocratic Central Powers. The United States fought again twenty-five years later to stop the expansion of fascist regimes in Europe and Asia, and it contained communism for another half century through a series of proxy wars and military alliances around the world. For the last sixty years, the United States Navy has replaced Her Majesty's Navy, but the goal remains the same: to keep open navigation and free commerce on the high seas. Great Britain and the United States did not act out of pure altruism. Both countries undoubtedly deployed their armed forces to achieve important national objectives. But they also advanced global welfare by spreading international trade and democracy and containing the spread of authoritarianism and bankrupt economic systems.

As great power conflict evaporated at the end of the Cold War, wars to provide global public goods have increased. Humanitarian intervention is the most prominent example. Western nations roused themselves to stop disasters that were not caused by nature but by the intentional repression of peoples by their own states, the collapse of centralized government authority, or religious and ethnic strife. They intervened to restore order or to end repressive regimes. Although the Charter forbids infringement of the territorial sovereignty and political independence of member nations, the Security Council authorized military action with regard to the internal affairs of Somalia, Haiti, Bosnia, and East Timor to stop human rights catastrophes. Even in cases where the UN would not act, nations have ignored the Charter and intervened, for example in Kosovo, Francophone Africa, and, arguably, Iraq.

A coalition of nations even supports a broader "responsibility to protect" doctrine to create a legal basis for humanitarian intervention. That principle would allow intervention in cases where a government is committing systematic human rights abuses. In 2006, the Security Council endorsed the responsibility to protect in a resolution.[33] Nonetheless, UN member nations have not amended Articles 2(4) or 51 to recognize this new responsibility, which is in tension with the Charter's core guarantee of territorial sovereignty. Perhaps more important, the UN may not be able to live up to this new responsibility. The Security Council acknowledges that the responsibility to protect will be enforced through regular channels, which means that the same institutional paralysis that has pervaded the United Nations for most of its history will likely continue unabated. Nevertheless, the "responsibility to protect" idea recognizes that the use of force can achieve valuable objectives that exceed the costs of war.

While preventing humanitarian disasters may provide the most vivid payoff, military force can advance the global good in other ways. Authoritarian regimes may pose harmful threats not just to the United States but also to other nations because of their coercive economic or political systems or aggressive plans for expansion. Opposing their threats can free millions and rebuild international stability. Nazi Germany presents an obvious example. Imagine if the Allies had intervened to remove Hitler from power by the time of the Munich Agreement or before the invasion of Poland. The use of force would have increased global welfare by preventing his genocidal campaign against Jews and other minorities and precluding the millions of battle casualties caused by his wars. Earlier intervention would have removed an evil regime with an ideology and expansionist goals that disrupted the international system and led to the most deadly war in human history. Imperial Japan presents another possibility. Suppose the United States had struck the Japanese Navy immediately before Pearl Harbor, or had strangled Tokyo's economic lifelines during its aggressive expansion in the 1930s. Halting Japan's plans could have saved millions of lives in China and forestalled the oppression of many Pacific nations.

World War II may offer too easy a case, so a better example comes from the Cold War. As the Grand Alliance dissolved, the Soviet Union imposed its communist economic and authoritarian political systems wherever its Red Army held sway. Accordingly, the United States formed a series of alliances around the Soviet bloc and waged proxy wars to contain it. After almost a half century of competition, the Soviet bloc collapsed and left the United States as the remaining superpower. The United States pursued its own national interest by containing the spread of Soviet influence in Western Europe and Asia, but America's containment policy also promoted global welfare by preventing the expansion of totalitarianism to new countries. The people of Western Europe, Japan, South Korea, and Southwest Asia surely were better off because of the American military and political assistance that prevented the rise of communist governments. American policy to protect its own security and interests also created a positive externality of spreading economic and political freedom to other peoples.

Rogue nations, as the Clinton and Bush administrations called them, or nations of concern in the Obama lexicon, present modern-day versions of the Soviet threat. Whatever their name, these states harm global welfare in two ways. First, they severely oppress their own populations both politically and economically. Take the two Koreas. At the end of the Korean War, South Korea was a small agrarian nation with a population of about 21 million. It went on a development boom that created the world's thirteenth largest economy and a vibrant democracy of 48 million. In the early 1960s, South Korea's GDP per capita matched the lowest levels in Africa and Asia; as of this writing, its GDP is estimated at $1.64 trillion.[34] North Korea, by contrast, has remained one of the most extreme dictatorships left on earth. It imposes a crushing economic system characterized by severe famines, malnutrition, and lack of basic services. Its population has stagnated for the past decade at around 24 million. Its barely functional economy is shrinking almost 1 percent a year. Its GDP sits at the bottom of the world at $40 billion per year.[35] Forceful overthrow of the North Korean regime, might not lead to an identical growth trajectory to South Korea, but it would save millions from suffering and dying under a deadly, misguided ideology.

Second, states such as Saddam Hussein's Iraq or present-day North Korea often pose a threat to the nations around them. These regimes refuse to abide by the basic principles of the international system and may seek to export revolution or disrupt the existing order. Nazi Germany, fascist Italy, and Imperial Japan present the obvious historical parallels, but more recent examples are at hand. North Korea has attempted to assassinate South Korean leaders, sparked border conflicts, and amassed a huge army along the demilitarized zone. And despite its poverty, North

Korea continues its quest to deploy nuclear-armed intercontinental ballistic missiles. As the last remnants of Cold War divisions, North and South Korea may pose a unique case. But some other countries that impose repressive domestic regimes have also pursued destabilizing foreign policies. Under Saddam Hussein's dictatorship, Iraq invaded Iran in the 1980s and attacked Kuwait in 1990. Under the Assad family, Syria has spent decades stoking civil war in Lebanon and supporting Islamic terrorist groups that attack Israel. Between the Communist Party's ascension to power in 1950 and its economic opening in the 1970s, China fought wars with many of its neighbors, including Russia, India, and Vietnam. After the breakup of Yugoslavia, Serbia combined internal ethnic cleansing with external warfare against other former provinces. Scholars suggest that repressive governments seek expansionist policies abroad to increase political control, distract unhappy populations, and placate supporting elites. Whatever the reason, these nations challenge the stability of the existing international order and threaten global harm by their external aggression and their internal repression.

Failed states, which will be discussed in greater detail in Chapter 7, also call out for military intervention. Failed states are territories where centralized authority has collapsed or has been hijacked by violent nonstate actors, such as terrorist groups or militias. Failed states cannot provide basic services to their populations nor stop conflict between ethnic, religious, or tribal groups—often triggering humanitarian disasters. States without an effective government may provide terrorist or criminal organizations with a safe haven to recruit and instruct fighters, to organize weapons and finances, or to establish transshipment points for illicit money, drugs, weapons, and personnel. Somalia, for example, not only gave rise to warlords who disrupted the delivery of basic necessities and abused the human rights of civilians, but it also became a breeding ground for al-Shabaab and other militant extremists who exported violence to other African nations and the high seas. Afghanistan allowed al-Qaeda to freely operate headquarters and training camps, from which al-Qaeda launched the offensive against the United States that culminated in the September 11, 2001, attacks. Without effective governing institutions, failed states remain powerless to prevent the use of their territory as a launching pad for attacks on other countries.

Such conduct within the borders of a failed state will decrease global welfare. A failed state might become a central operating position for a terrorist network to project power into nearby nations, which may in turn destabilize those governments and societies. The international system may benefit from the use of force in such circumstances not only because of the restoration of order in a state with a weak or nonexistent government but also because of the elimination of a base that results in destabilizing terrorist attacks in several nations. And it need not just be terrorist networks: failed states could provide a free zone for other groups whose activities harm global welfare and order, such as drug cartels, human traffickers, arms dealers, and anyone else engaged in conduct suppressed in other countries. A failure of internal government can present a threat to the international system.

III. Changing the War Calculus

Today's rules on war do not adequately confront these twenty-first-century challenges to international security. They remain rooted in a fear of the great power conflicts that brought such ruin in the last century. They rely on notions of criminal responsibility, which hope to stifle interstate war by reducing violence among nations to zero. But the international system today suffers far more from internal conflict than from great power competition. The goals of domestic law enforcement make little sense when transplanted to the higher level of world politics. Rejection of the criminal law framework can free us to develop an approach that meets the threats before us today while more accurately matching the rules to the realities of great power competition.

In international politics and economics, scholars have focused on the study of international public goods.[36] International public goods are, naturally, the global counterpart of domestic public goods. When domestic markets function properly, the uncoordinated actions of self-interested actors will result in the optimal production of goods and services. Prices represent the transmission of information that allows consumers to communicate the desired amount of goods or services. Producers will make a good or service until the marginal revenue falls to the marginal cost of the good or service, and at that point the market will clear.

Public goods, however, are those that benefit society but that the private markets do not produce at the optimal rate.[37] Public goods have two salient characteristics. They are nonrivalrous: one actor's consumption of a public good does not leave less for other consumers. And they are nonexclusive: it is not feasible to charge people for consuming the good. The costs of excluding nonpaying beneficiaries are so high that private firms will not supply the good.[38] Domestic examples include clean air and national defense. Clean air benefits all members of a community, regardless of whether they pay for it or not. This is even more the case for national defense. The military's protection of a nation benefits all living within the territory, regardless of whether they financially contribute or not. Public goods also suffer from the problem that producers and consumers do not fully internalize their costs and benefits. Because everyone enjoys the benefits of a public good, but few may bear its costs, producers will have little incentive to produce the optimal amount, and consumers will consume too much of it. In many cases, only the government can ensure the collective action needed to provide the efficient level of public goods, because of its ability to impose taxes and legislate for society as a whole.

Collective action can also produce similar effects by curing public harms. Government intervention, in other words, can correct market failures such as negative externalities or undefined property rights. A factory, for example, might pollute a river in one jurisdiction where the benefits of production are realized, but the pollution may then flow downstream into another jurisdiction, which suffers the harms. The factory will overproduce the good, because it does not take into account the pollution's harms, until it has fully internalized the costs of its production. Another related example is known as the tragedy of the commons. A commons like a fishery or an oil deposit may be overexploited because producers have a short-term profit interest in harvesting as much of a resource as possible, even though the resources would produce more in the long run with more moderate annual withdrawals. In this case, the public harm arises because of an inability to exclude producers, rather than consumers without clear property rights.

Such collective action problems are familiar concepts to domestic economic and legal scholars.[39] International law scholars have taken up the idea to analyze areas of interstate cooperation, such as the environment and health.[40] But both groups tend to overlook the classic public good of national security because its benefits are so obvious. National security is often provided as the quintessential public good, without the need for much analysis. Its international counterpart is peace and stability. The provision of international peace and security benefits all of the actors in the international system because it avoids the waste and destruction of war, reduces spending on arms and the military, and promotes mutually beneficial trade. Nations will suffer less from mass refugee migrations, while cross-border investment and exchange will improve, and greater certainty will allow markets to expand. International stability should come before all other public goods because without it, the international system is unlikely to achieve much progress with other collective action problems, such as the environment or public health.

As a public good, international stability will be undersupplied because it is nonexclusive and nonrivalrous. If one nation or a group maintains international security, then all nations benefit, even those that contribute little. One nation will find it difficult, though perhaps not impossible, to bar others from enjoying the benefits of international peace. One of the early public choice theorists, Mancur Olson, speculated that defensive alliances such as NATO might overcome collective action problems of international security by spreading the burden of its costs among many nations.[41] Joseph Nye has more recently argued that American power should maintain regional balances of power as a way to provide international stability.[42]

Nevertheless, rational states pursuing their national interest will have no incentive to supply more international stability than they individually need. A nation may pay for security, but only to the point where that security proportionally increases its own national welfare. Because nations may not capture the full benefits of the international security that they produce (because free-riding nations will benefit but not pay), they will always produce a suboptimal amount.

This dynamic equally applies to the use of force, which maintains international peace and security. Nations will go to war too little, rather than too much, to attempt to keep world order. The international legal system, therefore, should encourage nations to use force when the global benefits outweigh the global costs. Contemporary rules on the use of force, however, have the opposite effect. By demanding that the level of interstate violence fall to zero, the international legal system prohibits many wars and smaller-scale interventions that might improve overall global welfare.

The challenge presented by current international rules becomes even more profound when we consider the asymmetries in national resources, populations, location, and stages of economic development. As a result, states will have varying abilities to take the actions needed to promote stability while accruing different amounts of benefits. This makes nations even less likely to cooperate to supply the optimal amount of international security. Nineteenth-century Great Britain, for example, deployed a large navy that protected the freedom of the seas. Free navigation and commerce benefited Britain more than most nations, with its island location, dependence on commerce, and extensive but dispersed empire. Freedom of the seas, however, also helped other seafaring nations, most notably the United States. Britain's naval shield protected the United States from other European nations while its economy developed and its territory grew. Yet the British could not compel the United States to share the cost of maintaining the freedom of the seas, and when two nations pay for joint security, rational choice theory predicts that the nation that values security more will bear a disproportionate share of the costs.[43]

These values cannot be measured with precision. Nevertheless, there are some clearer cases. In Kosovo, Afghanistan, and Iraq, the threat of a future attack on the United States itself may have been relatively low compared to the costs of the war. Yet war ended broader harms to the international system that went beyond any threats to American national security. Here, war put a stop to humanitarian disasters and ethnic cleansing, drove international terrorists out of a safe haven, and overthrew authoritarian regimes that posed a military threat to their neighbors. While the United States benefited, it also bore the lion's share of the costs. The rest of the world benefited while paying far less. Whether these wars were purely in American self-interest is a difficult question, but regardless of how that question is answered, the wars benefited the greater interests of the world.

We must recognize an important cost of moving toward this new calculus of war. New rules could have a destabilizing effect on the international system. Less legal restraints on war might encourage the great powers to resort to force more often. Weaker nations may have greater fears for their own independence and territory. This greater uncertainty may cause nations to spend more on their militaries, resort to force more often by intention or mistake, and undermine the benefits of peace. Costs may also accrue from the wider impact of an intervention against a nation that fiercely and effectively resists attack. For example, human rights abuses, terrorism, and cross-border tensions between India and Pakistan no doubt add to the instability in Central and South Asia. But any military intervention by the great powers would create only more loss of life and instability, given the military strength of the contending states. Intervention to prevent human rights abuses might save many lives, but it also might cause nations to fear whether the great powers will intrude into their internal affairs. States might respond by building up their forces and engaging in their own hostile military conduct.

A new system, however, might create new opportunities to mitigate these costs. As the next chapter argues, the leading democracies might band together to form a loose alliance similar to the nineteenth-century Concert of Europe. Its members could refrain from force until a significant number lent their support. This mechanism would show that other nations, with different interests and power positions in the world, had reviewed the evidence and agreed that the calculus of global costs and benefits favored intervention. Their democratic systems might reassure other nations that they do not seek territorial conquest or spheres of influence. Indeed, the great powers would have an interest in developing new ways to reduce suspicions that their use of force advances their realist self-interests, rather than global welfare. Alleviating concerns about motivation will head off resistance to welfare-enhancing interventions, reduce costs to the system overall, and even yield more cooperation in solving threats to international peace and security. Committing to such a system would send an expensive "signal" to the rest of the world that a great power had more than its selfish conquest at heart.

As a matter of substance, the great powers could also commit to the economic restoration of weaker nations. Reconstruction costs would play the role of damages in the common law. If the great powers violate the global welfare rule and start an armed conflict where the global costs exceed benefits, they should compensate the injured party—just as in a tort action, the tortfeasor must pay an injured party when the former has acted negligently. To pursue the tort analogy even further, the great powers could establish their reconstruction policy as one of strict liability. Whether the great powers reach the right global welfare judgment or not, they should restore economic conditions to the status quo ante and attempt to repair the destruction of war. This would force the great powers to internalize more of the costs of an armed conflict and weigh heavier against a war's purported benefits. We can understand U.S. policy on Afghanistan and Iraq after the 2001 and 2003 invasions as movement toward this rule. In both nations, the United States went beyond removing the regime in power toward rebuilding the economy and society with efforts that cost billions of dollars, thousands of lives, and years of government focus. To be sure, the United States pursued reconstruction policies to establish a regime that would no longer pose a threat to its security, but it also had the broader, system-wide effect of forcing the United States to realize the costs of the wars and to put into place a government that would pose less threat to regional peace and security.

Costs of intervention can also be understood as a principal-agent problem. In domestic affairs, government allows citizens to cooperate to solve collective action problems. Nonetheless, public goods may still be imperfectly provided due to self-interested government officials, captured bureaucracies, or interest group rent-seeking.[44] Agents, in other words, may misuse the power delegated to them by their principals, a fact noted as long ago as Alexander Hamilton's *Federalist 78* and Chief Justice John Marshall's opinion in *Marbury v. Madison*. Hamilton argued, for example, that the Constitution had to be paramount law because it represented the grant of authority by the people (the principals) to the government (the agents). Without the basic proposition that the agents could only act within the power granted by the principals in the Constitution, the government, rather than the people, would be sovereign. Or, as Hamilton wrote, it "would be to affirm that the deputy is greater than his principal . . . that men acting by virtue of powers may do not only what their powers do not authorise, but what they forbid."[45]

At the international level, we can understand the rules on the use of force as a limit on the agent (the United States and other great powers) imposed by the principal (the world's people). Just as in domestic affairs, international institutions might see agents use their discretion to pursue their own advantage rather than acting in the best interests of the principal. The United States, for example, could claim that a war advances global welfare, when it actually provides Washington with benefits but at high costs for the rest of the world. Prevention of such self-serving wars can take several forms. For instance, international law could demand that great powers conclude a war by quickly restoring international stability, maintaining existing national borders, and removing their forces rather than installing a permanent military presence. This could demonstrate that the United States and other great powers remain faithful to the goals of the system.

International security depends on aligning the interests of the great powers with those of all nations. This impacts the choice of a rule or a standard to govern war. Principals should choose a rule when the distrust of the great powers is high. Recall that a strict rule will place more authority in the hands of those who enact a law beforehand. A more flexible standard grants discretion to future leaders who will interpret and apply a law. An anarchical international system only increases the possibility of abuse, because those who use force will often also be the interpreter and applier of the norm. In the international system, there is no truly effective third party, such as the courts in domestic affairs, that can enforce the terms of the delegations of authority from principal to agent. A standard, however, would fit better if other conditions hold. If there is less concern about powerful nations drifting from the purposes of a rule, it might be more appropriate to delegate authority to them. If the issue is serious or unpredictable, a standard may prove more appropriate because it shifts authority to the decision-maker of the future. Under a standard, the agent can more effectively tailor the use of force to unpredictable or unanticipated circumstances.

Wars among the great powers in pursuit of territorial gain have declined while new intrastate threats have increased. These developments should tilt the balance toward a standard. A stable international system divided between two hegemonic powers—such as in the Cold War—yields more predictable competition and thus is more amenable to a rule. The post-9/11 world, however, presents a greater kaleidoscope of challenges. Rogue nations, civil wars, terrorism, and WMD proliferation pose new threats to the United States and global peace for which there are no easy or clear answers. The more unpredictable the future crises, the more a standard should govern. With harm from these unconventional problems reaching or even exceeding those of interstate wars, the gains in international stability through the use of force outweigh potential principal-agent costs. This calculus could change, however, if the identity and goals of the stabilizing great power or powers were to change.

IV. War for Public Goods

Our public goods approach explains modern war more convincingly than the criminal justice model. Even though critics have sharply attacked the Kosovo and Iraq Wars, other nations in the system have been more careful in their responses. Kosovo, for example, is difficult to understand as self-defense, even under the more flexible standard of imminence outlined in Chapter 4. Some nations, such as Russia and China, protested. "Attempts to justify the NATO strikes with arguments about preventing a humanitarian catastrophe in Kosovo are completely untenable," Russia's ambassador to the United Nations declared. "Not only are these attempts in no way based on the Charter or other generally recognized rules of international law, but the unilateral use of force will lead precisely to a situation with truly devastating humanitarian consequences."[46] But after the conflict ended, Russia sent peacekeeping forces to Kosovo and declined to veto a Security Council resolution authorizing the entry of NATO troops and the withdrawal of Serbian forces.[47] Debates between international lawyers over whether the intervention was "legitimate" but not "legal" were beside the point. NATO carried out the Kosovo War, and the other great powers acquiesced. While postwar acceptance of Kosovar independence does not constitute ex ante approval, the Security Council's cooperation suggests that the other major powers accepted the war.

A flexible cost-benefit analysis accounts better for this turn of events. Although conflict involving the Albanian minority in Kosovo had been an internal matter of the former Yugoslavia, it threatened to become regional. In reaction to military operations by the Serbian military in 1998 and 1999, roughly 600,000 Kosovars had fled to neighboring states, and an additional 850,000—out of a total population of 2 million—had been internally displaced. When NATO air strikes began in March 1999, Serbian troops immediately tried to drive the rest of the Kosovars out of the country. The population outflow had a destabilizing effect on surrounding nations, which had to house refugees and might have become staging grounds for rebel attacks on Serbia. While the other former provinces of Yugoslavia immediately received refugees, the flow continued into Italy, Austria, Hungary, and Greece. The Balkans had already been the tinderbox for one European war, and NATO leaders were concerned that more instability might draw Russia into the conflict. War in Kosovo not only ended a humanitarian crisis, but it also restored stability in an important region of the world. While ending the Kosovo conflict no doubt benefited the United States and its European allies, it also benefited the international system by reducing the chance of a wider conflict.

Afghanistan provides another example of a war that has improved global welfare. Of course, the United States had a self-defense interest in attacking the al-Qaeda terrorist organization based there. Although the September 11 attacks were launched from within the United States, al-Qaeda planned, trained for, and financed the attacks from inside Afghanistan. With the Taliban's approval, al-Qaeda located its personnel, training camps, and headquarters in Afghanistan. But whether the proportional use of force included the replacement of the Taliban with a friendlier regime is less clear. Leading international legal scholars maintain that whether force can be used against a state that harbors terrorists "remains controversial."[48] After September 11, however, the Security Council condemned the terrorist attacks as "a threat to international peace and security" and "recognize[d] the inherent right of individual or collective self-defense in accordance with the Charter" but did not explicitly authorize the use of force against Afghanistan itself.[49] Nonetheless, after the overthrow of the Taliban regime, the United Nations gave its approval to the reconstruction of Afghanistan—a sign that the great powers accepted the outcome.

As with Kosovo, the Afghanistan intervention may have benefited the United States more than other nations, but it also contributed to the public good of international stability. Afghanistan had become a safe haven for terrorists groups, which could operate without being pursued by national police or military forces. Al-Qaeda could gather and train its forces without fear, base its infrastructure and support structure securely, and send out cells of terrorists to launch attacks unimpeded. In addition to striking American targets, al-Qaeda sought to destabilize different regimes in the Middle East and Asia, such as Saudi Arabia and Indonesia, and operate a terrorist network that reached into Europe and Africa. Terrorist groups are difficult to deter and negotiate with, and they use force indiscriminately against civilians. Al-Qaeda marked the emergence of an international nonstate terrorist organization that had the resources to engage in a level of destruction that, in the past, rested only within the hands of nation-states. Ending the unhindered terrorist operations in Afghanistan eliminated significant negative externalities experienced by the world.

Iraq raises a more difficult case. Arguments continue over whether Iraq constituted a direct threat of attack toward the United States. Prewar evidence of Iraq's WMDs was critical as a test not just of presidential truthfulness or the competence of the American intelligence community but also of the war's global benefits. Saddam Hussein certainly had the hostile intent to attack the United States and its forces abroad. The Bush administration viewed Iraqi links to terrorism as valid concerns that Hussein might indirectly attack the United States by transferring weapons to hostile nations or terrorist groups. While this may have once seemed unlikely, the September 11 terrorist attacks demonstrated that an enemy could project force without employing conventional armies, fleets, or aircraft. Nonetheless, self-defense as a justification proved extremely controversial, and as a result, the United States argued that it was primarily enforcing previous Security Council resolutions designed to contain Saddam Hussein.[50] Several nations, including three of the five permanent members of the Security Council, responded that an invasion of Iraq violated the UN Charter. While the dispute over the war's legality continues, with much of the international legal academy against it, the Security Council enacted three resolutions recognizing the occupation of Iraq.[51]

Even if Iraq did not present a case of direct attack on the United States, the war fits more comfortably within a framework of international peace and security than one of national self-defense. Iraq had destabilized the Middle East for decades. It had pursued nuclear weapons, fought a bloody eight-year war against Iran, and launched an unprovoked invasion of Kuwait. It had attacked Israel during the Gulf War in an effort to spark a broader Israeli-Arab conflict. It repressed its own population, used chemical weapons against both its own people and Iran, and supported terrorist groups that targeted Israel and the United States in the past (putting aside the later controversy over any links between Iraq and al-Qaeda). Since the end of the Gulf War, the United States and its allies had spent billions to contain Iraq and prevent it from restoring its WMD programs. Iraq had imposed significant costs on the international system. Only the constant application of countervailing force had maintained some stability in the region.

This accounting of Iraq's challenge to peace in the Middle East may have been enough to justify Western intervention. Whether Iraq posed an even greater danger depends, in part, on the advanced state of its WMD research and production. An Iraq armed with WMDs would have multiplied its own military power in the region and increased its ability to deter conventional responses to contain its aggressive moves. Standing alone, WMD capability may not pose enough of a direct threat to justify war. Some scholars argue that nuclear weapons might even reduce the chances of conflict by raising the costs of invasion.[52] Only when capability marries intention might a palpable threat emerge to regional peace and security. The character of the Hussein regime, armed with WMDs, increased instability and reduced global welfare. This conclusion overlaps with American self-defense claims for an invasion of Iraq. But while nuclear weapons may multiply the direct threat to the United States, they might have an even broader impact on international peace and security by sparking regional conflicts and a nuclear arms race.

We should not downplay the costs of turning to war to solve the problem of Iraq. Removing the Hussein regime and eliminating Iraq's WMD capabilities reduced a potential threat to regional peace. On the opposite side of the ledger, the war took thousands of lives, both military (about 4,500 U.S. armed forces) and civilian (estimates of 100,000 to 601,000 Iraqi civilians),[53] and cost the United States alone an estimated $800 billion in direct military appropriations, which does not include the hundreds of billions in longer-term expenses.[54] Broader costs should include the conflict's destabilizing effect. The Iraq War may have undermined the steadiness of nearby regimes, provoked a continuing domestic conflict that spiraled into more violence, and sent refugees fleeing throughout the region. It diverted American power and influence from the rest of the world and may have dealt U.S. prestige a serious blow in the region.

Determining the long-term effects of this invasion for the region will prove even more difficult. Some positive effects include the pacification of Iraq and the removal of the Baathist regime. The establishment of democratic government in Iraq may have inspired the spread of revolutions in Tunisia, Egypt, Libya, and Syria, which at least sought to overthrow authoritarian regimes, if not replace them with democracies. It may have led Libya to abandon its WMD programs, though it might have accelerated Iran's drive to acquire them. Negative effects could include an increase in terrorist activities in Iraq and the region, and a flare-up in the Israeli-Palestinian dispute.

Deciding on any war must include a consideration of system-wide costs. A more flexible legal regime may produce the optimal amount of force, but it may also allow too much force. Because there is no effective world government with a monopoly on force, collective action problems will remain acute. No nation can fully internalize the costs and benefits of using force in situations that go beyond self-defense. Nations have shown great reluctance to use force to stop purely humanitarian disasters, even if the commitment of troops required is relatively low. When the United States sent troops to Somalia in 1993 to solve a humanitarian crisis, the deaths of eighteen soldiers in a botched operation led to withdrawal. After the Somalia debacle, the Clinton administration refused to send a few thousand troops to Rwanda, which could have forestalled a genocide that killed nearly 1 million people. Intervention costs would have fallen mostly upon the United States, while the benefits would have accrued primarily to the rest of the world. Rational choice theory predicts that nations will rarely, if ever, intervene to provide such diffused public goods.

These collective action problems become more difficult when no single nation can act to shore up international security in several places at once. Even nations powerful enough to stop destabilizing problems may soon exhaust their resources and political will. Unlike the 1991 Persian Gulf War, nations may refuse to pay for the cost of wars that do not benefit them directly. For example, it is doubtful whether the United States received sufficient benefits in Kosovo, Afghanistan, or Iraq to outweigh its costs. Benefits may have accrued to the world as a whole, beyond those to the United States, but the other recipients of these benefits did not have to contribute. It is grounds for pessimism that the international system has no mechanism for compensating nations to engage in such conflicts. As with the British Navy in the nineteenth century, we can expect to see interventions only where the benefits will accrue in a greater proportion to the United States or other great powers that undertake them—and where these captured benefits outweigh the costs of intervention. Wars that benefit the world the most will also be the ones that are the most rare.

"Hegemonic stability theory," developed by economists and political scientists, provides support for this conclusion. It maintains that a single great power or small group of powers—the hegemon—can overcome the collective action problem created by large numbers of states in an anarchical international system.[55] Other nations permit the hegemon to exercise control over world affairs because, without its dominance, free-riding problems would doom the provision of international public goods. A hegemonic power, however, will not provide public goods unless it is able to realize benefits that either approximate or exceed the costs of keeping world order. Otherwise, over time, maintaining the international regime will exhaust its resources.

International relations theorists have questioned whether a hegemon is necessary for the maintenance of a stable international regime. Some suggest that nations can overcome collective action problems through international institutions without a single overweening nation.[56] Such post-hegemonic theories, however, require that nations trust each other to keep their promises in environments where no institutions compel compliance.[57] Without courts and police, private parties may well not trust each other enough to live up to their contracts. Still, it is not critical that an international regime, supported by a constellation of weaker powers, supply public goods. Rather, all that is needed from the theory is the conclusion that a hegemonic power could supply peace and stability, if it chooses to do so, and the conditions under which that may occur. Given that nonhegemonic powers and alliances have proven unable to directly address the problems posed by Kosovo, Afghanistan, Iraq, or Libya, international legal rules should be reconceived to encourage hegemonic powers to intervene to maintain international peace and security, rather than to discourage their intervention.

The great powers are unlikely to engage in purely humanitarian intervention unless regional or international security is at stake. While the wars in Kosovo, Afghanistan, and Iraq ended terrible regimes, the United States and its allies did not fight solely to stop oppression. Somalia and Rwanda demonstrated that the great powers would risk little to stop humanitarian abuses when their own national interests were not at stake. Whether the international system ultimately will accept humanitarian intervention under the analysis suggested here will depend on several factors. First, gross human rights violations create a negative externality that inflicts harm on others.[58] Second, intervention to stop human rights abuses, if widely adopted, may destabilize the international system. Nation-states may fear that humanitarian intervention is just a pretext for great power interference in their internal affairs. Third, overthrowing regimes that oppress their citizens may help improve international peace beyond saving the lives that were at risk. Nations such as Iraq, Afghanistan, Serbia, North Korea, and Libya, which systematically abused their own citizens, also engaged in destabilizing activities that threatened the international system. Even failed states that have no capacity for aggression against their neighbors, such as Afghanistan or Somalia, may still provide fertile ground for terrorist organizations that threaten other nations.

There is clear tension between a framework that allows the use of force to stabilize an international system founded on sovereignty and one that allows the use of force for humanitarian intervention. While the former acts to bolster nation-state sovereignty, the latter overrides sovereignty in the name of human rights. We need not resolve that tension here. Instead, we need only make the more modest claim that, putting humanitarian intervention to one side, the international system should still permit the use of force to address threats that destabilize world order. The main problem is not that the great powers will intervene too much but, as the theory of collective action predicts, that they will intervene too little. To be sure, there is a legitimate concern that the United States and other great powers may use military coercion to advance their own interests at the expense of global welfare. A nation on the receiving end of a great power war would likely resist on the basis of self-defense. Serbia, for example, opposed NATO's intervention in Kosovo, and Iraq resisted the 2003 American invasion in self-defense. If the international system operated according to the current doctrine, both Serbia and Iraq would be justified in using force. This would mean that both sides in the conflict would be acting properly, which seems paradoxical. It is even possible that the state producing the initial instability, such as Serbia or Iraq, might have a superior claim to legitimacy.

If we recognize a legal order, however, that promotes international peace and stability, states could not legitimately resist a welfare-improving war. Nations that illicitly produce weapons of mass destruction, kill minorities or drive them into nearby nations, give safe haven to international terrorist groups, or threaten neighboring countries should have no right to oppose force. While their conduct might not involve a direct cross-border attack—the traditional justification for war—they all work to destabilize the international system. Allowing a right to self-defense would only increase the costs of improving global welfare. Although a great power has the resources to successfully resist foreign assaults, many nations do not. But even the potential costs of intervention against a moderate, well-armed nation might be sufficiently large enough to weigh against war. Intervening to stop hostilities between India and Pakistan, for example, would likely not be militarily successful, and the intervention itself might increase instability in the region by expanding a conflict or increasing its destructiveness. All of these factors might tip the balance of costs and benefits against war. The resistance of nations with significant military capabilities would signal that war would not advance international stability. Comparing the costs of military intervention and its secondary destabilizing effects, however, against the benefits to global peace and security is the better way to judge the legality of the use of force.

V. Conclusion

Regardless of the international rules on war, nations may continue to act as they see fit. Without any enforcement mechanism, international law cannot restrain the United States or other countries that make decisions concerning the use of force. Constraints, if any, come only from the costs of undertaking military action and the countervailing power of other nations. This has long been the realist view of American foreign policy, as set out famously by George Kennan and Hans Morgenthau after the end of World War II.[59]

Even if international law had little, if any, impact on the decisions of the great powers, it still would make sense to develop new rules for war. In the wake of the conflicts in Kosovo, Afghanistan, and Iraq, other nations may fear that the United States has embarked on a campaign to increase its hegemonic power. It seems clear that recent American wars do not fall cleanly within the conventional rules. If the United States and its allies have no viable intellectual framework with which to modify or replace the UN Charter system, nations may believe that they only intend to use war purely for their own gain. Developing a new approach to war may help address the concerns of smaller nations, and of rivals, about the unrestricted exercise of power. A flexible cost-benefit approach would signal that war beyond self-defense can take into account developments in weapons, the rise of terrorism and rogue nations, human rights, and international stability. Adherence over time to this framework would show that the United States remains committed to the basic international system, founded on nation-state sovereignty, and that it seeks to change the legal rules to address threats to that order—but no more.

6 Great Power Security

AS THE UNITED Nations enters its sixth decade, it suffers from a crisis of ineffec-
tiveness and corruption. It has failed to reach a political resolution of the ongoing
civil war in Syria, though it did produce consensus on intervening in the Libyan
conflict. It has failed to prevent North Korea from acquiring nuclear weapons, and
it is unlikely to stop Iran's quest as well. It failed to produce a consensus on whether
the great powers should have used force to enforce Security Council resolutions on
Iraq, nor could it prevent the United States and its coalition of allies from invading
Iraq.[1] According to the Volcker Commission, it failed to avert corruption during its
administration of the Iraqi Oil-for-Food program.[2] It failed when it stood by in not
only Bosnia and Rwanda but also Darfur, Sudan, where government-backed militias have killed at least 400,000 people, with hundreds of thousands more at risk.[3]
And even when it has intervened, it failed to protect basic human rights when UN
peacekeepers in Congo and other African countries sexually abused children.[4] The
United Nations' promise to "save succeeding generations from the scourge of war"
rings hollow in the twenty-first century.[5]

Nevertheless, nations, policymakers, and scholars continue to rely on the UN
Charter's concentration of legal authority in the hands of the Security Council.
Even though the Security Council remains crippled by the veto of the permanent
members, the Obama administration supports its control of the international use of
force. Before the 2008 election, for example, Obama supporters argued that the Iraq
War was illegitimate without the Security Council's blessing. Yale Law School Dean

Harold Koh, who would become Obama's State Department legal adviser, argued before the invasion: "it would be a mistake for our country to attack Iraq without explicit United Nations authorization.... [S]uch an attack would violate international law."[6] Iraq was the bad war, and according to this line of thought, collective security methods, rather than great power politics, would have produced better outcomes for the United States and for global welfare. In contrast, the Afghanistan War was "good" because it received the Security Council's authorization. In keeping with this attitude, the Obama administration delayed American intervention in the 2011 Libyan revolution until the Security Council sanctioned the use of force.[7] The administration has since declared an intervention in Syria to aid the pro-democracy rebels to be off the table until the United Nations has given its approval.[8]

For other world challenges, the United States has turned to international institutions rather than unilateral force to achieve its aims. In its opposition to Iran's suspected nuclear weapons programs, for example, the Obama administration has relied on the International Atomic Energy Agency to detect illicit activity and on the Security Council to impose a tighter sanctions regime. Other nations would give even more responsibilities to the United Nations. A coterie of countries led by Canada, cheered on by scholars and outside advocates, proposed a right to intervene when a nation fails in its "responsibility to protect" its citizens.[9] In 2006, the Security Council unanimously adopted the "R2P" norm: the "international community, through the United Nations," would protect populations from "genocide, war crimes, ethnic cleansing and crimes against humanity."[10] But the underlying problem—the veto of the Security Council's permanent members—did not change.

In these recent moves, the Obama administration and other nations have followed academic efforts to bolster the United Nations. Many scholars of international law and politics share the conventional wisdom that strengthening the UN system will best advance international peace and security. Indeed, even with radically different security threats from those that prevailed in 1945, these scholars believe that the most effective way to control war remains the Security Council. Some academics, for example, maintain that even the use of force to stop human rights catastrophes must still run through the Security Council's monopoly—their contribution to UN Secretary-General Kofi Annan's proposal to reform the Charter. Expanding the Security Council permanently to include countries such as Japan, India, and Brazil remains the main issue for debate.[11]

At first glance, these proposals suggest a significant change in how the United Nations regulates war. These differences, however, are superficial. They do not alter the current legitimacy of the use of force by nations, nor do they move in the most effective direction to address the world's current problems. In fact, these changes have the unintended consequence of exacerbating international security problems.

Nations might become convinced that the United Nations has stronger methods at hand, even while its ability to act remains as deadlocked as ever.

Rejuvenating the UN Charter rules on the use of force, or even modifying them in the way suggested by various government officials and scholars, would have the perverse effect of making international peace and security worse off. Instead of enabling collective security, the UN Charter system only intensifies the collective-action obstacles to solving the challenges of the twenty-first century. The UN Charter system has never really worked. From the beginning, it represented a quixotic effort to end the great power rivalries that have roiled global stability since the Peace of Westphalia. Proposals to expand the Security Council's permanent membership would only aggravate the United Nations' problems—they would further inhibit the use of force even when *war* would promote international peace and security.

Broadening the mandate of the United Nations without removing the veto or curing the lack of military resources will only further push its reach beyond its grasp. Continued reliance on cooperation and coordination by the great powers, though imperfect, remains the better hope for managing contemporary threats to international security. The choice for the United States is whether it has sufficient control in the United Nations to promote advances in collective security, whether it ought to seek alternate rules to govern war, or whether it simply ought to ignore the United Nations and create a separate security framework—as it successfully did during the Cold War.

This chapter argues that the United Nations has failed as a mechanism for promoting international peace and security. It addresses the obvious question: what comes next? Rather than seeking more formal international institutions, constrained by ever tighter rules on national action, it argues that a less centralized system of cooperation should accompany more flexible rules for war. Instead of the government-like organization of the United Nations, this chapter looks to the Concert of Europe of the nineteenth-century as a model. It recommends that the world's advanced democracies form their own Concert today to act collectively in those instances when war could promote global welfare.

I. The UN Charter's Failed Promise

International law, as codified in the UN Charter, offers nations a bargain. If they give up war as a tool of international politics, a supranational government will prevent threats to their security. Made up of the world's great powers, the Security Council will assume the responsibility of maintaining international peace and order—as if Hobbes offered his escape from the state of nature to nations. But the United

Nations' recent performance should give nations little faith that it can live up to its side of the deal. Proposals for institutional reform will only compound the faults of a failed institution rather than provide a meaningful solution to the collective-action problems inherent in world security.

The United Nations' greatest mission—to respond to "any threat to the peace, breach of the peace, or act of aggression"—has proved its greatest failure. Perhaps the United Nations was stillborn because of a flaw in its very design. Under the Charter, the Security Council can use force to maintain international peace and security, and it is supposed to have a military staff made up of national units "available…on its call." From the start, nations disagreed over the size and shape of their contributions to the UN military. Instead of its own troops, the United Nations relies on the goodwill of its members to respond to its pleas under Article 51, which recognizes "the inherent right of individual or collective" self-defense.

Even the possibility of decision, without the reality of troops, has remained remote. Fundamental shortcomings in the United Nations' institutional design guaranteed that the international organization could not fulfill the promises of its charter. President Franklin Roosevelt hoped that the Allies of World War II would act as the world's "four policemen" and so reserved the power to use force for the Security Council. But his hopes could not survive the realities of great power politics that followed the defeat of the Axis powers. The war had exhausted two of the permanent members of the Council, Great Britain and France, which fell to the status of second-rank powers. China was torn by a civil war won by a communist dictatorship that remained isolated from the international system for decades. The Soviet Union took advantage of the defeat of Germany to sweep Eastern Europe into its orbit, and the ensuing superpower rivalry paralyzed the Security Council. During the Cold War, the Security Council authorized one intervention, the Korean War, and that only because the Soviet Union had boycotted the vote to protest noncommunist China's refusal to transfer control of its seat to Mao's government.

The record of practice shows that the new UN rules of collective security were every bit as ineffective as those of the League of Nations. With the Security Council paralyzed during the Cold War, the great powers continued to fight—for example, the United States in Vietnam and the Soviet Union in Afghanistan. The envisioned contribution of nations to an international militia under UN command never materialized. Once the Cold War ended, the United Nations did expressly authorize one significant conflict, the Persian Gulf War of 1991, and a variety of humanitarian interventions, such as those in Somalia and Haiti. But it failed to address other human rights crises in Rwanda, the Balkans, Darfur, and elsewhere with direct intervention.

The United Nations has sought a role mediating, rather than preventing, conflict because of deadlock among the great powers. UN troops, donated from member states, helped monitor peace agreements—acting as a tripwire, for example, should either party cross a negotiated boundary. The United Nations has also successfully served as a conduit for information as part of a peace settlement in nations such as Cambodia and El Salvador. But when the United Nations has pursued the more ambitious goal of peacekeeping—intervening in existing conflicts—it once again has displayed its shortcomings. In the former Yugoslavia, Serbs brushed aside UN troops protecting "safe areas" and massacred Bosnian Muslims from 1993 to 1995. Only the United States and NATO, acting without UN authorization, stopped Serbian aggression in 1999. In Somalia, the American-led UN intervention transformed from humanitarian aid to nation building, but forces hurriedly fled after the deaths of Army Rangers and other Special Operations Forces in a failed snatch-and-grab operation. In 1994, a UN peacekeeping force deployed in Rwanda stood by while Hutus killed nearly a million Tutsis. While the Security Council could come to limited agreement on these missions after the Cold War, the United Nations' reliance on the voluntary participation of its members stood in the way of success. Nations were unwilling to carry through when sustained fighting became necessary or when the great powers only allowed the Security Council to vest troops with narrow mandates.

The UN Charter's rules on the use of force also do not account for political and technological developments. As the September 11 attacks demonstrated, nonstate actors have emerged with the ability to wage armed conflict with a power that only nation-states once possessed. Yet international terrorist organizations, by their very methods of operation, may render self-defense rules obsolete. Terrorists deliberately disguise themselves as civilians, have no territory or populations to defend, and attack by surprise. These characteristics make it virtually impossible to use force in traditional self-defense once an attack is in motion, and there is no target to threaten in retaliation. Rogue states may share the character of terrorist organizations, because they have removed themselves from the international system and their leaders may have little regard for attacks on their territory or populations. Marrying these political developments with the proliferation of weapons of mass destruction has even further undermined the rules on the use of force. If rogue nations or terrorist groups can launch a sudden WMD attack, other nations have less time to defend themselves, the effectiveness of nonviolent measures decreases, and the benefits of preemptive action increases.

While UN and government officials have nodded to these developments, they have not proposed any serious responses. In 2005, Secretary-General Annan issued a report that proposed the most far-reaching official overhaul of the United Nations since its founding, based on the recommendations of a task force of leading international and government officials and scholars convened to study structural reforms to the United Nations. Annan's effort is worth sustained attention as the official statement of the conventional wisdom on the UN and the security challenges of the twenty-first century.

To his credit, then Secretary-General Annan recognized that the dispute over the rules governing the use of force has divided the United Nations. In his final report, *In Larger Freedom: Towards Development, Security and Human Rights for All*, he declared: "[Nations] have disagreed about whether States have the right to use military force preemptively, to defend themselves against imminent threats; whether they have the right to use it preventively to defend themselves against latent or non-imminent threats; and whether they have the right—or perhaps the obligation—to use it protectively to rescue the citizens of other States from genocide or comparable crimes."[12] Annan classified the use of force, beyond pure self-defense, into three types: (1) preemption, defined as a response to an imminent attack; (2) prevention, defined as a response to a latent but not yet imminent attack; and (3) protection, defined as force used to stop genocide or other humanitarian disasters.

In one promising sign, the secretary-general argued in favor of interpreting Article 51 to permit the use of force in self-defense to address imminent attacks. According to Annan, "imminent threats are fully covered by Article 51, which safeguards the inherent right of sovereign States to defend themselves against armed attack. Lawyers have long recognized that this covers an imminent attack as well as one that has already happened."[13] This put the secretary-general in agreement with scholars who have argued that Article 51 permits the use of force in anticipatory self-defense. But it does not represent a great change in the law, which the *Caroline* case established.

Unfortunately, for the second and third types of force defined by Annan—prevention and protection—the secretary-general was long on rhetoric but short on practical reform. Even though Annan's proposal recognized that force may constitute an effective remedy in situations ranging from the spread of WMDs to humanitarian crises, he still restricted the authority to use force in these situations to the Security Council. "Where threats are not imminent but latent, the Charter gives full authority to the Security Council to use military force, including preventively, to preserve international peace and security. As to genocide, ethnic cleansing and other such crimes against humanity, are they not also threats to international peace and security, against which humanity should be able to look to the Security Council for protection?"[14]

The academic study from which Annan drew his report restricted the right to use force for prevention military action to the Security Council. "If there are good arguments for preventive military action, with good evidence to support them, they should be put to the Security Council, which can authorize such action if it chooses to," the academics advised. "If it does not so choose, there will be, by definition, time to pursue other strategies."[15] For terms of humanitarian crises, the high-level panel explains that the Security Council should stay firm in the understanding that it can use Chapter VII powers to authorize collective military action, so long as it finds that the situation rises to the level of a threat to international peace and security.[16]

Rather than loosen the permanent veto, both Annan and his high-level panel provided new criteria to advise the Security Council on the use of its existing authority. According to Annan, the Security Council "should come to a common view on how to weigh the seriousness of the threat; the proper purpose of the proposed military action; whether means short of the use of force might plausibly succeed in stopping the threat; whether the military option is proportional to the threat at hand; and whether there is a reasonable chance of success."[17] His high-level panel provided more explanation for these standards. As the panel saw it, the problem is an absence of Security Council agreement about humanitarian intervention and a lack of trust by non-Security Council nations in the permanent members. By adopting these criteria, the panel sought "to maximize the possibility of achieving Security Council consensus around when it is appropriate or not to use coercive action, including armed force; to maximize international support for whatever the Security Council decides; and to minimize the possibility of Member States bypassing the Security Council."[18]

These reforms fail to address today's pressing challenges to international peace and security. And they do not provide any real change to the existing doctrine on the use of force. For example, these reforms recognize that the right to self-defense is not limited to cases where a cross-border attack is actually in progress, as some academics have argued. But state practice has recognized the imminence rule even before the Charter. Requiring that states receive the approval of the Security Council for all other uses of force is functionally the same as the current system, which already prohibits all uses of force except in self-defense or when approved by the Council. By continuing to tie the use of force to self-defense from an imminent attack, the United Nations will remain trapped in an outmoded framework that does not take into account the realities of terrorism, the conduct of nations such as Iran or North Korea, WMDs, or new forms of warfare, such as cyber- or drone attacks.

Annan's proposals also fail to recognize that the international environment and the means for protecting international peace and security have changed. The UN Charter system was designed to prevent large interstate wars through a criminal justice approach to the use of force. It sought to reduce international armed conflict to zero, much in the way domestic criminal law attempts to eliminate all killing. But the primary threats to international peace and security do not come from the great power wars of the first half of the twentieth century. Today, the threats come from the combination of rogue states, terrorist organizations, and humanitarian disasters.

Rather than reconceive the rules on war to address collective action problems, Annan's proposals continue to follow criminal law notions of liability.

Such UN reforms will only exacerbate the failure to solve the undersupply of global public goods. While the Security Council adopted the idea of a responsibility to protect, which could promote a collective good, it failed to initiate any institutional reforms that could enable the use of force. Annan's report recommended expanding the size of the Security Council, either by adding to the number of permanent members (but not expanding the veto) or by adding more rotating members. Under either proposal, the size of the Security Council will expand, which will only increase the transaction costs of authorizing force. David Caron and Thomas Weiss have expressed concern that increasing membership would not improve the effectiveness or legitimacy of the Security Council.[19] More Security Council members bring to the table more diverse foreign policy interests, which will make any consensus more difficult to achieve. An increase in the number of members will simply hinder the ability of Security Council members to negotiate and bargain to reach a decision. This is not to say, of course, that the Security Council will never authorize intervention in cases where a nation is producing negative externalities. Public choice theory, however, predicts that the increase in the size of the membership will further reduce the ability of the Council to reach decisions.

These institutional changes would not have a negative impact if the substantive rules themselves were loosened. For example, if nations could use force without Security Council permission when state authority has collapsed or when a human rights disaster has occurred, the international system still might encourage nations to provide more welfare-improving intervention. The world might even be better off under the status quo. Under the current system, nations have engaged in humanitarian intervention without the approval of the Security Council. These include India's intervention in Bangladesh, Vietnam's in Cambodia, Tanzania's in Uganda, and NATO's in Kosovo. Meanwhile, between the Korean War and the first Persian Gulf War, the Security Council never authorized the use of force. The international system may have been developing a norm in which nations can use force to prevent chaos in failed states or to stop humanitarian disasters without Security Council approval. Other great powers judged the legitimacy of these wars ex post by deciding whether to recognize the results of these interventions or to assist in bearing their costs. Nations, in effect, were developing a way around the literal restrictions of the UN Charter in order to address collective action problems.

The positive development of an international norm for intervention during crisis could be halted by reform that strengthens the United Nations. Official proposals go to great lengths to maintain the formal UN rule that nations may only use force in self-defense from an imminent attack or with Security Council approval. These requirements would prevent nations from developing, through the practice of the last few decades, a new international norm toward permitting intervention in discrete situations involving failed states and human right disasters. These proposals would also impose an unwieldy institutional process, made even more difficult by the expansion of the Security Council, on decisions to cure severe collective action problems.

The treatment of nations such as Iraq, which challenged the stability of the international order, may prove to be the test case for these different approaches to the use of force. Many scholars have focused on the threat that the United States' invasion of Iraq has posed to the Security Council. Michael Glennon argues that the Security Council's unwillingness to support the Iraq invasion demonstrated its inability to adapt to the "unipolar world" of American hegemony.[20] According to Glennon, the power disparities and differing views on the use of force between the United States and its fellow UN members have led to the Security Council's collapse. He does not foresee a multilateral institutional framework determining the use of force in the future. Thomas Weiss asserts that the central concern for the Security Council is "whether it can engage the United States, modulate its exercise of power, and discipline its impulses." If the Security Council continues to frequently disagree with U.S. foreign policy on central issues, it could end up resembling its "defunct predecessor, the League of Nations."[21] Thomas Franck and Anne-Marie Slaughter share a more supportive view of the United Nations. Franck emphasizes the necessity of maintaining the power of the United Nations' "jurying function" to restrain the United States' use of force.[22] Slaughter insists that the United States will need the United Nations "more than ever in the aftermath of war—to provide for refugees, to monitor human rights violations, above all to establish a transitional administration with genuine legitimacy...."[23]

According to UN officials and opponents of the war, the legality of the Iraq War ought to turn on whether the United States and its allies were under imminent threat of attack by Iraq. If an attack were imminent, then the United States could take preemptive action; if not, then the use of force was preventive and required Security Council approval. Without a claim of self-defense, the war in Iraq was illegal without the Security Council's ex ante approval. That approval was unlikely not just because of the difficulties of determining whether the benefits of intervention outweighed the cost but also because of the collective-action problem of forging a consensus among numerous Security Council members who may have had their own strategic interests in maintaining the status quo in Iraq.[24] Yet the Security Council's refusal to grant authorization to use force preceding the war did not stop the United States and its allies from invading Iraq and overthrowing the regime, just as the absence of Security Council approval did not prevent the many uses of force during the Cold War period.

On the Iraq War, the United Nations failed everyone. For realists concerned about Iraq's threat to the regional balance of power or humanitarians worried about oppressed Iraqis, the United Nations failed to stop Iraq. By the time of the 2003 invasion, Saddam Hussein remained in power, and Iraq was on the verge of breaking out of the sanctions regime that had been in place since the 1991 Gulf War. The United Nations proved ineffective as a means of cooperating to solve the negative externalities imposed by Iraq on the international system. For skeptics who believed the United States sought war for aggressive national interests and only cloaked its real rationale with talk of WMDs and human rights, the United Nations failed too. The United Nations' formal rules against the use of force did not prevent the U.S.-led coalition from invading a member state without the approval of the Security Council. Although the United States and its allies first sought Council approval, ultimately, they went forward without it. And neither the process for seeking approval nor the broader forum that is the United Nations persuaded the coalition to halt operations. The United Nations neither faced the challenges posed by Iraq nor stopped the United States and its allies from taking matters into their own hands.

II. The Legitimacy of Preventive Wars

If the Iraq War serves as the final proof that the UN framework has failed, what direction should the international system take? This book offers a global public goods approach that is better suited to today's international environment. Iraq provides a good argument for the superiority of a global welfare analysis over the self-defense or pure power understandings of war.

Even though the great powers could not reach consensus on war in 2002–2003, they all agreed that Iraq continued to threaten its neighbors and its own citizens. On November 8, 2002, the Security Council unanimously approved Resolution 1441 to address "the threat Iraq's non-compliance with Council resolutions and proliferation of weapons of mass destruction and long-range missiles poses to international peace and security."[25] The resolution "deplor[ed]" the absence of international inspections in Iraq since 1998 and Iraq's continued failure to renounce international terrorism and cease the repression of its civilian population. It offered Iraq "a final opportunity to comply with its disarmament obligations under relevant resolutions of the Council." It reminded Iraq that the Security Council has repeatedly warned that "serious consequences" would result from the continued violation of its obligations.

A global welfare analysis predicts that the great powers would be unwilling to intervene in Iraq, but not because of uncertainty over the Hussein regime's threat to international peace. Rather, nations would be reluctant to devote the significant resources required to provide security for the rest of the world. But if the United States and its allies could capture many of the gains from intervention, and those benefits outweighed the costs, then they might use force. If the ex ante estimates turn out to be incorrect, or if there are substantial gains to the international system that would allow the overall benefits to outweigh the costs borne by the intervening nations, the United States and its allies could seek assistance and contributions after the invasion. Conversely, other nations would already have an incentive to free-ride, so they would generally be unwilling to contribute.

If other nations disagreed with the invasion of Iraq, they could have launched a number of responses short of military force. First, they could have refused to provide ex post military or financial support to the U.S.-led coalition. Second, they could have refused to engage in economic transactions with Iraq's successor government and persuaded nations to leave the U.S.-led coalition. Third, they could have reduced trade and financial flows and refused to cooperate in other areas. Finally, they could even have withdrawn from political and military alliances and made clear that they would not provide aid in future wars. Failure by the coalition to receive support will lead great powers to be more reluctant to bear the concentrated costs of intervention in the future. A global welfare approach provides ways to regulate those who might abuse the system.

Conflicts of this kind are more "preventive" in nature than "preemptive," though both are just a species of waging war now to forestall threats in the future. To recall the definitions established in Secretary-General Annan's report on Iraq, preemption refers to wars that are undertaken to stop an attack that is certain or virtually so but has not yet occurred. The attacker has chosen the timing, not the defender. Prevention refers to wars that are launched to head off threats further in the future and hence less certain. The defender selects the timing. At times, we have seen preventive wars because of a coming, negative shift in the balance of power.[26] In the past, leaders of democracies did not shy away from the prospect of preventive war. In his memoirs of the Second World War, for example, Winston Churchill found "no merit in [statesmen] putting off a war" when "the safety of the State, the lives and freedom of their own fellow countrymen, to whom they owe their position, make it right and imperative in the last resort."[27]

Yet such thinking remains controversial, in large part because of the continuing disputes over the normative, strategic, and legal wisdom of what has been called the "Bush Doctrine." In 2002, the Bush administration announced:

Given the goals of rogue states and terrorists, the United States can no longer solely rely on a reactive posture as we have in the past. The inability to deter a potential attacker, the immediacy of today's threats, and the magnitude of potential harm that could be caused by our adversaries' choice of weapons, do not permit that option. We cannot let our enemies strike first.[28]

With this language, the Bush administration made clear that it would conduct wars of prevention in addition to preemption. Critics claimed that even if preemption were legal under theories of anticipatory self-defense, preventive wars were generally illegal and destabilizing. Political scientist Dan Reiter, for example, argues that "preventive attacks are generally ineffective, costly, unnecessary, and potentially even counterproductive tools for use in behalf of nonproliferation and counterterrorism."[29]

Yet, even critics of the Iraq War should acknowledge that preventive war ought to remain among the strategic options available to any American president. Reliance on the UN Security Council to combat terrorism, halt WMD proliferation, or prevent genocide and "ethnic cleansing" would be folly. The Council has proven to be impotent at confronting such challenges and, despite persistent calls for reform, will remain so. The lesson is that when "the Great Powers and relevant local powers are in agreement…the elaborate charades of the Security Council" are unnecessary, in the words of historian Walter MacDougall. "When those powers do not agree, the U.N. is impotent."[30] Although Security Council authorization for preventive war might well be desirable for policy reasons, dozens or even hundreds of conflicts have been fought since 1945 without its permission and in apparent violation of the UN Charter.

Preventive wars to stop an enemy's acquisition of WMDs, for example, and wars to forestall mass human rights abuses are fundamentally similar. Each falls within the UN Charter's ban on wars for reasons other than pure self-defense. In both cases, the purpose of the intervention is to protect. In the first case, a nation's objective would be the protection of its own people; in the second case, the objective would be the protection of another people. Next, in both cases, nations are employing force to counteract a threat of violence—a threat that is large in scale and grossly illegal. In the first case, the threat would involve intentional mass attacks on noncombatants from a foreign enemy. In the second case, the threat would involve severe and widespread danger to civilians from their own government. The targeted states in both cases would have wrongfully subjected others to unacceptable harm or risk of harm—either internally, by failing to protect their citizens from genocide and other gross human rights violations, or externally, by posing security threats to the citizens of other states, whether by acquiring WMDs themselves for aggressive purposes or by sheltering (or failing to control) terrorists willing to use such weapons. The aims of both the preventive and humanitarian interventions are to uphold the "strong global ethic" against the mass killing of civilians and other equally catastrophic events.[31]

The characteristic objections to both preventive war and humanitarian intervention are also essentially the same. According to critics, engaging in either activity will destabilize the international order by creating a dangerous precedent that will lead to further conflict, violence, and disregard for international rules. Critics argue that the justifications for such activity serve all too easily to conceal some other motive. Nations bent on imperialism or hegemony will use humanitarian intervention or preventive war as a pretext for conquest or control.[32] Even though these concerns are reasonable in some situations, the UN Charter does not provide an effective way to prevent the proliferation of WMDs or the spread of human rights violations. The Charter attempts to drive the level of international violence to zero, despite the possibility that the use of force can improve global welfare by stopping human rights catastrophes or heading off rogue states that are likely to cause greater harms in the future.

Viewed in this light, preventive war, in appropriate circumstances, can be justified for reasons that are closely analogous to those usually offered to justify humanitarian intervention. The key difference is that in preventive war, the nation initiating war protects its own population, whereas in humanitarian intervention, the nation at war protects another state's population. Although critics of preventive war tend to be sympathetic to humanitarian intervention, the underlying logic for both uses of force is substantially the same. Indeed, the rationale for preventive war is the stronger of the two. Even in the contemporary world, preventive war remains rooted in self-defense, whereas humanitarian intervention is rooted in the defense of others. Nations are more inclined to wage preventive war, which protects their own citizens first, and should be reluctant to engage in humanitarian intervention. As Jeremy Rabkin has argued, nations depend on the link with their citizens, as expressed in state sovereignty.[33] A credible objection to a U.S.-led preventive war cannot be that the war is chiefly about protecting the lives and safety of the American people.

The objection to preventive war cannot be that it is inconsistent with American practice. One prominent survey, however, describes the 2003 war in Iraq as the United States' "first preemptive [i.e., preventive] war."[34] Another diplomatic historian asserts that the Bush Doctrine has been "widely criticized" because Iraq "did not pose a direct and imminent threat to the United States." Instead, according to this account, "Bush chose to overturn more than 200 years of American foreign policy."[35] Arthur Schlesinger, Jr., was perhaps typical of some in his arguments against the Iraq War. He condemned the Iraq War as "illegitimate and immoral. For more than 200 years we have not been that kind of country."[36]

This criticism is severely mistaken. Historian John Lewis Gaddis argues that what he broadly calls "preemption" has been a constant facet of U.S. foreign policy. According to Gaddis, this practice led to a long series of interventions throughout the nineteenth and twentieth centuries against the Spanish Empire's possessions in the Americas and in the Latin American republics that succeeded them, including Mexico, Cuba, and Venezuela.[37] Historian Marc Trachtenberg concludes: "the sort of thinking one finds in the Bush policy documents is not to be viewed as anomalous. Under [Franklin] Roosevelt and Truman, under Eisenhower and Kennedy, and even under Clinton in the 1990s, this kind of thinking came into play in a major way."[38] Even more starkly, historian Hew Strachan argues that "[t]he United States has used preventive war regularly since 1945 to forestall revolutionary change. In the 1950s and 1960s, it employed military power once every eighteen months on average to overthrow a government inimical to its interests."[39] Colin Gray contends that even the Second World War—despite the Japanese first strike at Pearl Harbor—should be considered a preventive war. Gray characterizes several other major American wars as preventive, including the War in Afghanistan (2001); the Persian Gulf War (1991); the Korean War (1950); the First World War (1917); the Spanish-American War (1898); the Civil War (1861); and the many frontier wars the United States fought against Native American tribes, Mexico, France, and Spain.[40]

Consider the Second World War. Even after the outbreak of war in Europe in 1939, President Franklin Roosevelt pursued a policy designed to favor the anti-Axis powers in Europe and Asia, eventually bringing the United States into the war on their behalf. Roosevelt urged Congress to revise or repeal the Neutrality Act, provided Great Britain with desperately needed war materiel, waged a covert war against German submarines in the North Atlantic, occupied Iceland to prevent it from falling into German hands, and tightened the economic noose on Japan, seeking to strangle its efforts to continue its long war in China.[41] Consistent with his vision of the threat, Roosevelt deliberately pursued a policy of economic warfare with Japan for more than a year and a half before Pearl Harbor. The United States deliberately provoked and fought a war with Japan that it could have avoided for the sake of preventing the emergence of a grave strategic threat in the Pacific.[42]

World War II followed a series of preventive American wars, such as the First World War. Germany did not present any meaningful threat to American security in 1917. Rather, as Colin Gray has observed, the United States "chose to wage a preventive war as an Associated Power of the Allies. Wilson recognized that a German-dominated Europe must constitute a serious threat to U.S. national security."[43] In 1848, American claims that it acted in self-defense to pursue war with Mexico seemed far-fetched. President James K. Polk deliberately forced an armed incident over the location of the border on the Rio Grande River. After fighting broke out, the United States invaded Mexico, captured and occupied Mexico City, and took what is today California and the American Southwest. America used force to eliminate a competitor for influence on the continent rather than to defend the United States from Mexican attack.[44] Similarly, in 1898, there was no threat of a Spanish attack upon the United States. Yet the United States destroyed the Spanish Navy and took control over the Philippines and Cuba. American intentions again were preventive; the United States removed Spain as an obstacle to American expansion.[45]

Two other common criticisms of preventive war are misplaced. One is that democracies should not fight preventive wars because they run counter to democratic principles, which prize consensus and negotiation over armed conflict. Political scientist Jack Levy has argued that this assumption, though once widely accepted, is without empirical support. Indeed, Levy observes that democratic Israel fought a preventive war against Egypt in 1956 and that the United States fought a war in Iraq in 1990–1991 for preventive reasons broadly accepted by the American public. He writes that "[t]here is no evidence that normative beliefs that a preventive strike was immoral or contrary to American democratic identity played any role" in the Clinton administration's planning in 1994 for a possible air strike against North Korea's nuclear program.[46] The second criticism is that the preventive war against Iraq in 2003 is symptomatic of the policies of a "declining" hegemon, the United States.[47] Although this is a question for international relations theorists, empirical studies find that narrowing power differentials do not necessarily, or even usually, lead to preventive attacks.[48] In any case, the thesis that the United States is a "declining" power is itself doubtful.[49]

Obviously, preventive war is not always justified. Few defenders would be found today for all of the United States preventive interventions of the past, including some of those conducted during the Cold War. Likewise, wars undertaken by other great powers—China's intervention in the Korean War, for example—may also make sense strategically but hardly seem justified. Nonetheless, the Bush Doctrine has strong foundations in American political and diplomatic history as well as in international practice. We cannot outlaw preventive war, but we can seek to regulate its use.

Loosening the rules on the use of force expand the possibilities for pretextual uses of force. Critics of the Iraq War, for example, variously claimed that the United States sought to extend an "American empire" at home and abroad, advance Israeli interests, or capture more oil resources.[50] There are several reasons to believe, however, that an ex post approach to policing undesirable uses of force will prove superior to the current ex ante system. First, since the end of World War II, the costs of war have risen and the benefits seem to have fallen. Before World War II, claims of self-defense or humanitarian assistance served as pretexts for conquest. But territorial conquest may no longer provide the benefits that it once did, because the advent of nuclear weapons and other WMDs has made it easier for nations to impose costs on invaders, the costs of administering a hostile territory have greatly increased, and talented labor and capital have become more mobile. An invasion may also prompt a regional or global collective response, further increasing the costs of war. This suggests that an overinclusive rule that serves a prophylactic purpose—barring all uses of force out of concern over interstate invasions of territorial conquest—is unnecessarily broad because other circumstances will help enforce the prohibition on the use of force.

Using a strict rule does not prevent invaders from claiming false reasons for war. Invaders can always claim a pretext. Even Nazi Germany claimed that it was engaged in self-defense or protecting ethnic German minorities abroad. The question is not whether a rule on force will prevent nations from claiming pretexts, but whether it will discourage or encourage uses of force that are desirable from a global welfare perspective. It is difficult to see why an ex ante system—a strict prohibition on all nondefensive war—must be more effective across the board than an ex post approach in filtering good wars from bad ones. A strict rule designed to eliminate pretexts makes the most sense if most cases are fairly similar and require limited decision costs. An ex post system would be more effective in judging the legality of conduct whose legality is context-specific and depends on the weighing of many factors. Intervention in other nations is often, if not always, dependent on facts unique to each crisis.

Attempting to frame guidelines for evaluating interventions, in light of the overarching global welfare norm, is not easy. Nonetheless, five criteria may prove useful in flushing out pretextual claims and evaluating whether a potential preventive war would serve global welfare. These criteria are ultimately derived from classic *jus ad bellum* teaching and are closely modeled on similar criteria that may already be emerging in evaluating armed humanitarian interventions.[51] If, over time, the practices and opinions of states gradually conform to these criteria out of a sense of legal obligation, then a new norm of international law might be said to have emerged for regulating preventive military interventions.

First, a preventive war or armed intervention should only be undertaken after a nation has made clear why it is undertaking war. A nation should announce that another nation's statements and conduct has caused it harm. It should explain to other governments and the world media, consistent with the protection of intelligence methods and sources, the nature and gravity of the threat faced by the civilian population, which need not be that of the intervening nation. It should seek redress from the wrongdoing state or group if realistically possible as well as give its prospective target a reasonable opportunity to provide such redress.

Second, a nation must have the rightful purpose of protecting an innocent civilian population from a threat of mass killing or from a harm of a comparable severity and scale. Typically, this population will be that of the intervening nation or an ally. The expected benefits of intervention, viewed ex ante, should outweigh the expected costs, measured in terms of global welfare. To be sure, an intervener's stated purpose may disguise an improper motive. But there are various constraints on proposed interventions that can serve to screen out improper motives, such as a prohibition on annexing any part of the territory or exploiting any of the natural resources of the targeted state in the aftermath of war.

Third, nations may seek a criterion corresponding to "rightful authority" in the classic *jus ad bellum*. Some might argue that acting in a broad coalition, whether with other great powers, smaller regional powers, or both, is an important check on a pretextual use of force. If other nations reach the same judgment on a war, it might be thought that there is less likelihood that the intervening powers seek the gain of territory or resources. Moreover, having the support of foreign allies may generate greater domestic support in a democracy for the intervention. And, of course, acting in concert with allies will likely result in a more equitable distribution of the costs of the war's costs.

There is some truth to all of these points on the value of a coalition. But requiring regional support, or a great power consensus, cannot be an absolute and inflexible prerequisite for a justified war of prevention. Undoubtedly, the populations of the United States, Great Britain, Israel, and now India are far more exposed to transnational terrorist threats than those of other nations. The rights and duties of those nations to protect their civilians from such threats cannot hinge on the willingness of comparatively secure states to support them. A requirement of regional support, for example, would seem absurd in the case of Israel; its chief dangers come from several of its regional neighbors. As the Iraq War has shown, regional powers may be unable to reach consensus on war, or may even prefer to wait on the sidelines, hoping to free-ride off the great powers. In some circumstances, unilateral action by those states that are especially at risk would be justified.

Fourth, a nation should attempt nonviolent means to dispel the threat or otherwise reasonably conclude that peaceful methods will be unavailing. These alternatives include diplomacy, economic pressures or inducements, deterrence, and containment, and nations should invest sufficient time in them before force becomes an option. The intervening powers might suggest a third party to serve as a neutral power to measure compliance with any demands or to verify facts on the ground. Fifth, the preventive use of force should be proportionate to the threat. While the requirement of proportionality is hard to define with precision, it was traditionally regarded as a rule of *jus ad bellum* in all cases of war.[52] Proportionality requires that the use of force entail no more death and destruction than necessary to eliminate the threat. Furthermore, "proportionality" should require respect for the sovereignty of the targeted state to the extent that the situation permits. Thus, a preventive intervention may require an outcome as drastic as regime change (as in Iraq in 2003) but only in an extreme case where less intrusive measures cannot effectively remove the threat.

These criteria reject the move to place even more restrictions on the use of force in cases other than self-defense. They recognize that existing incentives discourage nations from undertaking wars that advance global welfare. These principles seek to create the right incentives for welfare-promoting wars, while ensuring that nations do not have ulterior motives and have accurately calculated the cost and benefits of war. Even if these criteria prove unsatisfactory on more sustained examination, whether because they are too lax or too restrictive, some other standards should, and eventually will, supplant the UN Charter's use-of-force rules. Rather than let international politics return to a no-holds-barred world of war, this proposal seeks to reorient nations toward cooperation that will advance global welfare by preempting threats to international security or civilian populations.

III. Toward a New Concert

Another challenge to a flexible rule on war comes from the perspective of institutions. The UN Charter's law enforcement approach, enforced by the Security Council's permanent veto, creates a one-size-fits-all, ex ante rule. In practice, this rule has done little to restrain great power war—while raising costs on smaller conflicts that could improve global welfare. But at least, a critic could say, the United Nations creates a neutral forum for nations to air disputes and exchange information. Discussion can lead to political approval, but this forum can exist without the ban on preemptive and preventive war. During the Cuban Missile Crisis, the United States presented its intelligence on the construction of Soviet missile sites to the Security Council and subsequently built political support for its blockade of the island. On the other hand, Middle Eastern nations have used UN institutions to harass Israeli measures taken for its self-defense, ranging from a deeply flawed Human Rights Commission investigation into Israel's southern Lebanon offensive to asking the International Court of Justice to stop the construction of a security wall between Israel and the West Bank. Quoting Alfred Tennyson's hope for world government, historian Paul Kennedy describes the UN as the Parliament of Man.[53] If it is a Parliament, it has none of the powers and all of the debate.

Even if the United Nations is powerless, critics might respond that discarding the UN system would deprive the world of any meaningful institutions for global security. A global welfare approach, they might say, would return the world to an anarchic system characterized by great power competition. Although a few customary rules prevailed, such as the immunity for diplomats or the prohibition on piracy, law did not govern the policies of nations. States could go to war for almost any reason, including conquest or retaliation. To unify Germany, for example, Prussia waged wars against a variety of other states, including Austria-Hungary and France. America expanded its borders by conquest in wars with Mexico and Spain. Great Britain and France fought for decades over North America, the Indian subcontinent, and ultimately Europe. Russia, Austria, and Prussia together eliminated Poland. Each great power sought to maximize its security by expanding its population and territory, maintaining significant armed forces, and, at times, waging war against its competitors.

Great power rivalries and international anarchy did not eliminate all international cooperation. Nations formed alliances when another country rose in power and threatened their security. Great Britain joined an alliance to stop the expansion of Louis XIV's France, and a coalition of Great Britain, Prussia, Russia, and Austria combined to defeat Napoleon. The United States, United Kingdom, France, and Russia joined forces in two world wars to contain a rising Germany. But under the conditions of international anarchy, nations concerned with their own survival do not fully trust each other, which sharply limits the potential for cooperation. Anarchy compels nations to compete, even those that harbor no aggressive designs toward each other.[54] Alliances tend to be temporary and opportunistic because of the temptation to free-ride off other countries' efforts and to bandwagon only after it is clear which side has the preponderance of forces. For example, Italy fought on the side of the Allies in World War I; then, after hesitating for over nine months after Hitler's invasion of Poland, it fought on the side of the Axis for much of World War II.

Yet even with its flaws, a great power system is not inevitably less stable than one regulated by international law. International relations scholars debate to this day the relative stability of systems that are hegemonic, such as the United States after 1991; bipolar, such as the United States and the Soviet Union during the Cold War; or multipolar, such as the period roughly from 1648 to 1945.[55] After the Napoleonic Wars, for example, the great powers created the "Concert of Europe," which coordinated their policies to prevent any significant outbreak of war on the continent. Aside from the wars of national unification for Germany and Italy, the mid-century Crimean War, and smaller early twentieth-century Balkan wars, the Concert helped to maintain relative peace in Europe for a century.[56]

The Great War, of course, changed all that. Its sheer destructiveness is difficult to comprehend even today. The overall death toll from the war amounted to between

9 and 10 million. France lost nearly one in every five men mobilized.[57] German, Austro-Hungarian, and British war losses, though less, were of similar dimension. The great battles of Verdun and the Somme resulted in an appalling level of casualties on both sides, and yet neither battle brought either side closer to victory; indeed, after the battles, positions at the front hardly changed.[58]

Collective security rejected the great power politics that had apparently brought World War I's horrifying destruction on the peoples of Europe. The postwar legal regime was largely the outgrowth of three seminal documents—Woodrow Wilson's "Fourteen Points," the Versailles Treaty, and the Covenant of the League of Nations. These documents embodied the American rejection of the European "balance of power" system as inherently unstable and prone to war in favor of a form of "collective security" designed to prevent and punish offensive war.[59] Instead of war, the international system would use permanent judicial and arbitral institutions to settle disputes. Collective security and judicial resolution would be supplemented by disarmament, such as the Washington Conference of 1922, which fixed the ratio of naval forces for the United States, Great Britain, Japan, France, and Italy. Altogether, the interwar disarmament process yielded six major naval treaties embracing five great powers that sought to demilitarize much of the world's oceans, limit the naval powers' fleets to defensive purposes, and reduce the risk of war by preventing naval alliances between those powers.[60]

Collective security in the interwar period, of course, failed. International politics did not change, even in the wake of the horrors of World War I. Nations continued to use force or the threat of force to resolve disagreements and to rely on alliances, such as the Anglo-French pact, for their security. International institutions could not deter war. In the early 1920s, Greece and Turkey, as well as Russia and Poland, fought wars in violation of the League of Nations. Japan's invasions of Manchuria and China, Italy's invasion of Ethiopia, and Germany's aggression under Hitler demonstrated the hollow hope of collective security.

Some believed that the fault lay in the design of the League rather than in the idea of collective security itself. One chief problem was the absence of the United States, which emerged from the war as the most powerful nation in the world. The League also lacked any real mechanism to enforce declarations to end fighting. But blaming the structure of the League obscures the root cause of its failure: changes in norms needed for collective security were not feasible. Conventional wisdom claims that Versailles' harsh terms, particularly the large reparations owed by Germany, made renewal of conflict in Europe inevitable. Marc Trachtenberg, however, convincingly argues that the deeper structural problem was Germany's unification, which had created a powerful nation in the middle of Europe.[61] The superpowers solved the "German Question" only by dividing the nation for the period of the Cold War.

Indeed, faith in collective security and the League of Nations diverted resources from more realistic measures that nations could have taken to avert World War II. As Trachtenberg suggests, the United States, France, and Britain could have preserved the peace by forming an alliance. A permanent American military presence in Europe would have balanced Germany's rise and reassured the French, and might have encouraged accommodation between Germany and her neighbors.[62] But such measures would have contradicted the theory of collective security: great power politics and the balance of power were responsible for war and had to be suppressed.

World War II should have proven that great power politics remained the fundamental mechanism in international relations. International law did little to affect nations' decisions to go to war. Neither the League of Nations nor the variety of interwar peace treaties prevented Hitler's Germany from rearming and then invading its neighbors. Nations at war pursued alliances and fought out conflicts regardless of shared values—Nazi Germany and the communist Soviet Union agreed to divide Poland, Germany then attacked the communist Soviet Union, and democratic, capitalist Great Britain and the United States allied with the communist Soviet Union. Even the apparent compliance with multilateral treaties, such as the ban on chemical weapons, can be explained by mutual deterrence rather than by regard for international law.

In the wake of even greater destruction in World War II, the Allies constructed yet another system of collective security. They resurrected the same basic idea that had motivated the League of Nations: that law could bring peace by "outlawing" the use of force to settle disputes between nations. They created a United Nations with a General Assembly, which, like the League of Nations, did not have any serious abilities to address threats to international peace and security. But they also added a Security Council, with the power under Chapter VII to deploy force, either through its own standing forces or by authorizing action by member states. The UN Charter created the possibility of a more effective enforcement mechanism than that of the League of Nations, though the Cold War would render it stillborn. Establishment of the NATO alliance for the mutual defense of the United States and its Western European allies only four years after the UN Charter was signed demonstrates how swiftly the faith in UN collective security collapsed. To take a more recent example, proposals to define and criminalize "aggression" under the Rome Statute for the International Criminal Court amount to an admission that the UN Charter's methods for constraining aggression have signally failed. International criminal law seeks to make good the Charter's defects—although the likelihood of success is no greater than it was under the Charter.

Great power politics in the twenty-first century may provide greater structure to international politics than feared. We should recognize that it is actually the great powers, rather than international institutions, that cooperate to maintain international peace and security. At the level of interstate armed conflict, it seems highly unlikely that the UN Charter's rules on the use of force have produced the steep post-1945 drop in great power wars. The world certainly came close to such wars several times during the Cold War period. In the 1950s, the armed forces of the United States and communist China fought in Korea, and the United States threatened its own allies, Britain and France, to withdraw from the Suez Canal. From 1948 to 1949 and again in the 1960s, the United States and the Soviet Union directly confronted each other in Berlin. The two superpowers came within a hair's breadth of nuclear war over Cuba in 1962. Proxy wars throughout the 1960s, 1970s, and 1980s in places like Vietnam, the Middle East, Africa, and Afghanistan kept alive the possibility of a major conflict between the powers. But none of these crises erupted into a major conflagration on the level of World War I or II.

Much of the explanation for the steep drop in great power war comes not just from nuclear weapons, which threatened extreme costs to escalating a conflict, but also from the balance of power between the United States and the Soviet Union. Both superpowers had an interest in preventing their allies from causing a destabilization of the international system, which might have invited a broader conflict. Their rivalry kept the peace, rather than any international legal injunction against the use of force. Indeed, if an international institution could ever reach such a level of influence, nations would have a strong interest in cheating or would worry about the gains that others would achieve at its expense.[63]

Great powers will be the central dynamic of any future system of international security. It is difficult to predict how the system will work in practice. From the end of the Cold War to the presidency of Barack Obama, the world faced something close to a unipolar system, thanks to the collapse of the Soviet Union. The United States' share of the world's economic and military power has allowed it to wield an almost hegemonic influence over world events. The United States was able to lead a coalition in 1991 that reversed Iraq's invasion of Kuwait. In the 1990s, the United States expanded NATO to the very borders of Russia. It led efforts to stop the proliferation of nuclear weapons to North Korea, Iran, and Libya. And in 2003, it invaded and occupied Iraq despite the opposition of many of the world's other major powers.

But the growth in the economic power of other nations, especially China but also Russia, Brazil, and India, signals that this state of affairs is temporary. The difficult question is whether this change will result in less warfare, or more. Any relative decline of U.S. economic and military strength in the years ahead may portend that the other great powers will combine to offset the power of the United States, either globally or regionally. Or, the United States might play the role of an offshore balancer, preserving its dominance in the Western Hemisphere while maintaining equilibrium among rival powers in Europe or Asia. "Asia seems to be moving toward a complex balance of power, something like the European system that emerged after the Congress of Vienna," Walter Russell Mead suggests. "In this system, an offshore balancing power—Britain in 1815, the United States today—can exercise great influence and protect its vital interests at low cost, even if other powers in the system have larger populations or economies, or even, by some measures, stronger military forces."[64] Mead foresees an Asia where China, India, and Japan will create a triumvirate of power, where two of them will ally to counterbalance any third that threatens supremacy. "With the United States as a second balancing power available to counter any aspiring hegemon, the path to Asian supremacy for India, China, or Japan seems difficult if not impossible to navigate—always assuming that the other powers, including the United States, recognize and act on their national interests."

In either case, we might see international peace and stability maintained by something similar to the nineteenth century's Concert of Europe, where the great powers attempted to manage conflict to maintain the status quo. The Concert, and the balancing it expressed, was relatively successful in keeping a general European peace from the end of the Napoleonic Wars to the start of World War I. Similarly, the United States, like other assumedly "declining" powers before it, may be tempted to launch a preventive war to thwart the rise of competitors or to forestall adverse shifts in the balance of power. Germany and Japan in World War II and Germany and Austria-Hungary in World War I provide examples of this kind of conduct. It would be a mistake to assume, however, that the emergence of a new dominant power must trigger a preventive war. With the exception of 1812–1814, the rising United States and the declining British Empire were able to resolve their differences in the Western Hemisphere without war.[65]

Relying on great power politics to provide international peace and security does not demand much in the way of international law. It is true that the formal structure of the Security Council provides a forum for discussion among the member states. But the territorial integrity of the great powers themselves does not need legal protection; the spread of nuclear weapons to the major military nations can guarantee their sovereign integrity. Great power balancing may well protect middling powers from larger ones. If Russia were to threaten Turkey, for example, other powers would aid Turkey to prevent Russia from expanding the resources under its control. For exactly these reasons, Britain provided the Turkish Empire with protection against Russian encroachments for much of the nineteenth century.[66] Such support would be far more valuable than a legal prohibition of aggression that lacked any reliable enforcement mechanism. The place for international law would not be to establish some type of nonintervention rule, but rather to regularize the means of coordination and cooperation among the great powers to prevent misunderstandings, transaction costs, and the like.

Great power cooperation would more effectively address the challenges of modern war. Since the end of the Cold War, rogue nations, international terrorist groups, humanitarian crises, and WMD proliferation have risen as threats as the prospect of great power war has declined. Great power cooperation has several benefits over the UN Charter system. First, it relies on those nations with the resources to actually intervene in a meaningful way. The performance of the United States in 1990–1991 provides a good example. Not only was it able to provide the military assets needed to reverse the invasion of Kuwait, but it also was able to cooperate with other nations, which provided financial and other noncombat support to the mission. The great powers also may benefit more than others from the trade and commerce that are facilitated by international stability. NATO members had a strong interest in solving the humanitarian crises in the Balkans in the 1990s because those crises created instability in Europe. While these considerations do not cure the collective-action problem, aligning the interests of the great powers with overall global welfare would move toward solving it.

A system that hearkens back to the Concert of Europe on a global scale could help ameliorate the collective-action problems that have beset the UN Charter system. International relations scholars distinguish between certain forms of the "balance of power" between states and what is genuinely a "concert" system. Some argue that the latter assumes "continuous coordination and collective decision making."[67] One historian theorizes that the success of the Concert of Europe in maintaining a general continental peace was not so much because it created a balance of power as because it achieved "a general equilibrium in which all the members of the European family of states would share in certain balanced advantages and duties... a balance of rights."[68]

One critical issue concerns the difficulties of moving from the more predatory kind of "balance of power" system postulated by some international relations theorists to a genuine "concert" system.[69] Under a great powers approach, no single nation would hold an absolute veto over action. Rather, five or even ten nations might have a say over whether to intervene to stop a rogue nation, for example, from acquiring nuclear weapons. There would be no formal vote in an international institution and no requirement of a majority vote. Rather, intervention would effectively be a function of the relative power of each of the nations—perhaps more similar to the weighted voting systems that characterize the decision-making of corporations. This might cure the paralysis imposed by the absolute veto of the Security Council's permanent members. This does not mean that any single nation, or perhaps a small group of nations, could not have the power to block collective action. If the most powerful nation was willing to use its resources to stop an intervention it opposed, that nation very well might have its way, though its relative power would have to be something near 50 percent of global economic and military power. This proposed system would only reduce global welfare if the current international legal rule against aggression has reduced the amount of interstate conflict (a proposition for which little or no evidence exists).[70]

Allowing the most powerful nation to block collective action would leave the world no worse off than the current situation, where permanent members of the Security Council can exercise an absolute veto. The real difference would arise where a group of nations representing more than 50 percent of the world's economic and military capabilities wanted to use force to intervene in a state. Under a great power system, they would be far more likely to prevail than under the Charter system, which allows a nation with a permanent seat such as France, which represents less than 3 percent of world GDP, to veto war. Under the proposed system, a decision on intervention will come far closer to the views of the median great power, rather than an extreme nation closest to the status quo position of inaction.

We cannot identify with precision the ideal level of intervention necessary to produce international peace and stability. It may be the case that a Concert might prompt a rise in undesirable interventions—that is, aggression for territorial conquest or influence. The same restraints that exist now on such interventions, however, would still apply with equal force under a Concert. The threat of great power intervention provides the sole means of deterring such wars under either system. But a Concert will have the important benefit of allowing the great powers to cooperate on more interventions, such as Rwanda and Darfur, than are currently possible under the formal UN Charter system, and therefore offers an advance for global welfare.

IV. Conclusion

The UN Charter system should be supplanted: its use-of-force rules are based on the assumption that the Security Council will provide collective security that will underpin a global peace. Not only has that system failed in practice, but it also is not designed to deal with the changing nature of warfare. The Charter's use-of-force rules were created to prevent armed conflict between states; they are no longer adequate to deal with the more contemporary problems of civil war, mass violence against civilians at the hands of nonstate terrorist groups, protecting populations from genocide or other atrocities inflicted by their own governments, or the violence that is bred within failed or failing states.

Relying on a Concert system to safeguard international peace need not spell the end of the United Nations. Despite its impotence in the security arena, the UN promotes international public goods in other areas through its specialized arms. In the United States, the World Health Organization's fight against disease or UNICEF's programs for children are perhaps the most widely known. Other agencies handle challenges such as refugees, disarmament, and education. The International Court of Justice plays an important role in settling disputes between nations. These agencies need not disappear under a Concert approach. They could continue their work within the current UN framework, or the United Nations could spin them off into independent international organizations. Turning to an informal coalition of the great powers to underwrite global security need not even mean the end of the Security Council, which could continue to serve as a forum for political debate and consensus. Giving up its failed mission on the security front might even free the United Nations to perform with more focus and effect in providing these other international public goods.

The world needs a new international legal regime to confront modern developments in warfare. The overarching goal of this regime should be the maintenance of international peace and stability as measured by increases or decreases in global welfare. Suppression of interstate conflict—which is the main goal of the UN Charter system—is no longer sufficient in itself. Instead, the international legal system should be designed to produce public goods, including the reduction of armed conflicts, the prevention of human rights catastrophes, the safety and security of civilian populations from both internal and external threats, and the nonproliferation of WMDs. Unlike the UN Charter system, which is designed to drive the use of force by states down to zero, a redesigned international legal system should seek to produce an optimal level of force, allowing armed interventions for the purpose of preventing catastrophic harms. Optimal need not mean ever-present. If threats to international security dissipated, or authoritarian regimes stopped engaging in mass human rights atrocities, the optimal level of force would be zero. A system with the correct incentives, such as the one described in this book, might create the conditions where the need for intervention would steadily decline.

The emergence and reemergence of great powers—such as China, the European Union, India, and Russia—have apparently begun to shift the post-Cold War world from unipolarity to multipolarity. Global peace and security in the future may no longer be underwritten by a "hegemonic" United States. Instead, the world may experience a return to the kind of great power politics that was prevalent in Europe before World War I and, arguably, throughout much of human history. Although the maintenance of peace and the possibilities of international cooperation are always problematic when rival great powers confront each other, the practice of the classical European "balance of power" suggests that even a long peace can be preserved in such circumstances. More specifically, the nineteenth-century's Concert of Europe might provide a useful analogy of how the great powers can identify common security interests leading them to cooperate in preserving peace and securing other international public goods. While the details of an emerging multipolar world are yet to be worked out, an explicit great power system could well ameliorate the collective-action problems unsolved by the UN Charter system, and thus advance global welfare.

7 Failed States

THIS CHAPTER APPLIES the international public goods approach to war to the critical problem of failed states. Failed states pose one of the deepest challenges to international peace and stability. They serve as an incubator for international terrorist groups, such as al-Qaeda. Their lack of government authority allows their territory to become transshipment points for illicit drugs, human trafficking, or weapons proliferation. In Somalia, Rwanda, Haiti, and the former Yugoslavia, failed states have become the breeding ground for gross human rights abuses. Since the end of World War II, far more lives have been lost to internal wars—many of which occurred in failed states—than to conflicts between nations. Military intervention in internal conflicts, often led by the United States and its allies, incurs high costs in terms of money, supplies, and lives. Finding a comprehensive and effective solution to the challenges of terrorism, human rights violations, and poverty requires a better understanding of failed states.

In the last decade, the United States has spent lives and treasure rebuilding nations on a grand scale. In Afghanistan, President George W. Bush initially deployed about 5,000 troops in 2002, rising to about 30,000 by the end of his presidency. In 2009, President Obama decided to deploy an additional 30,000 troops to Afghanistan—bringing the total number of U.S. troops there to about 60,000—to defeat the Taliban and al-Qaeda. In addition to fighting insurgents, the U.S. armed forces built schools and roads and trained local government officials. About 130,000 American troops participated in the 2003 Iraq invasion and the following occupation, which at its height rose to about 160,000 in 2007–2008.[1] Allied nations provided significant troop contributions as well, with Great Britain sending 46,000 troops to Iraq and 9,500 troops to Afghanistan.[2] Washington did not send the large force to fight a foreign enemy, which was defeated in relatively short order, but to stabilize the country. Along with other countries, the United States has also intervened in Haiti and Liberia to stop internecine wars. And to this day, U.S. troops remain in Kosovo to monitor the peace accords in Bosnia signed in 1995.

Some failed states are rogue nations that the United States invaded and has attempted to restore. But others are not. Regardless of the reasons for the original state failure, the response of the United States and its allies has remained consistent: rebuild the institutions of state control with the aim of planting a working democracy and a market economy. The United States and its allies seem convinced that international peace and security depend on the exclusive existence of independent states capable of controlling their territories, policing their populations, and discharging their obligations. States appear to be the most effective means to control conduct that threatens international order, at least in the dimensions of stability and security. Even when intervention in the affairs of malfunctioning states seems to depart from the principle of sovereignty, it may advance broader interests behind using the nation-state as the basic building block of world order.

Leading international law scholars, however, see such intervention as a fool's errand.[3] They believe that international law may permit the use of force for self-defense or a Security Council mandate, but not for rebuilding a state. To be sure, some observers support military force in the event of humanitarian disasters.[4] The concept of the "failed state," for example, traces its lineage to justifications to end civil wars in the former Yugoslavia and Somalia. Nonetheless, many scholars doubt the ability of individual nations—particularly the United States—to rebuild another's institutions and infrastructure. For these scholars, the problem is not failed states but nation-states. They believe that the nation-state is becoming obsolete, while various forms of subnational, regional, or supranational government emerge as better administrators of territories and peoples. These scholars seek solutions that erode the national exercise of traditional military and political powers in international affairs.

American and UN policymakers on the one hand, and critics of the nation-state on the other, are mistaken. Restoring a failed state to full sovereignty, but without reconsidering its borders, fails to address the causes of its failure in the first place. Viable states need not conform to the borders recognized by the United Nations or created during postwar decolonization. Yugoslavia, for example, contained several states that wanted to exist independently. Observers, however, who seek nonstate alternatives to the current world order offer no practical solutions. Supranational governments, trusteeships, or nongovernmental organizations, among others, do not possess the resources to fix failed states. Curing failed states still depends on the political, economic, and military resources of strong nation-states.

This chapter proposes an intermediate position based on what we know about state failure and recent interventions. It does not view the restoration of the status quo as the answer, nor does it endorse the replacement of nation-states with international institutions. Rather, it argues that nation-states remain the only actors with the capacity to fix failed states and the resources to increase global public goods and reduce global public "bads." Removing obstacles in international law and policy to intervention in failed states will allow nation-states to more effectively tackle the problem. This solution does not discard state sovereignty, but it may require accepting adjustments to the borders of failed states, possibly resulting in smaller, more numerous nations.

This chapter sketches a theory of why states are falling apart. Free trade and international security have accelerated the breakup of larger states because small states no longer need to combine for economic or defensive purposes.[5] While U.S. policy has promoted trade and security, it has also stood athwart the very fragmentation produced by those international public goods. But larger states might be more likely to fail in a globalized environment because ethnic, religious, and regional groups may be less likely to cooperate in the absence of external economic or security pressures. Current international rules do not ease the challenge of fixing failed states. Several factors create powerful disincentives, including the lack of direct benefit to an intervening state, the possibility of high costs in both military and civilian lives, the hard moral dilemmas involved in deciding whom to help and how, and the difficulty in exiting. International law only exacerbates these existing obstacles. This chapter ends by proposing reforms that would encourage, rather than deter, the great powers to intervene in failing states and to establish more flexible, appropriate governing arrangements.

I. The Problem of Failed States

The concept of a "failed state" first emerged in 1992.[6] Though scholars disagree on a precise definition, the term describes nations that cannot perform their domestic functions or meet their international obligations because of the collapse of government authority. Failed states cannot meet the Westphalian ideal, where a nation exercises full sovereign powers over a territory and population, monopolizes legitimate violence, provides public services, and keeps international obligations. In failed states, private groups control resources and population and rival the government for control over legitimate violence and public services; the economy has usually collapsed, producing famine, refugee flows, and human rights disasters.[7] Physical infrastructure decays, and living standards decline rapidly. Government usually has lost legitimacy and cannot stop internal wars, which are often rooted in longstanding ethnic, religious, or regional rivalries.[8]

No uniform consensus exists on which states qualify as "failed." Scholars initially focused on the successors to the former Yugoslavia and the Soviet Union. The end of the Cold War unleashed racial, ethnic, or religious animosities, or independence movements, which authoritarian dictatorships had suppressed. These states gave birth to more than two dozen successors, such as Serbia, Bosnia, and Croatia. Some turned on their neighbors, while others had difficulty governing themselves. Another set of failed states emerged after World War II in Africa and Asia, where decolonization tripled the number of states. Many of these states achieved autonomy without a tradition of democratic self-government. Superpower competition during the Cold War had kept some of these nations afloat, such as Somalia and Ethiopia. But the collapse of the Soviet Union largely ended great power interest in sub-Saharan Africa. In a third set of failed states, such as Haiti and Afghanistan, tribal rivalries and endemic civil wars have historically undermined fully functioning government.

Observers have created indexes to measure nations with the least functional governments. The World Bank, for example, issues a "Country Policy and Institutional Assessment" index that ranks states for purposes of allocating aid. It categorizes "fragile states" as low-income nations that have weak institutions, poor governance, and political instability, and suffer from frequent violence or the effects of past severe conflict.[9] In 2007, the World Bank listed thirty-four nations as "fragile" based on a review of their economic management (macro policy and fiscal policy), structural policies (trade and business regulation), social inclusion (gender equality, environmental and labor policies), and public-sector management and institutions (property rights, budget and revenue, public administration and corruption):

1. Zimbabwe
2. Eritrea
3. Comoros
4. Sudan
5. Central African Republic
6. Chad
7. Guinea-Bissau
8. Afghanistan
9. Cote d'Ivoire
10. Togo
11. Democratic Republic of Congo
12. Angola
13. Republic of Congo
14. Solomon Islands
15. Timor-Leste
16. Haiti
17. Sao Tome and Principe
18. Guinea

19. Burundi	27. Vanuatu
20. Sierra Leone	28. Uzbekistan
21. Djibouti	29. Mauritania
22. Tonga	30. Nigeria
23. The Gambia	31. Liberia
24. Papua New Guinea	32. Myanmar
25. Lao PDR	33. Somalia
26. Cambodia	34. Territory of Kosovo.[10]

According to the World Bank, these states experience high levels of extreme poverty, infant mortality, and deaths from disease. They have low levels of economic growth, savings and investment, and education. Violent conflict is endemic.

Foreign Policy magazine and the Fund for Peace publish the best-known ranking. Using similar factors to those of the World Bank, in 2009, they listed the twenty least-functional states:

1. Somalia	11. Ivory Coast
2. Zimbabwe	12. Haiti
3. Sudan	13. Burma
4. Chad	14. Kenya
5. Democratic Republic of the Congo	15. Nigeria
6. Iraq	16. Ethiopia
7. Afghanistan	17. North Korea
8. Central African Republic	18. Yemen
9. Guinea	19. Bangladesh
10. Pakistan	20. East Timor.[11]

Though there is a strong degree of overlap, some differences emerge. Professor Robert Rotberg identifies Somalia as a "collapsed state" and only seven other states as "failed": Afghanistan, Angola, Burundi, Democratic Republic of the Congo, Liberia, Sierra Leone, and Sudan. He considers roughly thirty-five other states as "weak" enough that they could become failed states. The Brookings Institution's "Index of State Weakness in the Developing World" contains most of the same states as the World Bank and uses similar measures of economic, political, security, and social welfare. Still, the Brookings Institution's index describes only Somalia, Afghanistan, and the Democratic Republic of Congo as "failed," followed by a larger group of twenty-eight "critically weak states" including Iraq, Burundi, Sudan, Central African Republic, Zimbabwe, Liberia, and Cote d'Ivoire.[12]

Efforts to grade failed states suffer from the same problems as other rankings, such as the annual declaration by popular magazines of the top-ranked law schools or the best places to live. There are inevitable subjective judgment calls. There are disputes about the dysfunctional nature of a government or the severity of a civil war. The rankings may also treat cases differently depending on the cause of a state's decline. Iraq, for example, was not considered a failed state until the 2003 invasion. Different rankings may also disagree about whether a nation with a strong, even tyrannical, central government can qualify as failed. In North Korea or Zimbabwe, for example, a small clique presides over widespread poverty and economic collapse but still maintains a public—albeit repressive—order. Nonetheless, these rankings show some rough consensus about the majority of states that have failed.

Whatever their precise definition, failed states present a challenge for both international law and policy. The 2002 National Security Strategy of the United States, for example, declared that failing states "pose as great a danger to our national interest as strong states." The European Union's 2003 security strategy found them to be an "alarming phenomenon," while the UN Secretary-General observed in 2005 that "[i]f states are fragile, the peoples of the world will not enjoy the security, development and justice that are their right."[13]

Failed states can generate three types of negative externalities. First, state failure can cause enough harm to a civilian population that refugees flee to neighboring countries. Failed states breed violence, produce starvation, and destroy the economy, which can convince the population to move elsewhere. In 1993, for example, the failure of state institutions in Somalia allowed armed bands to roam throughout the country, producing famine and demands for humanitarian relief. Haiti periodically has experienced similar problems, in which the absence of effective central government allows humanitarian crises to go unaddressed, producing waves of refugees bound for the United States. In both cases, the United Nations authorized intervention to assist in the delivery of humanitarian aid, with mixed results. Neither country has yet returned to a condition of political or economic stability. Similar problems elsewhere, particularly in Africa, suggest that failed states are becoming one of the most significant causes of humanitarian disasters.

Second, governmental collapse can unleash ethnic or religious conflict. In Yugoslavia, the end of the Cold War led Croats, Bosnians, and Kosovars to seek independence. Serbia sought to assert control over the other provinces using ethnic cleansing and population expulsion. One might also understand the genocide in Rwanda as the product of a failure of state authority in which a political assassination and the collapse of government allowed one ethnic group to attempt to destroy another. These internal conflicts can spread to neighboring countries, which might have similar ethnic or religious divisions, or which may be tempted to support one side or the other. Internal conflict in one country may weaken neighboring states or create pressure to increase armaments, which may further destabilize the region.[14]

A third type of negative externality came into focus after the September 11, 2001, attacks. States without a centralized government may become anarchic areas where terrorist groups can freely build resources, train operatives, and establish bases from which to launch attacks. Parts of Yemen, for example, appear to be ungovernable due to a weak central government, which has allowed the al-Qaeda terrorist network to take root there.[15] Afghanistan similarly witnessed the free operation of al-Qaeda within its territory. It appears now that either the Taliban could not control al-Qaeda or that al-Qaeda simply dictated to the Taliban; in either case, a stronger central government in Afghanistan might have prevented the large-scale, open operations of terrorist groups on its soil. In the wake of the September 11 attacks, U.S. government officials clearly believed that failed states—because of their potential use as bases for terrorist groups—presented as great a danger to American national security as the powerful national opponents of old. According to the 2002 U.S. National Security Strategy, "America is now threatened less by conquering states than we are by failing ones."[16] Terrorist groups are not the only problem. A lack of government authority allows nonstate actors to engage in other forms of undesirable activity, such as narcotics smuggling, human trafficking, and money laundering.

Beyond these concrete harms on their neighbors, failed states may also cause systemic declines in global welfare suffered by all. Even if the collapse of internal governance does not threaten world peace as directly as great power wars, it often triggers grave human rights violations. Philosophers vigorously debate the justifications for human rights, ranging from arguments that they are an essential feature of human dignity to claims that they result from choices made behind Rawls's veil of ignorance.[17] Utilitarians might conclude that severe human rights violations in one nation may cause psychological harm to the people of another nation. Our global welfare perspective calls for intervention when the lives saved from oppressive governments outweigh the costs of war. It also considers other global impacts of a failed state, such as economic disruption, interruption of resource flows, and environmental harms. Nations seem to recognize this principle in practice, if not in principle. The Security Council, for example, has authorized various actions to stop human rights violations that did not extend beyond a nation's borders, such as economic sanctions on South Africa, armed intervention in Somalia, and armed attacks in Bosnia. Coalitions led by the United States have also intervened in failed states such as Haiti, Somalia, and the Balkans to stop human rights catastrophes.

Human rights disasters in failed states may even present a more compelling case for intervention than violations that occur in well-functioning states. Failed states often lack the means to prevent ethnic or religious groups from coming to blows. Violence may not only reach genocidal proportions—as it did in Rwanda—but may also spread to nearby countries with similar tribal, ethnic, or religious fault lines.

Rwanda's genocidal killing, for example, spilled over into the civil war in Congo. Civil wars may spark widespread human rights violations, starvation, and disease that may prompt a destabilizing flood of refugees. Even if these systemic human rights abuses do not directly harm neighboring countries, severe catastrophes such as genocide cause harm to global welfare overall.

International law and policy have failed to grapple with the emergence of failed states. The former still rests on the nation-state as the primary actor in world affairs. As a general matter, for example, only "States" may legally engage in international relations. The Vienna Convention on the Law of Treaties defines a "treaty" as "an international agreement concluded between States in written form and governed by international law."[18] While international law recognizes that nonstate entities, such as international organizations, can become parties to treaties, states still remain the creators of international organizations, usually also by treaty, and the primary actors in international affairs.[19] Insurgents in control of particular territories have on occasion entered into agreements with governments, but even then, the rebels could be understood to represent an emerging state in the course of a successful move for independence.[20]

In determining whether a state exists, and hence whether an entity is entitled to the privilege of participating in international affairs, international law looks to a standard test. The 1933 Montevideo Convention rejects the "constitutive" theory in which recognition by existing states establishes the existence of a new state. Instead, it adopts a "declaratory" approach, which uses objective factors to determine statehood. A state must have (1) a permanent population, (2) a defined territory, (3) government, and (4) the capacity to enter into international relations.[21] The four factors test whether a state will be able to conduct international relations, both in making international agreements and in fulfilling its obligations. States have interests in forming treaties to ensure that other states do not invade their territories or harm their people. They have regimes that can be induced by promised benefits or threats of harm to comply with their international obligations. These costs and benefits can come from treaty partners or even third parties that have independent interests in securing treaty compliance. A state's breach of its treaty obligations may not only cause the injured state to retaliate by suspending performance of that treaty and others, but it may also cause third parties to alter their policies or sever diplomatic relations.

Absence of a state structure makes compliance with international law unlikely or even impossible. A terrorist organization like al-Qaeda, for example, has no territories or populations to defend. It provides no public services to a population, nor does it operate any traditional governmental institutions. Its apocalyptic vision and practices leave it unsusceptible to the ordinary pressures and incentives that characterize interstate relations. Instead, al-Qaeda is motivated by the perversion of certain religious doctrines, which permits or even encourages both the suicide of its own members and the mass murder of civilians. Finally, al-Qaeda engages in an asymmetric form of warfare that makes a state's military forces far less useful either offensively or defensively than such forces might be against a more traditional enemy. Given these characteristics, it would be absurd to expect al-Qaeda to show respect for treaty obligations and therefore pointless to attribute treaty-making capacity to it.[22]

International law once offered a way to govern new territories by limiting national sovereignty and allowing foreign powers to exercise high levels of control over domestic functions. Chapter XII of the UN Charter created a trusteeship system that allowed the United Nations to appoint an established nation to administer a territory and advance it toward self-government.[23] The trusteeship system applied to three types of territories: those still under a League of Nations mandate (which created a similar governance structure), those detached from the Axis powers at the end of World War II, and those voluntarily placed under the system by states already responsible for their administration (which generally applied to colonial powers). Ironically, given the recent rise of many failed states, the UN Trusteeship Council, created to oversee the system and composed of the permanent members of the Security Council, terminated its functions in 1994 after the independence of Palau, the last of the trusteeship territories. But even those scholars who support a rejuvenated trusteeship system, such as Gerald Helman and Steven Ratner, concede that Chapter XII does not reach the case of existing UN member states whose governmental institutions have failed.[24] Trusteeship addresses the unique situation that arose at the end of World War II with the redrawing of the map in Europe and Asia and the rapid decolonization of large parts of the world. The use of trusteeships in failed states would require an amendment to the UN Charter that would overcome the prohibition on interference with the internal affairs of states and the guarantee of the "sovereign equality" of all members.

Failed states produce negative externalities because internal groups do not bear the full responsibility for their actions. Actors within failed states will not curb their harmful actions because they do not fully internalize the costs. A warlord who drives out members of his rival ethnic group, for example, will not suffer the full costs of the refugee migrations, which are borne by neighboring countries. A rebel leader will not internalize the costs of allowing a terrorist organization or drug cartel to operate on territory under his control. He may benefit by receiving military or financial support without bearing the costs of terrorist attacks abroad or drugs smuggled to other nations.

These challenges produce a collective action problem. The negative externalities generated by failed states will often fall upon many nations or the international system as a whole. This collective action problem is especially evident with human rights catastrophes that affect only the inhabitants of the failed state or with the proliferation of WMD technology. No single nation may receive sufficient benefits to undertake the costs of intervening to rebuild governmental institutions and restore order in the failed state. As with other forms of international collective-action problems, nations must bargain in order to identify who will use force and who will shoulder the costs.

The international system has responded to these problems in several noteworthy, yet inconsistent, ways. First, the great powers have used military force to stop the negative effects of failed states on the international system or their regional interests. They have not always done so consistently or successfully, nor always with the formal approval of the Security Council. Usually, a major power with advanced military and organizational skills leads a coalition, though a state may act alone.[25] In Somalia and Haiti, for example, the United States and others used force to intervene to stop the human rights violations. The mission failed in Somalia but encountered some success in Haiti. In Afghanistan, the United States and its NATO allies overthrew the Taliban regime, which had allowed al-Qaeda to operate freely in its territory. Security Council resolutions authorized the use of force in Somalia, Haiti, and Afghanistan. In Kosovo, NATO successfully prevented Serbia from driving ethnic Albanians out of the territory. In Iraq, the United States and a coalition overthrew Saddam Hussein. The Security Council did not authorize the wars in Kosovo or Iraq. Smaller states have also unilaterally intervened in failing states, such as Tanzania's 1978 overthrow of Idi Amin in Uganda and Vietnam's 1978 invasion of Cambodia.[26] These interventions are likely to be less frequent than those by the great powers because smaller countries—unless they suffer concentrated costs from the externalities of a neighboring failed state—will have less incentive to spend their limited resources on restoring stability.

What may be just as significant, though less studied, is the absence of intervention. In some cases where the effects and consequences of a failed state are just as negative as the effects of Haiti or Somalia, no international intervention has occurred. The Kosovo intervention occurred only after Serbia had launched a three-year campaign, starting in 1992, of ethnic cleansing in Bosnia and Herzegovina, which ultimately resulted in the deaths of thousands of civilians and a partition of the territory along ethnic lines. No Western nation intervened to prevent the genocide that erupted in Rwanda in 1994, in which members of the Hutu tribe killed almost 1 million Tutsi.

Intervening nations have gone further than simply establishing minimal political and economic stability to end internal civil wars or human rights catastrophes. Instead, intervening nations have often sought to restore working governmental institutions and to return the failed states to full sovereignty. In Afghanistan, for example, the United States and its allies have promoted political parties, free elections, constitutional democracy, and rule of law with an independent judiciary. In Haiti, the United States has attempted to restore order by replacing a military junta with a democratically elected president. Such vigorous efforts to restore a failed state to a properly functioning nation-state are not inevitable. In some cases, no great power has emerged to lead the intervention, as was the case in Rwanda. Efforts to use the United Nations, rather than regional powers, have led to failed peacekeeping operations. Repeated state failure may actually signal not that existing state institutions have failed, but that a certain territory has never had a functioning state to begin with.

The nation-state is not a one-size-fits-all framework for governing certain territories or peoples. Both the League of Nations (mandates) and the United Nations (trusteeship) recognized certain forms of quasi-sovereignty in which a more powerful, developed nation takes charge in a territory that cannot quite govern itself and leads it toward full sovereignty and independence. Scholars recently have suggested that "neotrusteeships" could become a new form of institutional governance for failed states.[27] Historically, there have been alternate forms of governance other than the nation-state, such as multiethnic empires, federations, city-states, and colonies. In the recent interventions, however, the great powers have not seriously considered adopting alternate forms of governance. For the United States and its allies, it has been either the nation-state or nothing.

Intervening nations have made a determined effort to maintain existing territorial borders. The United Nations did not seriously consider dividing Rwanda into two nations—one for the Hutus and one for the Tutsis. Nor did the United States and its allies consider dividing Iraq into three different nations that reflected the different religious and ethnic groups there—Kurds in the north, Shiites in the south, and Sunnis in the middle—even though the WWI Allies arbitrarily drew Iraq's borders at the beginning of the last century. Maintaining the status quo, even at the price of forcing vastly different groups into one country, seems to be consistent American policy. At the end of the Cold War, for example, the United States did not support the fragmentation of the Soviet Union until confronted with a fait accompli. Even through the Clinton administration, American presidents kept arms-control agreements with the Soviet Union's successor states in full force on the fiction that the United State's treaty partner still existed.[28]

At other times, however, intervening nations have encouraged failed states to break up. In the former Yugoslavia, for example, the United States and its NATO allies prevented Serbia from maintaining its control over Kosovo. After years of NATO peacekeeping, it now appears that a political settlement will include substantial independence for Kosovo.[29] Similarly, neither the United States nor NATO intervened to prevent earlier conflicts in which groups split off from the former Yugoslavia. In these cases, the different preferences among internal groups were too great to maintain a single state; the price of the existing borders was too high.

International law mirrors this strong political commitment to the nation-state. In the wake of the U.S.-led invasion of Iraq, for example, the Security Council required that Iraq's borders remain intact and that Iraq be returned to full sovereignty in the future.[30] Nations have continued to recognize the borders of failed states such as Somalia and Afghanistan. When the issue of intervening in a failed state first presented itself in the case of Somalia, however, there was more uncertainty. The Security Council welcomed the United States' offer to lead an armed intervention, even though it might have been inconsistent with the UN Charter's prohibition on intervention "in matters which are essentially within the domestic jurisdiction of any state," by referring cryptically to "the unique character of the present situation in Somalia" and "its deteriorating, complex and extraordinary nature, requiring an immediate and exceptional response."[31] The Security Council was so strongly committed to the legal preservation of the nation-state that it resorted to ambiguities in order to avoid the fact that Somalia had collapsed as a state.

Iraq exemplifies these contradictory approaches. After the United States and its partners had successfully ousted Saddam Hussein's regime, they deliberately sought the status of "occupying powers." Under the Fourth Geneva Convention, the Hague Regulations, and customary international law, an occupying power acquires both power and responsibility. They can extract natural resources, take possession of state property, install friendly governments, and even rewrite constitutions. However, their powers are temporary. Occupying powers cannot abolish a defeated nation-state nor permanently reduce its sovereignty.[32] Thus, the U.S.-led coalition never moved to replace the Iraqi nation-state with something else, such as a protectorate, a colony, or an annexed territory. It kept Iraq whole and unified rather than splitting it into Kurdish, Shiite, and Sunni states. While the United States had its strategic reasons—a unified and friendly Iraqi nation-state could prove a useful bulwark against Iran and Syria—it also appears that current international law has no capacity to imagine anything short of a nation-state.

It would go too far to claim that a single explanation drove policymakers in all of these cases. But there are some common themes. In the case of the end of the Cold War, the United States opposed devolution because an intact Soviet Union or Yugoslavia would have proved better able to keep its international responsibilities and, as a result, maintained international stability.[33] In other cases, such as Africa, the United States may have defended existing state borders because it sought to reinforce state capacity or to reduce the prospect of ethnic, religious, or regional conflict. The breakup of these nations might lead to an unpredictable future filled with competing or even hostile regimes. In the cases of Iraq and Afghanistan, to signal its good intentions as liberators, not conquerors, the U.S.-led coalition pledged to keep borders unchanged. In all of these cases, however, the United States and its allies assumed that the benefits of larger nations for providing security, suppression of religious or ethnic conflict, or fulfilling international obligations outweigh the costs of imposing artificial borders on peoples who may no longer want them. Parts II and III of this chapter will show that the broader developments in world politics, driven by U.S. policy on international security and economics, frustrate American policies in discrete cases to keep nations intact.

II. Responses to Failed States

Scholars have responded to the rise of failed states by questioning the nation-state framework. In 1992, Helman and Ratner proposed that the United Nations authorize a new form of conservatorship for failed states. Robert Keohane finds that absolute de jure sovereignty could not account for failed states. Instead, he argues that mixed forms of sovereignty, in which other nations or international organizations control aspects of a failed state's functions, should be recognized. David Laitin and James Fearon argue that "neotrusteeship" has emerged, in which foreign countries and international organizations, rather than any single nation, exercise domestic political authority and manage governmental institutions within a failed state.[34]

International legal scholars, on the other hand, have criticized these neotrusteeship concepts. Early criticism, for example, responded to these proposals as susceptible to "neocolonialism" based on a "theory and system of subjugation, whose sub-text was racial and cultural inferiority."[35] Rosa Brooks has gone even further. She rejects the idea of restoring failed states because, she argues, these efforts attempt to cement the nation-state as the world's governing form. According to Brooks, the nation-state itself is tottering on eroded foundations, and failed states might be better off in "non-state arrangements." While the state is not "defunct," Brooks urges that "we should be more open to diverse forms of social organization—and that we should strive to create an international legal order that permits and values numerous different forms of social organization."[36]

Some practitioners also suggest that the solution to failed states lies in unpacking the sovereignty of the nation-state. Ashraf Ghani and Clare Lockhart argue that the state remains the "most effective form of organization of the polity." Nonetheless, they conclude that the international community should focus on strengthening specific government functions in economics, politics, and social domains. They recommend "a new legal compact" between government, citizens, and the international community and markets, rather than "a top-down imposition of the state." Current international organizations, in their view, present an obstacle because they assume that the primary actor in international affairs is the nation-state that enjoys absolute sovereignty within its territory.[37] On the other hand, a powerful scholarly movement has identified the fast-multiplying ways in which international organizations and regimes have opened opportunities for nongovernmental organizations, private groups, and even private individuals to participate in the development of public international law and affect world politics.[38]

These proposals to fix failed states encounter a significant obstacle: existing international law. International law, as expressed in the UN Charter and laws of war, does not provide a clear route to dividing states into bite-size pieces that can be administered by various international or regional organizations. Take, for example, the claims that the UN Charter's trusteeship provisions can provide the necessary framework for the existence of multiple, overlapping forms of sovereignty in failed states. International relations scholars, who sometimes favor this approach, display a reluctance to analyze whether the UN Charter actually would allow for the revitalization of the trusteeship process. At the same time, such proposals rely heavily on the United Nations, probably to assuage concerns that more unilateral moves to restore failed states could serve as a pretext for neo-imperialism.

Such worries, however, are misplaced. Recent interventions show little signs of colonialism or imperialism.[39] Western powers, for example, do not pursue territorial expansion or permanent political control of failed states as part of a competition for power and resources. The United States has intervened in places like Kosovo, Haiti, and Somalia, for example, where few, if any, direct economic benefits were to be had. It has displayed a desire to leave as soon as possible rather than establishing any significant political control—witness the hasty American exit from Somalia in 1994. It does not seem motivated by a desire to extract wealth from failed states— quite the contrary. Failed states often exist in territories with few natural resources or productive capital. Reconstruction may cost intervening nations more than any possibility of gain from operating the failed state's economy. Even American intervention in Iraq, criticized by some as motivated primarily by oil, may well have cost the United States close to $1 trillion, while Iraq retained full possession of its oil fields and revenues.[40]

Some international law scholars, on the other hand, too easily assume that new forms of political organization can replace the nation-state. Globalization is only the latest phenomenon to raise doubts about the longevity of the nation-state.[41]

But like Mark Twain's death, predictions of sovereignty's demise have been greatly exaggerated. Resistance to alternatives to the nation-state may originate from the international legal system itself, which continues to conceive of the nation-state as the basic unit of international affairs. Or perhaps people have come to accept nation-states simply because they have dominated recent history. History provides a means to understand how the nation-state came into being and became prevalent but not whether it should remain so. Accepting the nation-state solely because of history would be akin to requiring that all forms of business activity be organized along the lines of the modern corporation because it happened to become the most popular form. Rather, we must identify the benefits of the corporate form, compared to other alternatives, in the context of the contemporary global environment. So, for example, corporations are more effective at raising capital and reducing certain transaction costs (such as producing components for a product internally rather than buying all of them on the open market).[42] But the corporate form is not ideal for all types of business activity, which at times may be better served by sole proprietorships or partnerships.

As we have seen, nation-states have been more effective at organizing a population for internal security and national defense. Multiethnic empires became increasingly expensive to govern because of distances, the lack of loyalty on the part of subject populations, and a lack of innovation. Nation-states, by contrast, are better able to organize populations to defend against external threats in two ways: first, by using appeals to a common national origin to spur patriotic fervor and second, by providing efficient means of supporting large militaries. The idea of the nation-state assumed that the population of a "state" would consist, primarily if not solely, of a particular "people," understood in terms of a common historical consciousness or remembered collective past, and likely also in terms of commonalities in ethnicity, language, and perhaps religion.[43] Nation-states outperformed empires and other forms of governance in guaranteeing domestic peace and providing public goods such as markets, law enforcement, and security. Interstate conflicts may have led to much death and destruction, but nation-states also produced large increases in population and economic growth and longer stretches of international peace than under alternate forms of governance, such as the multiethnic empire.

Nevertheless, critics today often see the nation-state as the problem rather than the solution. Human rights advocates, for example, are apt to criticize nation-state sovereignty, which can be used to shield states from criticism over grave human rights abuses.[44] Globalization—the accelerated and cheap movement of goods, service, capital, and communication across national borders—is seen as another challenge to the ideal of nation-states. Nations, it is argued, cannot control worldwide changes that are occurring primarily outside their individual borders.[45] Efforts to solve problems arising from globalization in the areas of the environment, development, crime, terrorism, and trade, among others, are likely to view the nation-state and its sovereignty as an obstacle rather than an aid to cooperation.

But, as Jeremy Rabkin argues, it may be the case that the nation-state remains the best way to solve these problems.[46] Human rights abuses in the Balkans did not end because of the collective action of the international community, but because of the intervention of the United States and its NATO allies. European nations would not take decisive action in the Balkans until the Clinton administration decided to throw the weight of the United States military behind the war. Individual nations with historical or geographical ties to problem areas, such as the United States and Haiti or France and the Ivory Coast, have taken the lead to stop murderous civil wars. The United Nations has proven to be miserably inadequate at stopping genocide in Rwanda and, it appears, Sudan.[47] Regardless of one's opinion on the Iraq War, it is difficult to imagine a successful resolution to the challenge of rogue nations and the proliferation of WMDs that does not involve economic, political, or military action on the part of nation-states. Nation-states have not just become guarantors of their own security, but also have been better protectors of international peace and security than any currently existing alternatives.

If the nation-state framework were extended to failed states, the relationship between an intervening power and a failed state would be comparable to that of two nations in an alliance. Students of international relations have long viewed alliances as devices for "capability aggregation."[48] States form alliances in order to combine their strengths against a common foe or foes. The nature of the alliance depends on the relative power of the two nations and their strategic positions. The greater the military capabilities of a nation, the more attractive it is as an ally; on the other hand, a reduction in the common threat's capabilities or in an ally's abilities makes an alliance less useful. Work on these themes suggests that alliances represent a trade-off between security and autonomy.[49] Powerful allies can offer improved security but are more likely to expect substantial autonomy in the partnership; conversely, smaller nations with fewer capabilities will be willing to provide greater control to their larger and more capable partners. A larger partner may be willing to enter such an alliance because greater control over a smaller ally can allow it to devote resources elsewhere.

Another way of seeing this point is to view a traditional strategic alliance, such as NATO or the Australia, New Zealand, United States Security Alliance (ANZUS), as a species of international governance that provides a fairly high level of autonomy to its members. Other relationships in which the weaker party has low levels of autonomy approach that of an empire; various forms of federations, colonies, or protectorates lie somewhere in between. For example, one can view the Warsaw

Pact as a relationship between a stronger power and weaker ones that fell some-where between the high autonomy of NATO and the low autonomy of an outright empire.

Some have likened alliances to relational contracts in which the level of control in the relationship depends on the level of opportunism to shirk or abrogate agree-ments by the smaller power, to entrap the larger power in unwanted conflicts, or to renegotiate the level of contributions to the joint enterprise.[50] The more likely that an ally will act opportunistically in these ways, the more likely that the more powerful partner will demand greater control over the alliance. Less autonomy, in turn, means higher governance costs for the greater power. Monitoring the activity of the smaller power will distort the allocation of resources available for security. Greater powers could act opportunistically too by exploiting the weaker power once an alliance is formed; safeguards necessary to protect against such exploitation will also increase governance costs. The threat deterred by the aggregation of capabilities (or, to put it differently, the costs created by going at alone without an alliance) will define the benefit of the alliance. The total cost will be the sum of the cost of oppor-tunism and the governance costs to prevent it.

Alliance theory can help us understand why the great powers are so quick to restore failed states. They need to create other nation-states as a prerequisite to form-ing alliances or more hierarchical relations. Nations will seek to rebuild nation-states when the benefits from an alliance with the failed state are very high. In Kosovo, the benefit was the prevention of warfare in a territory on the border of Europe, in an area where previous conflict had produced a continental war and where humani-tarian catastrophes could have led to destabilizing refugee flows. In Afghanistan, a capable, central government could suppress infighting and prevent al-Qaeda from slipping in and establishing a base of operations.[51] The September 11 attacks demon-strated that American policymakers had underestimated the benefits of restoring a nation-state in Afghanistan. A larger nation cannot reap the benefits of an alliance, however, without a nation-state across the table.

On the cost side, a failed state presents the greatest opportunity for rogue actors to undermine international stability. Without a central government, the United States is left only with private or quasi-public entities, such as warlords or ethnic leaders, with which to cooperate. Without a government to enforce laws, these groups may have little incentive to uphold their end of the bargain. Such groups may also lead to unwanted entanglements in local affairs, as they may have more scores to settle with other groups within a failed state. Building nation-states in the former Yugoslavia or Afghanistan can simply be understood as incurring very high governance costs in order to control extremely high levels of opportunism. Nation building represents a particularly expensive method for monitoring whether a partner is going to live up to its end of the bargain, whether it be maintaining peace and stability in the former Yugoslavia or hunting down al-Qaeda terrorists in Afghanistan.

Balancing these benefits and costs may explain the haphazard meanderings of policy and the presumptions built into international law. Nation-states appear to be the most consistent means for guaranteeing law and order within a territory. With a functioning government, a territory is less likely to become a base for terrorists. It may be less likely to cause humanitarian catastrophes (although this is not true in every case, as demonstrated by North Korea). However, the governance costs of establishing a functioning nation-state can be high. Hence, we would not expect to see the great powers undertake state building except when the expected benefits are large. Perhaps this explains why the West launched its expensive state building efforts in Kosovo, Afghanistan, and Iraq, but not in other places, such as Somalia or Congo, which seem to pose less of a threat to Western security. The success of nation-states in restoring security seems so consistent that it may even make sense to embody the policy in a legal rule.

We should also recognize that our modern age lacks sufficient experience with other forms of governance. Alternative means of social organization might provide much higher levels of control, at lower cost, and still sufficiently prevent a territory from producing negative externalities. For example, some form of joint sovereignty between local provinces and NATO nations may prove a more effective long-term solution to the former Yugoslavia than undertaking the expensive task of ensuring that each can survive as an independent state. Similarly, some form of governance greater than the rule of warlords but less than a fully independent nation-state might track down al-Qaeda in Afghanistan just as effectively, at a lower cost.

International legal rules, however, discourage states from intervening in territories that witness serious human rights catastrophes or serve as a base for terrorist operations. If nations that intervene in a failed state must receive UN permission to use force and must also shoulder the costs of restoring a functioning government, they will be discouraged from intervening in the first place. Continued occupation will raise the costs of intervention, especially if insurgent groups arise. While the intervening nation may benefit by halting human rights violations or avoiding a terrorist attack, it eventually loses control over the territory and the confidence that such harms will not return.

The blanket rule against intervention runs against our global welfare approach. Failed states present a collective action problem—they impose costs on the international system, but the diffuse effects do not give any single nation the incentive to take action to restore order. The welfarist approach favors international legal rules that encourage nations to intervene to prevent human rights catastrophes or the spread of international terrorism, rather than rules that discourage them, as do the current international rules that guarantee the sovereignty of even failed states. If the global welfare approach is correct, then the international legal system should distinguish between interventions to address negative externalities, establish internal stability and security, and restore a functioning state.

In fact, the international legal system creates exactly the wrong incentives. If failed states create negative externalities by allowing human rights catastrophes or terrorist activities, it is an international public good to restore order in those territories. By imposing on intervening nations a duty to restore a territory to the status of an independent nation-state, the international legal system makes it less likely that intervention will occur. Two ways that the international legal system can address this collective action problem are spreading the burden or reducing the cost. Rather than impose all of the costs of repairing a failed state onto a few nations, the international legal system could allocate the costs of intervening and restoring order among many nations. Bargaining failures, free-riding, and administrative issues may interfere with efforts to reach a deal to share the burdens. Alternately, the international legal system could assist by reducing the overall cost of intervention. This could be accomplished by relieving intervening nations of the legal responsibility of bringing a failed state to independence and instead allowing intermediate forms of governance short of full sovereignty.

As we have seen, there are two main criticisms against loosening the rules on the use of force. First, some maintain that allowing nations to determine whether to use force, without a showing of self-defense or authorization by the Security Council, will provide an easy pretext for aggression. Second, a more subtle argument claims that requiring Security Council authorization will weed out uses of force based on poor reasoning or information. In the case of failed states, these concerns are misplaced. Concerns about pretextual uses of force may have little purchase here, as a number of factors—independent of any force exerted by international law—already deter the threat of aggression by the great powers. The value of territorial expansion has declined due to the rise in the cost of conventional warfare and the reduction in the gains from conquest because of the easy mobility of human talent and capital. Aggression by a powerful nation for purposes of extracting wealth or expanding its territory, even if cloaked in claims of humanitarian intervention, may prompt counterbalancing moves by regional or global powers. Failed states may also lack any natural or territorial resources that would make them attractive takeover candidates. Nations intervening in failed states will likely spend more resources than they will gain—hence the collective-action problem.

Relying on the Security Council to force better decisions is similarly inappropriate with failed states. Permanent members on the Security Council may veto intervention into a failed state because it might alter the regional balance of power, even if military action would enhance global welfare. Russia blocked resolutions authorizing the use of force in Kosovo, for example, because of its long-standing ethnic and religious ties to Serbia. Reform of the Security Council, such as enlarging the permanent membership while replacing the veto with a supermajority rule, might better allow interventions that enhance global welfare while filtering out pretextual uses of force. But even the last round of UN proposals to enhance the options for humanitarian intervention still preserved the veto of the permanent members, and the United States, Russia, China, Great Britain, or France are unlikely to give it up.

Relying on the Security Council does not solve the collective-action problem posed by failed states. If anything, it exacerbates it. Even assuming that loosening the rules on the use of force might permit more pretextual conflicts among nation-states, that cost to the international system must be balanced against the benefits from a reduction in the harms caused by failed states. As discussed earlier, the rate of interstate conflicts and their casualties have fallen significantly since the end of World War II, while the deaths due to internal armed conflicts have risen dramatically. To be sure, international and internal armed conflicts do not always cleanly distinguish themselves. Over time, internal armed conflicts may draw in foreign involvement, whether financial or military, or expand to involve the movement of personnel or resources across borders. Nonstate terrorist groups at war with nations, as we saw with the 9/11 attacks, also blur the clean distinctions. But even accounting for these questions on the margins, not all internal armed conflicts occur in failed states, but failed states often allow high levels of violence and indiscriminate civilian casualties to flourish.

III. Dividing Failed States

Dividing failed states into smaller, more governable parts may provide a more durable solution than keeping them whole. This may reduce internal conflict by separating warring ethnic or religious groups and muting centrifugal forces that might undermine government authority. While less common, consolidation of smaller nations into larger units has occurred in certain cases, such as the unifications of Germany and Italy. Since the end of World War II, however, the trend has clearly run in the other direction. In this part, we consider two explanations for the increase in the number of smaller states—one at the level of the international system and one internal to failed states—and ways in which the United States and other great powers can advance these developments.

A. Big is Not Always Better

American foreign policy has not charted a consistent path on the size of nations. Initially, for example, the first Bush administration supported efforts to keep the Soviet Union together but then chose to accept its disintegration.[52] At first, the United States chose not to promote decentralization in the former Yugoslavia, but later intervened to prevent Serbia from restoring its control over Kosovo. More recently, the United States has decided to support keeping Afghanistan and Iraq whole, despite possible alternatives that would break up the countries. In its recent history, the United States has fluctuated between decentralization and the status quo.

International law blindly follows a presumption against the breakup of states. Under the doctrine of *uti possidetis*, the international system mandates that the administrative borders drawn by previous colonial regimes should continue to hold for their successor states, but with little explanation for when or why.[53] This default rule has even governed where decolonization or imperial collapse did not occur. The United Nations, for example, commanded that Iraq continue as one nation rather than a division into three independent countries.[54]

Automatically keeping the status quo prevents consideration of the breakup of failed states or their merger with others to form a larger nation. Economists Alberto Alesina and Enrico Spolaore have proposed a new way to think about the problem of the ideal size and number of nations.[55] They argue that the size of a nation is determined by the trade-off between the benefits of scale for larger nations versus the heterogeneity of preferences within the nation. Nations can benefit from larger size because expansion reduces the cost of supplying public goods, such as defense, law and order, and infrastructure, among others. While the cost of some public goods may increase at a steady per capita rate, others may require initial high investments that can be more cheaply spread among a larger population. National security may be the best example. Purchasing weapon systems or building fixed defenses may require high initial investments, but after a certain point, economies of scale come into play that make the projects affordable. Larger nations, Alesina and Spolaore argue, also benefit from the creation of larger markets. If territorial borders provide nations with the opportunity to establish trade restrictions on imports, then a larger nation can create a larger internal free trade area.

On the other hand, nations contain their own built-in limits. The larger a country becomes, as Alesina and Spolaore argue, the more factions will come into conflicts over policies. A larger nation will likely contain more diverse cultural, religious, and ethnic groups. As the nation grows, central government decisions will fully satisfy fewer and fewer of these groups.[56] At some point, national policy and local wishes will become so different that groups will want to break away. Nations can attempt to use transfer payments to overcome these centrifugal forces—Canada can send more federal funds to Québec to undermine secession movements—but they come at a cost. Larger countries will also encounter greater agency costs. As the electorate becomes larger, it becomes more difficult to elect good leaders who act in the public interest rather than their own. Larger size makes it harder for the people to monitor elected officials to discover cases of corruption. Larger size makes it easier for the agents to play interest groups off against each other, which opens more space for the pursuit of their own agendas.

One caution is in order. It is not clear whether the theoretical link between nation size and group heterogeneity bears out empirically. Some large nations include many ethnic, religious, or social groups but remain stable, such as the United States and India. Meanwhile, internal instability has occurred in nations dominated by one or two relatively large minority groups, such as in the former Yugoslavia, Kenya, or Sri Lanka. James Madison may have offered an explanation. In *Federalist 10*, he criticized Montesquieu's claim that republican government could only succeed over a small territory. Madison responded that a larger number of groups in a larger nation would actually lead to greater political stability, because the groups would tend to cancel each other out. "Extend the sphere, and you take in a greater variety of parties and interests; you make it less probable that a majority of the whole will have a common motive to invade the rights of other citizens," Madison wrote. "Or if such a common motive exists, it will be more difficult for all who feel it to discover their own strength, and to act in unison with each other."[57] Madison believed that the transaction costs of political organization among a larger number of groups would produce more stability than decentralization into smaller units. Empirically, the number of nations has increased dramatically since the end of World War II, and the number of deaths due to internal conflict has risen.[58] Madison may well have been right.

National size can also depend on the nature of a country's political system. Dictators may pursue more territory because they seek larger populations and resources from which to extract rents for their personal benefit. Dictators, however, are likely to encounter more resistance as their countries grow in size; hence, they may engage in efforts to create an artificial sense of national unity. Because democracies seek to represent the preferences of their citizens and are less likely to use force to restrain them from leaving, they are more likely to devolve into smaller nations.

Two additional developments, according to Alesina and Spolaore, have produced the recent surge in the proliferation of nations. First, economic openness in the form of the General Agreement on Tariffs and Trade (GATT), the World Trade

Organization (WTO), and regional economic integration (such as the European Union) have created large markets that are not constrained by the territorial boundaries of a single state. Entry into a worldwide or regional market reduces the need to be part of a large nation-state with its own market. As international trade becomes more open, smaller states become more viable.[59]

Second, a larger nation will have more resources to field a larger military and provide defense in a more cost effective manner. As the need for security falls, the more viable smaller states become. A number of causes can reduce the need for a large military: less conflict between nations, a larger power guaranteeing regional security, or international institutions offering to resolve disputes. On the other hand, the greater the number of nations, the more international interactions that will occur. According to Alesina and Spolaore, more interactions will raise the possibility of war and the need for defense—though this assumes that the rate of conflict per international contract remains permanent or even increases. It is possible that greater international interactions could increase opportunities for cooperation and a resulting drop in the rate of conflict. Finally, the spread of democracy may actually lead to lower levels of international conflict because of the "democratic peace" and therefore produce smaller, viable states.

Another cautionary note arises from the debate over whether separating hardened ethnic groups can help reduce conflict. Chaim Kaufmann has suggested that partition could solve the problem of ethnic groups that cannot live together peacefully in a large state.[60] He argues that separating relatively homogeneous groups into compact territories would allow them to settle differences and defend themselves more effectively. Critics respond that division of a state will transform a domestic conflict into an international one, that an artificial border will not diminish ethnic rivalries, and that lives would be lost as populations migrate as a result of border changes.[61] The record, however, remains mixed. Croatia went to war with Serbia after the 1991 dissolution of Yugoslavia; Eritrea fought a border conflict after seceding from Ethiopia in 1993; and India and Pakistan have fought three wars since their 1947 partition. On the other hand, conflict ended after the division of Greeks and Turks in Cyprus (though the dispute remains unresolved), and no war occurred after the 1971 separation of Bangladesh from Pakistan. It is fair to say that, at this point, empirical studies do not show one way or the other whether partition increases or decreases the chances of war.[62]

Thus, there is no compelling reason why the United States and its allies, or the United Nations, should seek to maintain the preexisting borders of failed states. Their policy attempts to hold back the current of recent history. In the last sixty years, the number of nations has nearly tripled. Policies of the United States and its allies, in fact, have supported the trend. By pressing for trade liberalization through the GATT and then the WTO, the Western democracies have made it possible for smaller territories to survive, and even prosper, as independent nations.

As a hegemonic provider of global peace and security, the United States has further established the conditions for the survival of smaller, militarily weaker nations. Since the end of World War II, the United States has guaranteed the peace in Europe, both from external attack and from internecine warfare. As NATO's first Secretary General Lord Ismay famously quipped, the purpose of the Atlantic alliance was "to keep the Americans in, the Russians out, and the Germans down."[63] Since the end of the Cold War, the United States has continued to spend large amounts on its military, which has allowed Europe to reduce its own defense expenditures. In the 1990s, when the United States was spending $280 billion a year, Europeans discussed an increase in their collective defense spending from $150 billion to $180 billion a year.[64] Ultimately, they decided against it. There was little political desire to come within shouting distance of the United States; in the wake of the September 11, 2001, terrorist attacks and the wars in Afghanistan and Iraq, Washington even stepped up its defense budget to $600 billion a year.[65]

By providing security (to advance its own interests certainly), the United States allows small countries to survive in Europe. The same might also be said of the Americas, where the Monroe doctrine has led the United States to play a hegemonic role in blocking outside interference. Washington has played an additional balancing role in East Asia, where it has stabilized the security environment, deterred any territorial ambitions of the regional powers, and suppressed old rivalries.

If peace and free trade are public goods, the international legal system ought to promote their supply. By seeking to maintain existing national borders, however, the international legal system has the effect of supporting the existence of larger nations, which will press in the opposite direction. Larger nations will have less of an interest in public goods because they benefit from the trading blocs and from the efficiency of scale of providing security to a larger population. Better rules would eliminate the presumption in favor of the status quo. The United Nations could promote global welfare by allowing the breakup of nations along ethnic or religious lines, rather than by requiring the postwar restoration of a nation's original borders.

B. Failed States and Foreign Intervention

Our perspective can also address the failed state problem at the micro level: how do we encourage intervening nations to restore failed states to some level of sovereignty, though at times within smaller borders? The rules and practice of occupation place relatively heavy burdens on nations that intervene in failed states. Occupying powers are forbidden from altering most domestic laws, cannot change borders, and presumably must leave most domestic institutions in place, except when they threaten the security of the occupying forces. At the same time, occupying powers are responsible for maintaining order and basic social services, even when conflict with insurgents is ongoing. For this reason, military officers estimate that maintaining security in an occupied country demands high troop levels. Pacifying Kosovo required 50,000 troops, or one soldier for every forty inhabitants. Extrapolating from the Balkans experience, General Eric Shinseki in 2003 testified that occupying Iraq would require "several hundred thousand" coalition troops, a number considered politically infeasible at the time.[66]

Such manpower demands will often render impractical the restoration of failed states to full sovereignty. Western powers have had difficulty establishing adequate government in Haiti, not to mention harder cases like Somalia. Nonetheless, the United States and its allies restored stability and functioning governmental institutions in Iraq with troop levels that—even at the height of the "surge"—still fell far short of the original estimates for a comprehensive occupation. Understanding why the surge in Iraq succeeded will point the way to a reorientation of international rules on occupation.

One way to conceive of the fundamental problem in Iraq, and the ultimate solution, is to view it as a dispute between Shiites and Sunnis over sharing power. This was caused in part because each side, but particularly the Sunnis, misunderstood their relative power. The political science literature on crisis bargaining is helpful here. Because war is so devastating, rational actors with complete information should always prefer a negotiated settlement to armed conflict. Wars, for example, often conclude with bargains—in the form of treaties—that both sides prefer to continued fighting. Both sides would have been better off by simply agreeing to the peace settlement initially and avoiding the costs of war. So the question arises: why don't rational nations always avoid war?[67]

Imagine, for example, that a government and a rebel group dispute control of a territory. The rebel group issues a threat that it is willing to use force unless the government withdraws. The government must decide whether to accede to the demand or to resist with force. Both the government and the rebel group have an expected value of going to war, which is a function of the probability that each will win the conflict and the value of controlling the territory minus the expected cost of fighting. If the government knows that the expected value of controlling the territory is lower for the rebel group than the likely cost of any conflict, it will not back down because it knows that a rational rebel group will refuse to fight. Likewise, if the government knows that the expected value of controlling the territory is higher to the rebel group than the likely cost of war, it will withdraw or reach some negotiated settlement. In both cases, both the government and the rebel group avoid the dead-weight loss of warfare. The only difference is whether the territory remains within the control of the rebel group or the government.[68]

But even if both sides act rationally, war may still result. Incomplete information can cause the groups to incorrectly estimate important variables. For example, the government may not know the rebel group's expected value of going to war. It may know the value of the disputed territory to the rebels, but perhaps not the probability that the rebels will prevail in a war. The government may not know the rebels' military and political capabilities, its support among the population, or the levels of outside support. This information is likely to be known only to the rebel group. The government might lack intelligence, for example, on the size of rebel units, their armament, or their fighting effectiveness. Similarly, the rebels may have little information on the true capability of government forces in the territory, its abilities to deploy reinforcements, or its internal and external political support.

Both sides could reduce the chances of unintended war by revealing private information. But a few problems stand in the way. First, they might feed each other misleading information to exaggerate their strength and hence their chances of winning a conflict.[69] Bluffing, in other words, could prevent a deal. Second, the sides must find a way to signal their honesty. One way is to issue a threat or a promise that will incur domestic political costs if unfulfilled. If a political leader makes a public threat of war, for example, but then backs down, she may experience a loss of political support at home. Another is to make significant expenditures, such as building bases or local infrastructure in a disputed region, which would be wasteful if she later changed course.

In the case of a failed state, the difficulty of credibly revealing private information can be acute. Regional, ethnic, and religious tensions may make different groups particularly distrustful of each other. An insurgent group that has suffered abuses at the hands of the government may view any move by the authorities as a deception. A government in the middle of a bitter war may believe that a rebel group is attempting to bluff its way to a better deal, or that its irregular tactics make it untrustworthy.

Both sides could try to send credible signals through a third party. They must trust the third party to provide accurate, reliable, unbiased information. Some multilateral arms-control agreements, for example, create a body that operates beyond the control of any single state or group of states. The Secretariats of the Chemical Weapons Convention and the International Atomic Energy Agency conduct inspections that generate information on whether states are upholding their promises not to develop WMDs. Joining an intrusive inspection regime, one managed by an international organization, can be a costly signal by intruding on a sovereign's freedom of action, raising the chances of discovery of violations, and by increasing the negative consequences of violations in domestic politics.

Commitment problems pose a second obstacle to a peace deal. Full information allows each party to identify the acceptable range of outcomes and commonalities and hence find a bargain. But even if opponents have full information about their rivals, they may have no confidence that the other will keep its promise.[70] This is not a problem that arises so much with private contracts; individuals ultimately can rely on the courts or administrative agencies to enforce their bargains. But in an environment with weak institutions, such as international affairs, parties to an agreement may not trust their partners to keep their promises. James Fearon and Robert Powell have argued that the lack of supranational institutions capable of enforcing international agreements will make it more difficult for states to reach such bargains in the first place.[71]

A failed state will lack the power to enforce agreements between contending groups. By definition, failed states have already experienced a collapse of central authority. If state failure has arisen from conflict between two or more ethnic, religious, or regional groups, government institutions are usually not strong enough to force them to comply. If conflict instead has arisen between the state and a rebel group, no third party is likely to exist within the state powerful enough to enforce an agreement between the two.

Commitment difficulties can become worse in struggles over territory and natural resources. Winning a valuable resource could give one side an advantage in future wars, or economically. Suppose, for example, that a government and rebel group could settle a territorial question by agreeing to a division of the land. Suppose that the division would give the rebels a distinct military advantage by providing them with additional resources, such as oil, or geographic tactical advantages, such as mountain retreats. The government cannot rely on the rebels to keep the agreement in the future rather than take advantage of the relative shift in power to seek even further gains in the next round of fighting.

These problems point the way to a reworking of international law. International rules should allow outside nations to intervene in failed states to help overcome these informational and commitment obstacles to a peace deal. When a larger power intervenes in a failed state, it will often find different groups vying for political and economic control. An intervening nation can begin to establish political stability by facilitating a power-sharing agreement between the different domestic groups. The bargain must reflect the actual distribution of power among the competing groups; otherwise, groups that are shortchanged either will not agree to it or will work to undermine it. To reach agreement, each group will want reliable information on the expected value for other groups of continuing to fight. Intervening nations can advance this process by serving as an impartial conduit for information, such as each group's military strength, willingness to fight, probability of prevailing, and value placed on winning. Without this knowledge, groups might refuse to reach a deal and fight on because they underestimate their opponents' strength or determination.

Even with accurate information, groups may still fail to reach a bargain because of a weak institutional environment. Two groups, for example, might agree to a division of territory, which reflects the current division of power. Imagine, for example, two ethnic groups, A and B, which hold roughly a 60–40 balance of power. They would agree to a division of disputed territory along the same 60–40 lines, but only if they were confident that the other would obey the agreement in the future. If either side grows stronger as a result, it will have a strong incentive to renege or cheat. A guarantee against breaking the deal can only be provided by an outsider.

An intervening nation could play the role of deal broker. But it must have the trust of both sides. It must have the power to identify violations, sanction cheaters, and reward the faithful. It must have the freedom to shift economic and political support, change regional borders, or even change political or constitutional institutions. An outside nation, for example, could reduce the territory, population, and resources of a group that violates a power-sharing agreement. Ultimately, such moves must be backed by the threat or actual use of force.

International law, however, does not clearly grant intervening nations the necessary flexibility. It is even uncertain what law governs a failed state. A conventional approach would consider territory held by an outside power to fall within the law of occupation, a subset of the laws of armed conflict. But an intervention may not rise to the level of an armed conflict if the outside power does not conduct hostilities against any of the groups. In authorizing the 1992 Somalia intervention, for example, the Security Council did not specify whether the laws of armed conflict applied or whether the laws of occupation would govern. By contrast, the Security Council's resolution in the wake of the 2003 Iraq invasion specifically called upon "all concerned to comply fully with their obligations under international law including in particular the Geneva Conventions of 1949 and the Hague Regulations of 1907."[72] Those treaties set out the positive laws of occupation.

If the law of occupation applies, great powers may have some limited authority to play dealmaker. Under the customary laws of war, an occupying army enjoyed broad discretion to administer a defeated enemy.[73] A victorious nation was once considered to be the absolute owner of occupied territory, but by the nineteenth century, customary practice had narrowed an occupier's power to temporary control until a peace treaty was reached or complete subjugation occurred.[74] But while a territory remained under occupation, the army held the legal authority to change the laws and institutions in force. According to the 1863 Lieber Code, issued by President Lincoln to guide the operation of Union forces during the Civil War and the first document to compile the customary international laws of war, the army could impose martial law, which included "the suspension by the occupying military authority of the criminal and civil law, and of the domestic administration and government in the occupied place or territory," the "substitution of military rule and force for the same," and the "dictation of general laws."[75] These changes to the occupied nation's laws had to be justified by "military necessity" and no more. The Lieber Code defined military necessity as "those measures which are indispensable for securing the ends of the war, and which are lawful according to the modern law and usages of war."[76]

Codification of the laws of war tightened limits on the occupying power. The 1907 Hague Convention, known as the "Hague Regulations," allows the occupier to "take all the measures in his power to restore, and ensure, as far as possible, public order and safety," but also requires it to "respect[], unless absolutely prevented, the laws in force in the country."[77] The Fourth Geneva Convention expressed a similar presumption in favor of preexisting laws and institutions, except where they threatened security. Article 64 of the Convention declares that the "penal laws of the occupied territory shall remain in force," but allows for their repeal or suspension "where they constitute a threat" to the security of the occupying power or the implementation of the Geneva Conventions.[78] It allows the occupying power to establish new laws when necessary to implement the Conventions, "maintain the orderly government of the territory," and "ensure the security of the Occupying Power." Article 64 is more generous to the occupying power than the Hague Regulations in that it creates a presumption only for criminal laws and implicitly allows for changes in constitutional, administrative, and civil laws when necessary for security.[79] This reading comports with state practice, which recognized an occupying power's authority to alter laws, including government institutions, in order to maintain the security of military forces, preserve its gains, and keep order.[80]

These rules might allow the role demanded by failed states, if we consider the settlement of internal conflicts as critical to the occupier's responsibility to maintain security. An occupying country would want to access a broad spectrum of possible measures, including the alteration of institutions and constitutional arrangements, to enforce a power-sharing agreement. To fall within the formal rules of Hague and Geneva, an occupying nation's actions to create, enforce, or modify governance agreements would have to maintain public safety or protect its own forces.[81] This standard should be satisfied in cases where a previous regime took the form of a hostile dictatorship. Keeping in place Iraq's government and constitution from the Saddam Hussein era would have presented an obvious threat to public order and military security after the April 2003 invasion.

Other situations, however, pose difficulties for the Hague and Geneva standards. An intervening nation may want to create a power-sharing agreement that is not necessary to maintain order or to protect the security of its forces, but instead will provide political stability for the post-occupation future. Such a pact would seek to guarantee stability once the occupier withdraws, rather than security and order during the occupation itself. For example, the United States and its allies may want to make territorial changes among different provinces controlled by Afghan warlords because of their noncompliance with a provisional constitution. In Somalia, on the other hand, an intervening nation that has already established a secure environment would have difficulty showing the necessity of a constitution that would divide authority among competing ethnic groups. International law leaves uncertain whether an intervening nation may make permanent changes to domestic laws and institutions in order to enforce such a governance agreement.

IV. Conclusion: The Iraq Surge

Clarifying the authority of the great powers in failed states is critical. Of the strategies that have been tried, enforcement of power-sharing agreements seems to be the most effective way to rebuild. The "surge" of American forces in Iraq in 2007–2008 illustrates this theory. Until 2007, the United States had responded to growing sectarian violence between Shiites and Sunnis by concentrating its forces in large bases outside major cities and deploying troops as a reaction force. American strategy built up the Iraqi military and police to provide security. Holding democratic elections and establishing a constitution would convey the necessary political legitimacy for the Iraqi central government to exercise authority. Maintaining a light "footprint," American leaders believed, would keep U.S. forces from becoming a lightning rod for attacks by either Sunnis or Shiites.

As U.S. casualties rose, the Bush administration switched course. In 2007, it increased U.S. forces in Iraq by about 24,000 troops. A sharp change in strategy accompanied the surge. Troops moved off their bases to secure Baghdad and other cities and provinces where insurgent activity had peaked. American soldiers entered neighborhoods to provide security for the Iraqi population, gain intelligence, and conduct counterinsurgency operations. Sunni volunteers formed "Sons of Iraq" units that provided security in their regions and helped American troops fight al-Qaeda. Violence dropped quickly within the year. Monthly Iraqi civilian deaths from violence, which had risen from 700 in November 2003 to 3,450 in November 2006, fell to 650 in November 2007 and 550 in May 2008. Daily attacks by insurgents, which had risen from 35 in November 2003 to 180 in November 2006, fell back to 80 in November 2007 and 45 in May 2008. The number of American troops killed per month, which had fluctuated between 69 and 137 before the surge, fell to 40 in November 2007 and to 19 in May 2008.[82]

Historians and strategists will argue for years over the link between the surge and the sharp decline in violence. A leading argument credits the focus on protecting the Iraqi population rather than conducting search-and-destroy missions.[83] According to this account, restoring security allows civilian authorities to build infrastructure and provide public services, encourages the local population to cooperate against insurgents, and boosts government forces. American counterinsurgency doctrine focused on "clear and hold": pushing rebels out and then holding territory, providing time for the government to win the loyalty of the local population. Championed by General David Petraeus, the U.S. Commander in Iraq (and later Afghanistan), this population-centric approach could only succeed with the higher troop levels provided by the surge and influenced a similar surge of 33,000 American troops in Afghanistan in 2010.[84]

Our analysis suggests that U.S. troops played a more modest role. The counterinsurgency strategy may have worked, though it is unclear whether adding 24,000 troops, in addition to the roughly 140,000 already present in 2006 (and 323,000 Iraqi security forces), was sufficient to secure a population of 24 million Iraqis spread over 437,000 square kilometers. Baghdad itself is home to a population of roughly 6.5 to 7 million inhabitants in 1,134 square kilometers. By contrast, the New York City police department requires about 38,000 officers to control crime for 8 million inhabitants in a space of 783 square kilometers, without the additional challenge of controlling political violence.

A better explanation may lie elsewhere. Rather than improving security throughout Iraq, the troops provided by the surge may have performed the enforcement function described here.[85] We can understand part of the ongoing violence in Iraq as a result of asymmetric information. If we simplify the civil war as a struggle between Shiites and Sunnis, the Sunnis controlled the main instruments of power in Iraq for decades despite their smaller population. The destruction of Saddam Hussein's regime opened the door for a renegotiation between the two groups over their relative shares of power. The Sunnis likely overestimated their advantages because of their historical dominance of the government and military. Civil war ensued because the Sunnis did not fully understand Shiite resources and willingness to fight, perhaps materially distorted by Iranian financial and military support for Shiite political groups in Iraq. Al-Qaeda attacks further disrupted bargaining by confusing the information on each side's capabilities and undermining trust to reach agreement.

The information problem would have gradually shrunk as the civil war proceeded. Military setbacks showed the Sunnis that their population and resources were smaller than before; their efforts to restore control over the Iraqi government failed. A durable power-sharing agreement placed the Sunnis in a minority role, in line with their share of population, territory, and resources. Similarly, the results of the civil war revealed to the Shiites that their numbers and resources would not support complete control of Iraq's governing institutions. Each conflict and its result would reveal more information about each side's strength, which would permit an agreement that more closely matched the actual balance of power.

But even with that problem overcome, Sunnis and Shiites still had to build trust. A long history of Sunni oppression of the Shiite majority made Shiites unlikely to trust Sunnis. Uncertainty over demographic trends and their effect on the balance of power would raise fears that the Shiites would renege on the deal. If the Shiite population, for example, continued to grow while Sunnis would continue to leave the country, Shiites might just wait until their numbers allowed them to seize even more power. Without an external enforcer, Sunnis and Shiites could not credibly commit to a power-sharing agreement.

Under these conditions, the American surge may have provided more than security. It may have given the Sunnis and Shiites the confidence to reach a deal. The necessary military contingents need not have been as large as those required to police Iraq's major cities. They need only have been large enough to create confidence that the United States had the strength to enforce an agreement. The surge did this in two ways. First, it increased the units available to carry out missions imposing sanctions on either side for violating the agreement. Ideally, those sanctions would be calibrated to counterbalance any gains achieved by the cheating party. Second, the American show of force represented a costly signal by the United States that it was committed to seeing Iraq become a stable nation. High-profile, regular U.S. military patrols in neighborhoods in Baghdad and other cities sent visible signals of that commitment, in addition to their value in reducing insurgent activity.

It will not be known for many years why the surge reduced violence in Iraq from 2007 to 2009. But if this account is correct, it indicates a narrower but deeper role for the great powers. President Bush's "Freedom Agenda," whatever the merits in philosophy or politics of spreading democracy, cannot take credit for stabilizing Iraq. Several of the ambitious efforts to remake Iraqi society were not crucial to ending the civil war. Building infrastructure and public services may have their own virtues, but they go well beyond what is necessary to restore a failed state.

This vision could reduce the scope of intervention by the great powers and reduce their interference with existing cultural and social norms. International mandates to occupy and temporarily govern a nation may reach too far by placing democratic goals on the same plane as restoring security and brokering governing arrangements between locals. This is not to say that democracy itself cannot produce enforceable bargains between groups in a failed state. A smaller elite with control over a large sector of resources, for example, may have difficulty convincing a larger, poorer majority that it will redistribute a stream of wealth in the future. Agreeing to the introduction of democratic governing structures that transfer more power to the population might send a credible signal of commitment.[86] This could allow the elites and the population to escape a vicious cycle in which the inability to commit creates the conditions for warfare and coups. Democracy, however, does not seem to explain the success of the Iraq surge, in which the majority Shiite population already held the majority after the fall of Saddam Hussein.[87]

While international law and policy may sweep too wide, they may also dip too shallowly. Occupation law presumes that domestic laws must remain intact. This rule seems to apply not just to the conventional case of a nation temporarily occupied during an interstate war but also to the unconventional case of a failed state. Different circumstances require different rules. In the case of failed states, there is no preexisting normal regime to which an occupier must return a territory. A great power, therefore, should have broader authority to establish permanent, effective government. In order to do that, the outside power needs to facilitate and enforce political bargains between competing groups. While the United States may have exercised relatively broad authority in remaking Iraq, international law did not clearly grant it. If the international system is to enable the rescue of failed states, it should provide the great powers with the leeway to reshape domestic political and economic systems.

Failed states create a broad range of negative externalities. The collapse of central authority can create the conditions for human rights catastrophes or exploitation by international terrorist organizations or WMD proliferators. Even though states that attack these problems provide a public good, the international legal system continues to protect national sovereignty and place strict limits on the use of force. In fact, international legal rules create the wrong incentives by discouraging intervention, requiring that interveners restore a nation to full independence and maintaining failed states within their preexisting borders.

This chapter applied our theory of war to this problem. International rules must encourage the great powers to fix failed states, which will promote global welfare, and explore alternate forms of governance beyond the nation-state. International law can advance the restoration of government in a failed state by focusing intervention more narrowly. Rather than attempting to remake failed states into parliamentary democracies, intervening nations should focus their efforts on enforcing power-sharing agreements between competing ethnic, religious, or regional groups. This would narrow the broad claims made on behalf of intervening nations to spread democracy to failed states, but it would require a broadening of the authority to put into place less democratic but more durable regimes. Reaching for more modest goals may prove to be the better way to address the challenges of failed states and solve one of the central security challenges of the new century.

8   Conclusion

THE TOUGHEST TEST for any theory of war is to apply it to the real world. No plan of operations "survives collision with the main body of the enemy," said Helmuth von Moltke, chief of staff of the Prussian and then German army.[1] Similarly, an abstract theory about *jus ad bellum* could fall apart when applied to real wars and contemporary crises. Our approach will only improve upon the UN Charter's system if it provides satisfying results in a consistent manner. This concluding chapter will compare our global welfare analysis with current law by taking up recent examples and suggesting ways that new methods and modest goals can reduce the costs of intervention. It will finish by addressing the circumstances of the United States during a time of potential decline.

Transforming the rules of war responds to deep changes in the nature of international conflict. Although it has not approached anything near zero, the prospect of great power war in the twenty-first century has sharply declined. Since the end of World War II, interstate war has virtually disappeared in the arenas where the great powers once struggled. Europe, North America, and South America (aside from the Falklands War) have not witnessed open conflict between states for almost seven decades. Since 1945, none of the European nations, the United States, the Soviet Union/Russia, or Japan has fought each other. The decline in war has spread beyond the great powers to the rest of the world. Since 1945, the rate of armed conflicts between nation-states has fallen by an order of magnitude from the pace that prevailed in the three centuries before.[2] Despite fears of mutually assured destruction, superpower rivalry, and an anarchic international system, the end of World War II ushered the world into an era of long peace.

But war itself has not disappeared from the world. It has just moved indoors. Since World War II, civil wars now account for over half of all wartime deaths.[3] These wars, such as those in Rwanda, Congo, and Sudan, are killing hundreds of thousands, even millions.[4] Nine out of every ten of the deaths from internal armed conflicts are non-combatants.[5] While the fighting seems concentrated in the undeveloped world, with the greatest number of deaths occurring in Africa,[6] it has effects on the international system as a whole by creating negative externalities. Other threats to international stability come from WMD proliferation and aggressive nation-states that oppress their own populations, but which fall short of interstate war.

A global welfare approach demands that we shift the international system to encourage intervention to prevent these new, destructive challenges. Despite the changes in global politics, however, international rules still aim to prevent a World War III. Force today remains outlawed except for self-defense against attack or missions approved by the UN Security Council,[7] whose veto-wielding permanent members have few reasons to consent. The system already remains stacked against wars that will reduce the harms of internal conflicts and increase international stability. Great powers have precious little incentive to risk their militaries to prevent global harms, especially when many other countries can free-ride on their efforts. The rules of the international system only compound the obstacles to wars that might increase global welfare by halting potential or actual human rights catastrophes, stopping WMD proliferation, preventing terrorist attacks, or removing oppressive regimes.

This is not an argument for reducing current U.S. conventional and strategic force levels. While theorists argue over the causes for the long peace of the postwar period, the United States' nuclear and regular armed forces surely deterred the expansionist designs of the Soviet Union. The North Atlantic Treaty Organization brought America and Europe together to preserve peace on the Continent. Reforming global rules to address the security challenges of the twenty-first century will not affect the relationships between the leading nations, where the resort to use force will depend on their relative power and the costs and benefits of war. An adequate military and the political will to use it will deter great powers from attacking each other far more than international law. Any change in the international rules should not affect the level of defense spending needed by the great powers to balance each other. It is doubtful that international law could head off any conflict between the great powers themselves.

American decisions on defense spending, however, would have a profound effect on the world conditions that allow a focus on global welfare. American military and diplomatic policies have maintained the long postwar peace and global stability that foster the production of international public goods. Falling U.S. defense budgets might have the reverse effect. A weaker American military and less resolute diplomacy could invite the more aggressive designs of other great powers, such as China and Russia, and revisionist regional powers, such as Iran or Venezuela. Without the United States to guarantee the peace, the great powers might reignite their military struggle for territory, influence, and resources. A return of great power war would both increase the death and destruction from interstate conflict and divert resources and attention away from curing the ills of internal wars.

Nor must a global welfare approach lead to more force in every case. Weighing the costs and benefits of an intervention will involve uncertainties and imperfect information that may create a presumption in favor of the status quo. An intervention, no matter how noble the goal, may produce more harm due to the resources and will of the weaker nation. A determined opponent, especially perhaps if it is authoritarian, may feel little reluctance to sacrifice civilians or to widen a conflict to its neighbors if its governing regime is threatened. Unintended consequences may trigger greater instability or loss of life even if a great power fulfills its immediate plans. Even the stability imposed by an authoritarian regime might outweigh the costs that might arise from a collapse of governmental authority in a state. All of these factors, and more, should guide national decision-makers in deciding on intervention and should determine whether the international system should support it.

Current cases will help illustrate these different factors at work.

Libya. The 2011 war in Libya should have been a good one. Bringing down Colonel Moammar Gadhafi's tyranny should have been a major strategic and humanitarian victory in the Middle East. Gadhafi had imposed an authoritarian military regime since taking power in 1969. He had reserved much of the nation's oil wealth for his family and supporters, suspended the constitution, and established a police state in which political dissent was a crime.[8] Freedom House ranked Libya as "not free" continuously throughout Gadhafi's reign.[9]

Beyond its internal repression, Libya also posed a threat to regional peace and stability. In 1973, Libya provoked a border war with Chad and did not withdraw until 1994;[10] it fought Egypt in 1977;[11] and it sought to break Darfur away from Sudan in the late 1980s.[12] Gadhafi supported a variety of international terrorist organizations, such as the Palestine Liberation Organization and the Irish Republican Army, and conducted his own attacks abroad.[13] Libya's terrorist campaign culminated in the April 1986 attack on a German club popular with U.S. servicemen[14] and the 1988 bombing of the Pan Am airliner over Lockerbie, Scotland, which provoked U.S. military action and UN sanctions.[15] Libya also engaged in WMD proliferation by seeking to acquire or develop nuclear and chemical weapons. Despite joining the Nuclear Non-Proliferation Treaty, Libya attempted to purchase nuclear weapons and technology and only gave up its program in 2003 after the U.S. invasion of

Iraq.[16] Gadhafi also ordered the production of chemical weapons such as mustard gas, which international inspectors discovered and destroyed in 2004.[17]

Ending Gadhafi's threat to international stability as well as freeing the Libyan people from oppression carried obvious benefits for global welfare. The costs, however, of regime change would have been high but for the opportunity presented by the "Arab Spring." Inspired by popular uprisings against authoritarian regimes in Tunisia and Egypt, a rebellion against Gadhafi erupted in February 2011.[18] Civil war would substantially disrupt the nation's economy and society regardless of external military involvement. Popular support clearly fell on the side of the rebels, and the beginning of the revolt witnessed significant defections by Libyan army officers and units.[19] Gadhafi's army had a mere 50,000 poorly trained and poorly equipped troops at the start of the rebellion (half of them draftees).[20] Gadhafi kept his military "deliberately weak," seeking to avoid a coup d'état like the one that brought him to power in 1969.[21] In the first weeks of the civil war, most major Libyan cities other than the capital, Tripoli, reportedly fell to the rebels.[22] But Gadhafi bolstered his forces by hiring mercenaries (allegedly paying them from the large gold reserves held in Libya's Central Bank).[23] He also had available several elite brigades, such as the Russian-equipped "Khamis Brigade," commanded by his Russian-trained son Khamis.[24] But in size, equipment, and quality, the regime's military assets could not hold a candle to NATO.

Western intervention would not add significantly to the loss of human life but could influence the outcome and might even reduce civilian casualties by helping shorten the conflict and install a more democratic regime. The relatively small size of the Libyan armed forces called for a relatively minor exercise of force that ultimately did not require ground troops. Without Western aid, however, Libyan rebels fought at a significant disadvantage against Gadhafi's armored units and air force. By early March 2011, loyalist forces had driven the rebels to retreat across the country into a small pocket around Benghazi.[25] U.S. political and military leadership, or at least the extensive use of U.S. forces in combat, were essential to NATO's success. In March, American fighters and bombers destroyed the Libyan air defense network and air force, and NATO's concomitant air superiority blocked any ground advance by Gadhafi's units.[26] Libyan units retreated before the rebels throughout the summer until Tripoli fell in late August,[27] and in October 2011, rebels killed Gadhafi and took Sirte, the last loyalist city.[28]

While Western intervention turned the tide in Libya, it was a close call. A misguided faith in the United Nations Charter almost doomed the rebellion. The Obama administration refused to intervene in the civil war until the UN Security Council gave its authorization to do so. America and its allies could make no plausible claim of self-defense, and they were unwilling to claim a right under international law to intervene for humanitarian ends or to prevent a threat to regional peace and stability. Due to Russian and Chinese reluctance, UN approval did not come until Gadhafi's forces had closed around a last rebel stronghold in Benghazi.[29] Even when the UN Security Council adopted Resolution 1973, which formed the basis for the subsequent intervention into Libya, it authorized the use of "all necessary measures" only to protect Libyan "civilians and civilian populated areas under threat of attack."[30] Resolution 1973 did not explicitly authorize the Western coalition to bring Gadhafi down. Yet the United States, Britain, and France pursued precisely that policy objective. For the sake of obtaining the Security Council's (partial) approval, the Obama administration denied itself and its coalition partners the full use of the military instrument to achieve its core policy goal.

As a result, the United States and its allies were left either to hamstring its means or go beyond the UN Security Council authorization. Resolution 1973, for example, did not authorize NATO or the coalition to train the rebel forces or supply them with weaponry. Some coalition members questioned whether they could lawfully provide aid.[31] NATO did not authorize its forces to join with the rebels if they advanced on cities in western Libya that were still in Gadhafi's grip. The Security Council decision even seemed to require NATO to resist any rebel attacks on Gadhafi's forces if those attacks were likely to bring about collateral civilian casualties. Media accounts even reported that a "senior U.S. administration official" "did not rule out the possibility of an attack on the rebels if they were to go on the offensive and strike cities with civilian populations, now held by pro-Gadhafi forces."[32] Under the terms of the resolution, if rebel forces were poised to attack Gadhafi's stronghold in Tripoli, NATO may have had to take sides against the rebels if (as is inevitable) their attack endangered the city's civilian population.

Resolution 1973 also displayed other, less visible flaws. For instance, it did not authorize an attempt to seize Libyan oil fields still under Gadhafi's control, although there was a serious risk that he might destroy them in a desperate attempt to punish his Western enemies. Gadhafi threatened to turn the entire Mediterranean Sea into a theater of war and had the example of Saddam Hussein's destruction of Kuwait's oil fields in 1991 before him. Yet the UN gave no permission to guard against this obvious threat. Resolution 1973 also did not authorize NATO to take out Gadhafi's stockpile of chemical weapons (unless, perhaps, he signaled the intent to use them against his own people). Even if Gadhafi had lacked the means to deliver these weapons, their destruction ought to have been a primary objective, not only for the sake of the Libyan people but also for the safety of the region. If a democratic government succeeded Gadhafi, it would not need chemical weapons; if Islamic radicals succeeded him, the United States would have to ensure that these weapons did not fall into their hands.

Considering Resolution 1973's handcuffs, the United States eventually either ignored it or construed it disingenuously. UN approval has virtually no offsetting benefits, except for a thin veneer of international legality for a no-fly zone, an embargo, and limited efforts to protect Libyan civilians. Although neither Russia nor China decided to veto the resolution, both promptly condemned the coalition air attacks, and both are opposed to any expansion of current military actions.[33] Germany, Brazil, and India, nonpermanent members of the Security Council, abstained from voting on the resolution, and BRIC countries (along with South Africa) subsequently criticized the coalition's attacks on Gadhafi's forces.[34] Nations representing about half the world's population (and several of its most dynamic economies) either did not support Resolution 1973 or have since condemned the efforts to implement it.

At the same time, the resolution constrained the United States' methods at the price of the long-term stability of postwar Libya. President Obama announced that the United States would not introduce ground troops into Libya.[35] Even if the United States was not planning to take that step, it was a mistake to say so publicly. As simple international bargaining theory demonstrates, the threat of escalating a conflict by a party with superior resources should lead to a more favorable settlement. The threat of invasion could have convinced Gadhafi to leave power or encouraged his generals to remove him. An announcement that troops were off the table only strengthened Gadhafi's resolve to hang on by informing the enemy of U.S. limits, undercutting the coalition's position.

If the U.S. strategic goal was to overthrow the Libyan regime, it may well have needed to introduce ground forces to maintain a successful transition. Air power is far more likely to succeed if combined with significant military operations on land—as it was in the two Iraq wars. NATO's air power did not bring down Milosevic. It may have forced Serbia's withdrawal from Kosovo, but even there, it was supported by the land forces of the Kosovo Liberation Army. Without the use of land forces—whether provided by the rebels, defectors from Gadhafi's side, NATO, or the United States—successful regime change seemed unlikely. Without substantial U.S. involvement, the British, French, and other nations would have less incentive to aid the transition to a more stable government. As a result, actors that could provide manpower on the ground, such as al-Qaeda and other similar extremist Islamic groups, enjoyed a corresponding increase in their influence among the rebel groups. Those groups have destabilized Libya in the two years since Gadhafi's departure, as evidenced by the September 2012 al-Qaeda attack on the U.S. consulate in Benghazi.

Syria. Syria's civil war presents an even more compelling example of the harms of delay. Earlier involvement by the United States and its NATO allies might well have reduced the amount of force and the loss of life, and thereby produced greater gains for global welfare. Protests against the authoritarian rule of Bashar al-Assad began only a month after unrest hit Libya. By April 2011, civil war in Syria had broken out, with many high-ranking officials and officers eventually defecting to the rebels.[36] For the next two years, the rebels enjoyed significant gains, but have proved unable to wrest control of the country from the regime in Damascus. By summer 2013, the Free Syrian Army and other loosely allied groups had gained control over about 60 percent of Syria's territory and 40 percent of its population, but the major cities of Damascus and Aleppo remained in government hands.[37]

During these two years, the great powers have remained divided on Syria. Russia and China have systematically protected the Assad regime and have vetoed proposals in the UN Security Council to impose heavy sanctions.[38] According to the Stockholm International Peace Research Institute, Russia has delivered heavy arms to Syria since the outbreak of the civil war, such as air and naval defense systems, large stocks of ammunition, aerial missiles and bombs, and perhaps helicopters and aircraft.[39] Although the United States and its NATO allies imposed arms embargoes on Damascus and declared that Assad should step down, they limited their support for the rebels to nonlethal economic and humanitarian aid. Regional powers have filled the vacuum, with Saudi Arabia and Qatar apparently providing arms and funds to the rebels and Iran supporting Assad.

Allowing the civil war to continue inflicts both short-term and longer-term costs, both internal and regional. In the short term the fighting in Syria has cost a reported 100,000 civilian lives or more.[40] It has displaced 4 million civilians and driven about 1.4 million refugees into neighboring countries,[41] a humanitarian crisis that has prompted terrorist groups such as Hezbollah to fight on the side of the government and has drawn in regional powers such as Turkey, Saudi Arabia, and Iran. Israel has conducted air strikes on targets within Syrian territory against a sophisticated weapons system for fear of their transfer to terrorist groups, and some unrest has spread beyond Syria to Lebanon and Jordan. In the longer term, Assad's authoritarian regime has long oppressed Syria's population by arresting and executing thousands of political opponents, such as the massacre of 10,000–25,000 civilians in Hama in 1982.[42] The civil war has only redoubled the government's efforts. Syria has long pursued efforts to destabilize the region, including attacking Israel in the 1973 Yom Kippur War and the 1967 Six-Day War, using the civil war in Lebanon as a pretext to send military forces to occupy territory,[43] supporting insurgents in Iraq during the last war,[44] and acquiring chemical weapons and seeking nuclear weapons.[45] With one of the largest confirmed stockpiles of chemical weapons in the world, Syria is suspected of using sarin gas during its recent civil war (though there are also claims that the rebels have used chemical weapons to draw in the United States).[46] While Syria forestalled a threatened U.S. air strike by agreeing to destroy its chemical weapons stockpile, the infrastructure for its recreation may still exist and the Assad regime's broader threat to internal and regional stability remains undiminished.

As with Libya, U.S. and NATO intervention could have shortened the fighting and removed the Assad regime's threat to its own people and the broader regime. At the outset of the civil war, the rebels enjoyed significant gains in territory[47] and population despite their lack of air, armor, and centralized command and their dependence on light infantry units. The Assad regime succeeded in halting the rebel's momentum by relying on heavy armor, artillery, and air supremacy.[48] Western imposition of a no-fly zone, combined with military aid to the rebels, could have blunted the regime's advantages and allowed the popular uprising to succeed. Instead, according to recent reports, the Obama administration refused to send any direct military aid—or take more aggressive steps such as attacking Syrian air defense units—due to concerns about international law. Apparently, administration lawyers argued that the lack of UN Security Council authorization for aid or the use of force would render any U.S. aid illegal.[49] As in Libya, the Obama administration's allegiance to the UN Charter's view on war introduced a critical delay into Western intervention. While great power air strikes in Libya turned the tide at the last minute and led to Gadhafi's fall, the Assad regime has used its advantage in heavy weapons and air support to stop rebel gains and shore up its strategic and political position. Fealty to the UN Charter has kept the Obama administration off the sidelines and the Assad regime in power—though in July 2013, the United States allegedly decided to send military aid covertly to the Syrian rebels and may have been doing so already in more limited form earlier.

Relying on the UN Security Council system, a critic might respond, still proves superior for global welfare by avoiding any wider great power conflict. UN Security Council approval of the Libyan intervention implied that neither Russia nor China would attempt to block Western attacks on the Gadhafi regime. Without such a guarantee, U.S. military aid or action in Syria might risk direct conflict with other great powers. Russia might counter a NATO no-fly zone by sending sophisticated ground-to-air defense systems to Assad. Moscow might arm Damascus with top-rank anti-ship missiles to hamper U.S. naval operations in the eastern Mediterranean supporting the rebels. Russia and China might send ships carrying arms, or Iran might continue an air route for aid, risking direct military conflict with U.S. forces. Syria and Iran might respond to U.S. force by launching attacks on Turkey and Israel to impose higher costs on the West. A threat to escalate the Syrian civil war into a broader conflict involving the great powers—which could end the long peace that has prevailed since 1945—could far outweigh the gains of replacing Assad with a regime that respected the human rights of its population and disavowed a revisionist agenda toward its neighbors.

Balancing these competing costs is difficult and calls for a fair amount of pre-diction and educated guesswork. In my view, the more concrete benefits of removing the Assad regime outweigh the more speculative harms of Russian or Chinese resistance or great power conflict. This calculation turns on both the costs of using force and the likelihood of Russian or Chinese military hostility, as the magnitude of benefit of a peaceful Syria and the magnitude of the harm of a great power conflict can be estimated and will not change under different scenarios. Deploying air assets to Syria would certainly entail greater risks to Western air forces and would require more intensity to tilt the balance toward the rebels. Syria in 2013 could field a far more sophisticated air defense network and a larger air force than Libya could have in 2011. Syria appears to have about 450 Russian-made aircraft and more sophisti-cated Russian surface-to-air missiles (SAMs).[50] According to U.S. military officials, Syria has an air defense network that is five times as effective as Libya's covering one-fifth the territory. Nevertheless, Syria's air defenses should prove no match for the United States and its allies. In 1982, the U.S.-equipped Israeli air force confronted the Syrian air force in the Bekaa Valley and destroyed eighty-seven Russian-made MIGs and nineteen SAM batteries while losing a few helicopters and two aircraft.[51] In 2007, Israeli air units slipped through Syrian air defenses undetected to destroy a suspected nuclear reactor site without any loss of aircraft. Costs would clearly exceed those to establish a no-fly zone over Libya, and might rise even higher if the United States and its allies decide to intensify their operations—as ultimately occurred in Libya—and conduct direct attacks on Syrian armor and artillery units.

Even assuming the possibility of a higher loss of U.S. aircraft than over Libya or Serbia, the benefits of regime change in Syria would still easily outweigh the costs of intervention. Removing the Assad regime would immediately increase global wel-fare, both domestically and regionally. It would end the ongoing and indiscriminate attacks on civilians, halt the widespread internal and cross-border displacement, and improve the future lives of the Syrian people. It would also remove a destabilizing agent in the Middle East, one that has supported terrorism in Iraq, sought conquest in Lebanon and Israel, and served as a vital link between Iran and terrorist groups. One factor, however, that could change this analysis would be the chances of events spiraling out of control and leading to a confrontation with Russia and China or regional powers such as Iran. Such an outcome would cost far more harm than any gain to global welfare. Fearing the loss of its last ally in the Middle East, Russia might take more steps to counter—in addition to selling Assad advanced SAM systems (though perhaps still delaying their delivery) and jet fighters. It also decided in June 2013 to station a permanent Mediterranean fleet at the Syrian port of Tartus.[52] Russian leaders may view support for Assad as part of a policy to contain Islamic ter-rorism and to arrest the decline in their country's superpower status.[53]

Despite that potentially dire scenario, the probability of a direct conflict still remains quite low. Russia, for example, also opposed the NATO air war in Serbia, where Russia's strategic and political interests were even stronger. Russia did not resist and even sent forces after the end of the war to protect civilians in Kosovo. While it might have an interest in increasing the costs of Western intervention by supplying Assad with arms, the Kremlin would gain little by interposing Russian military units against a no-fly zone. Russia is reducing the size of its conventional military as its budget has fallen along with oil and gas prices, and it seeks Western cooperation on strategic weapons and commodity sales. While Russia and China may have felt that the United States and its allies went beyond the UN Security Council Resolution on Libya, neither took any steps to keep Gadhafi in power. China also seems highly unlikely to pursue any military response because, as Julian Ku has observed, its foreign policy finds its roots in general support for territorial sovereignty against international activism.[54] China would have little incentive to risk military confrontation to defend the sovereignty of Syria in the Middle East. Unlike Russia, China does not have the capability to project military power in the Middle East, and it appears to be focusing its current buildup to deny access to the United States in the seas around East Asia instead. The great powers still have a greater interest in maintaining a stable peace among themselves than in preserving the status quo in Syria.

We must also take another, secondary variable into account in making the judgment on intervention. While removing the Syrian regime would bring benefits both internally and externally for Syria, the aftermath could cancel those gains. An equally or perhaps even more oppressive government could succeed Assad. Or central authority might crumble, with more civilian death and destruction to follow and the possible dispersion of Syria's conventional and WMD arsenals beyond its borders. Arguably, the first scenario developed in post-Mubarak Egypt, while the second may have occurred after the fall of Gadhafi in Libya. As some have argued, regime change may even prolong the duration of a civil war, increase the civilian death toll, and provoke regional instability.[55] The problems of a failed state would replace the threat of a rogue nation. Here, this book's argument on failed states might help address the uncertainty over this factor. As in Iraq and Afghanistan, the great powers might spend blood and treasure to rebuild Syria in the image of a market democracy. Postwar occupation increases the costs of the use of force and creates another obstacle to intervention. Or Western nations could allow Syria to devolve into more compact, ethnically homogeneous units that would not require an expensive military occupation and civilian reconstruction. Smaller, more numerous national units would increase utility for the people living within, and they would reduce the threat to the peace of the region.

Others might calculate these probabilities, costs, and benefits differently. They depend on the prediction of uncertain events and the evaluation of hidden motives and resources. But it seems clear that the real choice is between the improvement to global welfare from a change of regime in Syria and the expected harm of a great power conflict. Here, the chances of the latter seem too low to veto the modest Western action needed to bring about the former.

North Korea. Lest the Libyan and Syrian cases suggest that a global welfare analysis always comes out on the side of military force, North Korea sounds a clear cautionary note. The North Korean regime combines perhaps the world's worst domestic tyrannies with one of the most dangerous foreign policies. Its 25 million people live under one of the "most centrally directed, and least open economies.[56] According to the CIA's World Factbook, North Korea's gross national product amounts to only $28 billion, or $1,800 per capita, which counts as 197th out of 229 countries in the world.[57] Starvation and famine are prevalent. North Korea still operates one of the last totalitarian communist dictatorships, where a military elite props up a single leader, Kim Jong-un, who is the third in his family line to rule. No political dissent is tolerated, and hundreds of thousands are political prisoners. A change of regime would free 25 million Koreans[58] to join their fellow 49 million Koreans in the South's vibrant market democracy.[59] It is difficult to think of another place in the world where a change in government could produce such a large, immediate gain in human welfare.

Removing the Kim regime would also lance a long-festering cancer on international security. No peace treaty ended the Korean War in 1953. Pyongyang still considers itself at war with the United States and South Korea, and its national goal has remained the expulsion of American forces and the forcible unification of the peninsula.[60] It has conducted covert attacks on the South, including a 1983 attempt to kill the South Korean President and cabinet[61] and has even launched open military strikes, such as the 2010 sinking of a South Korean naval vessel.[62] Of deep concern is North Korea's quest for nuclear weapons, which has proceeded since the early 1990s with the construction of nuclear reactors capable of generating material for a bomb. In 2006, North Korea conducted an apparently failed test of a weapon of below 1 kiloton,[63] but in 2009, it successfully exploded a bomb of between 2 and 7 kilotons.[64] It has also sought to develop a launch capability that could deliver a nuclear warhead to targets in the United States and Europe. In December 2012, Pyongyang tested the necessary technology for an intercontinental ballistic missile by launching a satellite into low-earth orbit.[65] Intelligence reports indicate that North Korea has shared its nuclear and ballistic missile expertise with others, such as Pakistan, Iran, and Syria.[66] Replacing the North Korean leadership would probably produce greater gains to international peace and stability than the removal of Libya's Gadhafi or Syria's Assad.

Nevertheless, intervention in North Korea would run prohibitive risks. North Korea fields the world's fourth largest military, estimated by some at more than 1 million active duty soldiers and many million more in reserve.[67] It is armed with a large but aging arsenal of Soviet-designed tanks (4,100) and armored vehicles (2,100), artillery (8,500), aircraft (1,300), and several hundred theater ballistic missiles.[68] According to the U.S. Defense Department, North Korea has stationed 70 percent of its ground forces within 100 kilometers of the demilitarized zone with South Korea.[69] This forward deployment seeks to deter attacks on the regime by promising immediate retaliation against Seoul, home to one-fifth of South Korea's population. Pyongyang's history of covert attacks and military provocations conveys the message that the regime would have little reluctance to resort to force to defend its control of the North.

North Korea's military raises the costs of any intervention in two ways. First, it increases the difficulties of using force against the North. Unable to overthrow Kim through aerial power alone, the United States and its allies would have to transport heavy armor units across the oceans to conduct a ground invasion on difficult, prepared terrain. Current U.S. ground forces stationed in Korea, which amount to about 28,500 soldiers,[70] might slow a North Korean advance but could not stop it. The American deployment acts as a tripwire that would trigger massive American air and naval retaliation. Losses in any direct military conflict would be high. Second, once the great powers undertook any campaign, North Korea would likely launch an attack on civilian targets in South Korea, with high casualties all but certain. North Korea might even respond to any military intervention by using nuclear weapons and ballistic missiles to attack nations in the region, such as Japan or even the United States. While ending the Kim regime's oppression of North Korea's people could dramatically improve the lives of 25 million, it would risk with high probability the deaths of hundreds of thousands and could invite Chinese military intervention.

In contrast to the Libyan and Syrian cases, however, the postwar occupation cuts the other way. Military intervention in the Middle Eastern countries could spark a collapse of public order that prolonged the fighting and increased civilian casualties. Western removal of Kim might not trigger the same problems due to the unique presence of South Korea. A wealthier, more populous nation, the South could extend its political and economic system to northern territory, provide refugee aid, and reconstruct the north. Instead of an Iraq, the collapse of government in North Korea would bear more resemblance to the 1990 reunification of Germany. Koreans view themselves as one people, with the post-1945 separation as temporary and artificial, unlike the cases of Iraq, Afghanistan, and Syria, where the West has used force to keep different peoples bound together in single nations with outdated colonial borders. Nevertheless, the absence of deep costs for postwar reconstruction does not outweigh the high probability of widespread losses from any military action against North Korea.

Iran. Iran presents perhaps the most difficult case for a global welfare approach. Since its 1979 revolution, Iran has pursued a revisionist agenda in the Middle East. It supports the Hezbollah terrorist group in Lebanon,[71] has supplied weapons and training to insurgents in the Iraq War,[72] and props up the Assad regime in Syria in its civil war.[73] If the International Atomic Energy Agency has reported accurately,[74] Iran will soon join the ranks of the world's nuclear powers.

So far, the Obama administration reluctantly confronted this looming threat. It fell to Obama's 2012 Republican presidential challengers to press for a case for a military strike to destroy Iran's nuclear program. Former Massachusetts governor and Republican nominee Mitt Romney promised that Iran "will not have a nuclear weapon" under his presidency.[75] Economic sanctions and aid to internal opposition come first, said the former Massachusetts governor, but "if all else fails...[and] there's nothing else we can do besides take military action, then of course you take military action."[76] Former Republican House Speaker Newt Gingrich, also a candidate, proposed covert operations, including "taking out their scientists" and "breaking up their systems," and a Cold War-style strategy "of breaking the regime and bringing it down."[77] But the former House speaker "agree[d] entirely" with Romney that, should pressure fail, "you have to take whatever steps are necessary" to stop Iran from acquiring nuclear weapons.[78]

In this game of diplomatic poker, the Republicans would go all in where the last and current Presidents have checked. Though he has declared that he "will take no options off the table," President Obama has avoided explicit military threats.[79] Instead, he seeks to "isolate and increase the pressure upon the Iranian regime."[80] At the start of his term, President Obama hoped to negotiate a settlement with Tehran (and Moscow, Venezuela, Cuba, and North Korea), but he has ended up in the same place as his predecessor. President George W. Bush also declined to attack Iran's nuclear infrastructure, even when the United States had significant numbers of troops and military assets deployed next door. Bush also passed on striking a suspected Syrian nuclear facility (the Israelis destroyed it in 2007).[81] Like Obama, he pursued economic sanctions and applied political pressure to foster Iranian regime change.

President Obama has done more than merely delay the inevitable day of reckoning with Iran. He has left the public unprepared about the nature and possible consequences of military action, which must be serious and sustained enough to destroy complex, protected, and dispersed facilities—in other words, pinpoint bombing of a single facility will not end Iran's nuclear program. Iran might respond by attacking Israel, Arab allies such as Saudi Arabia, and oil shipments in the Persian Gulf. President Obama has also failed to explain the heavy costs of alternatives such as containment, which would involve a constant, significant conventional and nuclear military presence on Iran's perimeter.

Nor has the Obama administration built the political or legal case for attacking Iran. Instead, the administration has tethered American national security to the dictates of the United Nations. In Libya, Obama delayed launching the air war until the Security Council approved the intervention, allowing a popular revolution to metastasize into a prolonged, destructive civil war. It has so far refused to intervene in Syria without the approval of the Security Council, too.

The same craving for international approval may lead the administration to put off military action against Iran until it is too late. The UN Charter guarantees the "territorial integrity" and "political independence" of each member nation,[82] and prohibits the use of force except in self-defense,[83] which many scholars and international officials interpret to mean that force is prohibited except when an invader either has attacked or is about to attack across a border. It does allow an exception for war to prevent threats to international peace and security,[84] but only if approved by the Security Council (where the United States, Russia, China, Great Britain, and France have a veto). Not surprisingly, UN authorizations to use force are rare. China and Russia, both Security Council members, generally oppose intervention in what they consider "internal" affairs, including policies that repress political and economic freedoms. They can usually be counted on to protect other nondemocratic regimes by blocking UN approval for war, as they did in Iraq in 2003.[85]

If President Obama were to go beyond the UN Charter for military action against Iran, he would have to make a case based on the human welfare grounds of this book. The administration could argue that destroying Iran's nuclear weapons rests on a combination of protecting self-defense and international security. Nuclear weapons in the hands of an obvious enemy would constitute a grave threat to American interests. Even without them, Iran has fomented conflict in the region, supported groups hostile to Israel through its client state Syria, supported terrorists who target American allies such as Saudi Arabia, and attacked American troops in Iraq. It has also supported attacks on U.S. embassies and military bases in places such as Saudi Arabia and Lebanon, planned to kill ambassadors on American soil, and, of course, taken U.S. diplomatic officials hostage. Nuclear weapons would allow Iran to escalate hostilities with little fear of any large-scale American military response. If Saddam Hussein had succeeded in his drive to build nuclear weapons, would the United States have gone to war in 1991 to protect a small, oil-rich sheikdom?

A President need not wait until an attack is imminent before taking action. Iranian nuclear capabilities would cause a radical reversal of the balance of power. During the Cuban Missile Crisis, President John F. Kennedy imposed a blockade, which is an act of war, though his legal advisers merely claimed it was a "quarantine."[86]

Soviet nuclear missiles were not fueling on the launch pads, but President Kennedy used force because the Russian deployment upset the superpower equilibrium in the Western Hemisphere. Even realists who criticize a pro-democracy agenda should support the prevention of Iranian hegemony in the Middle East. Iran seeks to export a fundamentalist revolution, with the brutal suppression of individual rights and free markets, throughout the region. It stokes the Israel-Palestinian conflict. Iran's past president, Mahmoud Ahmadinejad, publicly hoped to wipe Israel from the map.[87] It undermined reconstruction and reconciliation in Iraq. It is tied to terrorism throughout the world, including the bombing of the Israeli embassy in Argentina[88] and a plan to kill the Saudi ambassador to the United States.[89] It threatens to close off the Straits of Hormuz, through which 20 percent of the world's oil exports travel.[90] It has attacked shipping in the Persian Gulf.[91] A nuclear Iran could expand its asymmetric warfare against it neighbors or even escalate into conventional warfare, with little fear of direct retaliation.

An attack on Iran might trigger the same response, but worse. Iran could close the Straits of Hormuz, which would lead to a spike in world oil prices and might plunge the global economy into recession. The United States Navy would have to undertake costly operations to reopen the channel. Tehran could order its Hezbollah allies in Lebanon to attack Israel, or it might conduct its own covert operations to attack Americans abroad or even the continental United States. Iran might even launch direct conventional attacks on U.S. allies in the region, such as Israel and Saudi Arabia.

An attack on Iran would also inflict significant costs to the United States and its allies. An attempt to remove the ruling Iranian regime would require a ground invasion for which the United States has not prepared. President Obama completely withdrew American forces from Iraq, which could have carried out such an effort, and is in the process of recalling U.S. troops from Afghanistan, where they still fight against the Taliban. Even if President Obama were to make such a fateful decision, it could take months to move the massive armored and ground divisions to a nearby nation where they would need permission to establish a base of operations. During the buildup, U.S. forces would remain vulnerable to direct and asymmetric attack from Iran and its allies in the region. An eventual invasion might prove as swift and decisive as the 1991 or 2003 wars with Iraq, which on paper fielded a more sophisticated military. As Samuel Huntington observed long ago, militaries that devote their resources and training to oppressing their own populations quickly lose their ability to carry out their original purpose of fighting a war against an external foe.[92] While the outcome might be in doubt, the level of casualties and the length of a postwar occupation are highly uncertain.

But military action need not go so far as an invasion or even a no-fly zone. American forces would have to destroy Iranian air-defense sites, but otherwise, thanks to precision-guided missiles and drones, they could concentrate on a few choke points in the Iranian nuclear chain: the centrifuge facilities where uranium is enriched, the assembly points for weapons, and perhaps missile and air-delivery systems.

The surgical nature of such strikes would make them "proportional" to the military objective, which would be not the overthrow of the Iranian regime but the destruction of its nuclear capability. Nuclear-weapons infrastructure is a legitimate military target, even if some strikes may kill civilians. If casualties result because facilities are located beneath cities, the fault rests with the Iranians for deliberately using civilians to shield its military—a move long forbidden by the laws of war.[93] Unlike Iranian-supported terrorist groups, the United States should do everything possible to keep civilian loss of life to a minimum.

The United States has assumed the role, once held by Great Britain, of guaranteeing free trade and economic development, spreading liberal values, and maintaining international security. Though it risks serious costs in human lives and political turmoil, an attack on Iranian nuclear facilities would serve these interests by preventing the rise to nuclear status of one of the most destabilizing nations in the region, if not the world.

* * *

These cases provide a useful test of the global welfare approach developed in this book. Others may disagree with the evaluation of the expected magnitude of the benefits and costs of conflict, which involves difficult judgments on the responses of different regimes, the military resources at hand, and the after-effects of fighting. Even if there were agreement on these variables, observers and government officials may still differ on the weighing of these costs and benefits and the allowances to be made for unpredictable future events and unintended consequences. But these are the right questions to ask when judging war, because the ultimate measure should rest on its effect on global human welfare, rather than whether it violates an ineffective legal ban on the use of force. Limiting armed conflict only to self-defense or UN approval may reduce the amount of interstate war in the world, but it does so blindly. As World War II and Rwanda demonstrate, there can be things worse than war. A properly designed international legal system should encourage intervention that improves global welfare in such circumstances and discourages wars that harm it. This book seeks to begin the critical rethinking of the international order necessary to align legal rules with the world's security needs.

Notes

CHAPTER I

1. Virgil Hawkins, Stealth Conflicts (2008).

2. John Lewis Gaddis, The Long Peace: Inquiries into the History of the Cold War (1989).

3. For a general overview of cost-benefit analysis, see Matthew D. Adler & Eric A. Posner, New Foundations of Cost-Benefit Analysis (2006).

4. On the changes wrought by globalization, see Julian Ku & John Yoo, Taming Globalization: International Law, the U.S. Constitution, and the New World Order (2012).

5. Philip Bobbitt, The Shield of Achilles (2003).

6. Henry Kissinger, Diplomacy (1994).

7. See John Yoo, Fixing Failed States, 99 Cal. L. Rev. 95 (2011) (describing phenomenon of failed states).

8. Quoted in Michael Byers, War Law: Understanding International Law and Armed Conflict 47 (2005).

9. Thomas M. Franck, What Happens Now?: The United Nations After Iraq, 97 Am. J. Int'l L. 607, 610 (2003).

10. Lori Fisler Damrosch & Bernard H. Oxman, Editors' Introduction: Agora: Future Implications of the Iraq Conflict, 97 Am. J. Int'l L. 553, 553 (2003).

11. George Kennan, American Diplomacy, 1900–1950, at 95 (1951).

12. Thomas Hobbes, Leviathan 90 (Richard Tuck ed., 1996).

13. Anthony Clark Arend, Pursuing a Just and Durable Peace: John Foster Dulles and International Obligation 57 (1988).

14. See Kennan, supra note 11, at 95.

15. Robert H. Bork, The Limits of "International Law," 18 The Nat'l Interest 3, 10 (Winter 1989–1990).

16. See, e.g., Raymond Aron, Peace and War: A Theory of International Relations (Daniel J. Mahoney & Brian C. Anderson eds., 2003); E.H. Carr, The Twenty Years' Crisis 1919–1939: An Introduction to the Study of International Relations (1939).

17. See, e.g., Frederick H. Russell, The Just War in the Middle Ages (1977); Thomas Pangle & Peter J. Ahrensdorf, Justice Among Nations: On the Moral Basis of Power and Peace (2002).

18. See, e.g., John Rawls, The Law of Peoples 92–105 (1999); Michael Walzer, Just and Unjust Wars: A Moral Argument with Historical Illustrations (1976).

19. Rome Statute of the International Criminal Court, July 17, 1998, Annex 11, U.N. Doc. A/CONF. 183/9 (1998) (amended June 10–11, 2010), art. 8 bis [hereinafter Rome Statute].

20. Id. art. 8 bis.

21. There is still the issue of whether the ICC could exercise jurisdiction over non-States Parties. For ways countries could exempt themselves from the ICC's jurisdiction over the crime of aggression, see Stephen Eliot Smith, Definitely Maybe: The Outlook for US Relations with the International Criminal Court during the Obama Administration, 22 Fla. J. Int'l L. 155, 175–77 (2010).

22. See, e.g., Jack Donnelly, The Relative Universality of Human Rights, 29 Hum. Rts. Q. 281, 292–93 (2007); Amartya Sen, Elements of a Theory of Human Rights, 32 Phil. & Pub. Aff. 315, 317 (2004).

23. See Eric A. Posner, Human Welfare, Not Human Rights, 108 Colum. L. Rev. 1758, 1761–62 (2008); Eric A. Posner, International Law: A Welfarist Approach, 73 U. Chi. L. Rev. 487 (2006).

24. Posner, Human Welfare, supra note 23, at 1781–84.

25. Robert Cooter & Thomas Ulen, Law and Economics 42 (3d ed. 2000) (defining public goods).

26. For discussion of international public goods, see Joseph S. Nye, Jr., The Paradox of American Power: Why the World's Only Superpower Can't Go It Alone 137–71 (2002); Inge Kaul, Isabelle Grunberg & Marc A. Stern, eds., Global Public Goods: International Cooperation in the 21st Century (1999); Todd Sandler, Global Challenges: An Approach to Environmental, Political, and Economic Problems (1997); Charles P Kindleberger, International Public Goods without International Government, 76 Am. Econ. Rev. 1 (1986); Robert O. Keohane, After Hegemony: Cooperation and Discord in the World Political Economy 49–64, 107–08 (1984).

27. David Armitage, ed., Hugo Grotius, Mare Liberum (The Free Sea) (2004) (1609).

28. See, e.g., Alan O. Sykes, The Economics of Public International Law, in Handbook of Law and Economics (A.M. Polinksy & S. Shavell eds., 2007).

29. Daniel Webster, Letter to Henry Fox, British Minister in Washington (Apr. 24, 1841), in 1 British Documents on Foreign Affairs: Reports and Papers from the Foreign Office Confidential Print (Part I, Series C) 153, 159 (Kenneth Bourne & D. Cameron Watt, eds., University Publications of America 1986).

30. The National Security Strategy of the United States 15 (2002).

31. Marc Trachtenberg, The Iraq Crisis and the Future of the Western Alliance, in The Atlantic Alliance Under Stress 201 (David M. Andrews, ed., 2005).

32. Peter Baker, Obama Puts His Own Mark on Foreign Policy Issues, N.Y. Times, Apr. 13, 2010, at A10.

33. The National Security Strategy of the United States 3 (2010).

34. Remarks by the President at the Acceptance of the Nobel Peace Prize (Dec. 10, 2009), http://www.whitehouse.gov/the-press-office/remarks-president-acceptance-nobel-peace-prize.

35. Remarks by the President at United States Military Academy at West Point Commencement (May 22, 2010), http://www.whitehouse.gov/the-press-office/remarks-president-united-states-military-academy-west-point-commencement.

36. For a discussion of the U.S. legal justifications for the Vietnam War, see John Norton Moore, Law and the Indo-China War (1973).

CHAPTER 2

1. See generally Charles Tilly, Coercion, Capital, And European States (1992).

2. Philip Bobbitt, The Shield of Achilles: War, Peace, and the Course of History 333–42 (2002).

3. See John J. Mearsheimer, The Tragedy of Great Power Politics 21 (2001). For classic statements of realism, see Kenneth Waltz, A Theory of International Politics 111–28 (1979); Hans Morgenthau, Politics Among Nations (1948).

4. See, e.g., Andreas Osiander, Sovereignty, International Relations, and the Westphalian Myth, 55 Int'l Org. 251 (2001); Leo Gross, The Peace of Westphalia, 1648–1948, 42 Am. J. Int'l L. 20, 22 (1948).

5. See Edward V. Gluck, Europe's Classical Balance of Power (1967).

6. As Philip Bobbitt observes, the two concepts were slightly different. Machiavelli understood reason of state to mean the "rational, unprincipled justification for the self-aggrandizement of the State," while for Richelieu, reason of state "achieved a parallel justification through the personification of the state, and leveraged the imperatives of this justification to impose obligations on the dynastic ruler." Bobbitt, supra note 2, at 108.

7. See generally John Lewis Gaddis, Strategies of Containment: A Critical Appraisal of Postwar American National Security Policy (1982); John Lewis Gaddis, We Now Know: Rethinking Cold War History (1997).

8. UN S.C. Res. 1973 (Mar. 17, 2011).

9. Factbox—Libya Oil Production, Outage, Export, Customers, Reuters, Mar. 16, 2011, available at http://www.reuters.com/article/2011/03/16/libya-oil-idUSLDE72F22G20110316.

10. Id.

11. K.J. Holsti, The State, War, and the State of War 24 (1996).

12. Bureau of Intelligence and Research, U.S. Department of State, Independent States in the World Fact Sheet, Jan. 3, 2012, http://www.state.gov/s/inr/rls/4250.htm.

13. Holsti, supra note 11, at 24.

14. Cf. Steven Pinker, The Better Angels of Our Nature: Why Violence Has Declined (2011).

15. Nils Petter Gleditsch et al., Armed Conflict 1946–2001: A New Dataset, 39 J. Peace Res. 615, 620 (2002).

16. Holsti, supra note 11, at 21 (stating 77 percent).

17. Eric Hobsbawm, The Age of Extremes: A History of the World 1914–1991 (1994); Zbigniew Brzezinski, Out of Control: Global Turmoil on the Eve of the Twenty-First Century 7–18 (1993).

18. Milton Leitenberg, Deaths in Wars and Conflicts in the 20th Century, Cornell University Peace Studies Program Occasional Paper #29, at 9 (3d ed., June 2006).

19. Id.

20. Robert S. McNamara, The Post Cold War World: Implications for Military Expenditure in the Developing Countries, Proceedings of the World Bank Annual Conference on Development Economics 1991 (1992).

21. Human Security Centre, Human Security Report 2005: War and Peace in the 21st Century (2005) (90 percent of all war-related deaths are "indirect" civilian deaths).

22. James D. Fearon & David D. Laitin, Ethnicity, Insurgency, and Civil War, 97 Am. Pol. Sci. Rev. 75, 75 (2003).

23. Leitenberg, supra note 18, at 15.

24. See Stephen Biddle, Military Power: Explaining Victory and Defeat in Modern Battle 14–27 (2004) (critiquing various methods for measuring military power).

25. Mearsheimer, supra note 3, at 5.

26. The President's News Conference, 515 Pub. Papers 13 (Nov. 20, 1962), available at http://www.presidency.ucsb.edu/ws/index.php?pid=9020&st=&st1=#axzz2jiSwgY3x. I am grateful to Marc Trachtenberg for the reference.

27. See generally Abram Chayes, The Cuban Missile Crisis: International Crisis and the Role of Law (1974); but see Norbert A. Schlei, Memorandum to the Attorney General re: Legality under International Law of Remedial Action against Use of Cuba as a Missile Base by the Soviet Union (Aug. 30, 1962), reprinted in 6 Green Bag 2d 195 (2003).

28. See, e.g., Michael Glennon, Limits of Law, Prerogatives of Power: Intervention after Kosovo (2001) (arguing that international law has failed to prevent nations from waging war); Thomas Franck, Who Killed Article 2(4)?, Am. J. Int'l L. 809 (1970) (arguing that the UN Charter's restrictions on the use of force had died in 1970); Arthur Weisburd, Use of Force: The Practice of States Since World War II (1997) (arguing that states have regularly gone to war since 1945 in violation of the UN Charter).

29. Thomas Franck, What Happens Now?: The United Nations After Iraq, 97 Am. J. Int'l L. 607, 609 (2003).

30. See, e.g., Louis Henkin, How Nations Behave 47 (2d ed. 1979); Harold Koh, Review Essay, Why Do Nations Obey International Law?, 106 Yale L.J. 2599 (1997).

31. John Lewis Gaddis, The Long Peace: Inquiries into the History of the Cold War 219–37 (1987).

32. Kenneth N. Waltz, Nuclear Myths and Political Realities 84 Am. Pol. Sci. Rev. 731, 740 (1990).

33. Id. at 744.

34. See generally Scott D. Sagan & Kenneth N. Waltz, The Spread of Nuclear Weapons: A Debate Renewed (2d ed. 2002).

35. See, e.g., Karl Deutsch & J. David Singer, Multipolar Power Systems and International Stability, 16 World Politics 390 (1964); Kenneth N. Waltz, Theory of International Politics 170–93 (1979).

36. Mearsheimer, supra note 3, at 338–44.

37. Kenneth N. Waltz, Theory of International Politics 170–76.

38. David Hume, Of the Balance of Power, in Essays Moral, Political, Literary (1987) (arguing that the "balance of power" is not a modern policy but is rooted in the ancient empires of Greece and Persia); Jean-Jacques Rousseau, The State of War, in A Lasting Peace through the Federation of Europe and the State of War (C.E. Vaughan trans., 1917); Jean-Jacques Rousseau, A Lasting Peace through the Federation of Europe, in A Lasting Peace through the Federation of Europe

and the State of War (C.E. Vaughan trans., 1917); 1 Jean-Jacques Rousseau, Jugement sur la Paix Perpetuelle, in The Political Writings of Jean Jacques Rousseau (Charles Edwyn Vaughan ed., 1915); 21 John Stuart Mill, A Few Words on Non-Intervention, in The Collected Works of John Stuart Mill: Essays on Equality, Law, and Education (John M. Robson ed., 1984); 21 John Stuart Mill, Treaty Obligations, in The Collected Works of John Stuart Mill: Essays on Equality, Law, and Education (John M. Robson ed., 1984).

39. John Rawls, Law of Peoples (2001).

40. See, e.g., Dan Reiter & Allan C. Stam, Democracies at War (2002); Bruce Russett, Grasping the Democratic Peace: Principles for a Post-Cold War World (1993); Bruce Bueno de Mesquita et al., An Institutional Explanation of the Democratic Peace, 93 Am. Pol. Sci. Rev. 791 (1999); David A. Lake, Powerful Pacifists: Democratic States and War, 86 Am. Pol. Sci. Rev. 24 (1992). But see Joanne Gowa, Ballots and Bullets: The Elusive Democratic Peace (1999) (arguing that "democratic peace" is not a result of common polities, but rather a product of the shifting-interest patterns after the Cold War); Michael C. Desch, Democracy and Victory: Why Regime Type Hardly Matters, 27 Int'l Sec. 5 (2002); Sebastian Rosato, The Flawed Logic of Democratic Peace Theory, 97 Am. Pol. Sci. Rev. 585 (2003).

41. Bueno de Mesquita, supra note 40, at 791.

42. Michael W. Doyle, Kant, Liberal Legacies, and Foreign Affairs, in Debating the Democratic Peace 10 (Michael E. Brown, Sean M. Lynn-Jones & Steven E. Miller eds., 2001).

43. See, e.g., Henry S. Farber & Joanne Gowa, Common Interests or Common Polities?: Reinterpreting the Democratic Peace, 59 J. Pol. 393 (1997).

44. Immanuel Kant, The Metaphysics of Morals, in Kant: Political Writings 171 (Hans Reiss ed., H.B. Nisbet trans., 2d ed. 1991).

45. Immanuel Kant, Perpetual Peace: A Philosophical Sketch, in Political Writings 105 (1795).

46. Daniel Goldhagen has recently argued that nondemocratic regimes today "have a built-in propensity—a real one, and not just a hypothetical one—to adopt eliminationist policies, including their lethal variant." Daniel Jonah Goldhagen, Worse Than War: Genocide, Eliminationism and the Ongoing Assault on Humanity 280 (2009). On U.S. democracy promotion, see G. John Ikenberry, America's Liberal Grand Strategy: Democracy and National Security in the Post-War Era, in American Democracy Promotion: Impulses, Strategies, and Impacts 103, 124–26 (Michael Cox, John Ikenberry & Takashi Inoguchi eds., 2000).

47. This is not to say that democracy can or should be imposed by military intervention. Economist Christopher Coyne has studied U.S. attempts since 1898 to impose democracy after military intervention. See Christopher J. Coyne, After War: The Political Economy of Exporting Democracy (2007). Coyne found a success rate of only 28 percent after five years and of only 36 percent after twenty years. Id. at 15–16. Moreover, the most significant successes of coerced democratization were the post-Second World War cases of Nazi Germany and Austria, fascist Italy and Imperial Japan—where traces of pre-War liberalism had not been wholly effaced, and where the American military victories had been absolute. In general, Coyne found that "political, economic, and social change that is imposed at the point of a gun is more likely to be met with resistance and is less likely to 'stick' once occupiers exit the country." Id. at 28.

48. George W. Bush, Second Inaugural Address (Jan. 20, 2005), http://avalon.law.yale.edu/21st_century/gbush2.asp.

49. Robert O. Keohane, After Hegemony: Cooperation and Discord in the World Political Economy (1984).

CHAPTER 3

1. See, e.g., Michael Walzer, Arguing About War 3–4 (2004).

2. Stephen C. Neff, War and the Law of Nations: A General History 279 (2005).

3. See Sophocles, Antigone 24–42 (Richard Braun trans., 1973).

4. See, e.g., Adriaan Lanni, The Laws of War in Ancient Greece, 26 L. & Hist. Rev. 469, 471–72 (2008).

5. See Donald Kagan, The Peloponnesian War (2004); Donald Kagan, Thucydides: The Reinvention of History (2009); see also Victor Davis Hanson, Introduction to the Landmark Thucydides, A Comprehensive Guide to the Peloponnesian War xiv–xxxiii (Robert R. Strassler ed., 1998) [hereinafter Landmark Thucydides].

6. Landmark Thucydides, supra note 5, at 5.89.

7. Id. at 5.90.

8. Id. at 5.105.

9. Antigone, supra note 3, at 24.

10. Coleman Phillipson, The International Law and Custom of Ancient Greece and Rome 179 (1911); cf. Arthur Nussbaum, Just War—A Legal Concept?, 42 Mich. L. Rev. 453, 453 (1943) (criticizing Phillipson on this point).

11. Aristotle, Politics, bk. I, at viii (Benjamin Jowett trans., 2000) (c. 350 BCE).

12. Nussbaum, supra note 10, at 476–82.

13. Landmark Thucydides, supra note 5, at 4.98; Lanni, supra note 4, at 477.

14. Lanni, supra note 4, at 479.

15. Antigone, supra note 3, at 24.

16. W. Kendrick Pritchett, The Greek State at War, pt. V, at 205–19 (1991).

17. Landmark Thucydides, supra note 5, at 3.36–3.49.

18. Id. at 3.52–3.68.

19. Neff, supra note 2, at 19.

20. Phillipson, supra note 10, at 32–33; David Bederman, International Law in Antiquity 33–34 (2001).

21. Plato, 4 Dialogues of Plato 156 (Benjamin Jowett trans., 1892).

22. Victor Davis Hanson, A War Like No Other: How the Athenians and Spartans Fought the Peloponnesian War 299 (2005); Victor Davis Hanson, The Western Way of War 14–18 (1989).

23. Lanni, supra note 4, at 484–85.

24. See, e.g., Henry Wheaton, History of the Law of Nations in Europe and America 21 (1845).

25. Neff, supra note 2, at 34.

26. Cicero, De Officiis, bk. I, ¶ 11 (Andrew Peabody trans., 1887) (c. 44 BCE).

27. Id. ¶ 23.

28. Alan Watson, International Law in Archaic Rome: War and Religion 2–3 (1993) (quoting Dionysus of Halicarnassus).

29. Phillipson, supra note 10, at 339.

30. Cicero, supra note 26, ¶ 11.

31. Watson, supra note 28, at xii–xiii.

32. Cicero, supra note 26, ¶ 11.

33. See William V. Harris, War and Imperialism in Republican Rome 327–70 B.C. 163–75 (1985).

34. Id. at 182–90, 234–40.

35. Cicero, De Officiis, bk. II, ¶ 8 (Andrew Peabody trans., 1887) (c. 44 BCE).

36. Bederman, supra note 20, at 234.

37. On this point, Henry Maine is mistaken in arguing that the *ius gentium* was a subset of *the ius fetiale*. See Bederman, supra note 20, at 236.

38. Cicero, supra note 26, ¶ 11.

39. See, e.g., Thomas L. Pangle & Peter J. Ahrensdorf, Justice Among Nations: On the Moral Basis of Power and Peace 73 (1999); see also G.I.A.D. Draper, The Just War Doctrine, 86 Yale L.J. 370 (1976); James Turner Johnson, Ideology, Reason, and the Limitation of War (1975); Nussbaum, supra note 10.

40. Frederick H. Russell, The Just War in the Middle Ages 12–15 (1975); see also Maurice H. Keen, The Laws of War in the Middle Ages (1965).

41. Nussbaum, supra note 10, at 455.

42. Draper, supra note 39, at 372.

43. See, e.g., Russell, supra note 40, at 17–18; M.H. Keen, The Laws of War in the Late Middle Ages 66 (1993).

44. Russell, supra note 40, at 18; Paul Ramsey, The Just War According to St. Augustine, in Just War Theory 8 (Jean Bethke Elshtain ed., 1992); Herbert A. Deane, The Political and Social Ideas of St. Augustine 154–71 (1963).

45. Russell, supra note 40, at 22–23.

46. Id. at 19.

47. Id. at 23.

48. Nussbaum, supra note 10, at 455.

49. Russell, supra note 40, at 26–39.

50. Id. at 44–45.

51. Laurent Mayali, Droit, Raison et Nécessité dans la Théorie de la Guerre au Moyen Age, in Le Gouvernement des Communautes Politiques a la Fin du Moyen Age: Entre Puissance et Negociations: Villes, Finances, État 451, 466 (Corinne Leveleux-Teixeira et al. eds., 2010).

52. Russell, supra note 40, at 126.

53. Id. at 138–55.

54. Mayali, supra note 51, at 467.

55. Neff, supra note 2, at 59–62.

56. Id. at 60–61.

57. Russell, supra note 40, at 195–212.

58. See, e.g., Pangle & Ahrensdorf, supra note 39, at 80–81.

59. St. Thomas Aquinas, Summa Theologiae, in Aquinas: Political Writings 240–41 (R.W. Dyson ed., 2002).

60. Id. at 240.

61. Id. at 240–41.

62. Russell, supra note 40, at 261–62.

63. Francisco de Vitoria, Vitoria: Political Writings 264–76 (Anthony Pagden & Jeremy Lawrence eds., 1992).

64. Pangle & Ahrensdorf, supra note 39, at 98.

65. As a matter of principle, Vitoria held that war could not be just on both sides; he used a penal model of war. See Oliver O'Donovan, The Just War Revisited 22–23 (2003). But he also

taught that "invincible ignorance" could excuse the party in the wrong, and in that sense believed that war might be just on both sides. See Nussbaum, supra note 10, at 460.

66. Nussbaum, supra note 10, at 461–62.

67. Francisco de Vitoria, De Indis I, no. 3, ¶ 2 (1952).

68. Nussbaum, supra note 10, at 463.

69. See Antonio Cassese, Realism v. Artificial Theoretical Constructs: Remarks on Anzilotti's Theory of War, 3 Eur. J. Int'l L. 149, 149–50 (1992); see also C.A. Pompe, Aggressive War: An International Crime 301–02 (1953).

70. David Kennedy, International Law and the Nineteenth Century: History of an Illusion, 17 Quinnipiac L. Rev. 99, 127 (1998).

71. John Westlake, International Law: Part II—War 4 (1907); see also Amos S. Hershey, The International Law and Diplomacy of the Russo-Japanese War 67 (1906).

72. For studies of Grotius, see Karma Nabulsi, Traditions of War: Occupation, Resistance, and the Law 128–76 (1999); Pangle & Ahrensdorf, supra note 39, at 125–61; Richard Tuck, The Rights of War and Peace: Political Thought and the International Order from Grotius to Kant 78–108 (1999); David J. Bederman, Reception of the Classical Tradition in International Law: Grotius, 10 Emory Int'l L. Rev. 1 (1996). An earlier study is G.I.A.D. Draper, Grotius' Place in the Development of Legal Ideas about War, reprinted in Reflection on Law and Armed Conflicts: The Selected Works on the Laws of War by the Late Professor Colonel G.I.A.D. Draper, OBE 48 (Michael A. Meyer & Hilaire McCoubrey eds., 1998).

73. See Walzer, supra note 1, at 4; Julius Stone, Aggression and the World Order: A Critique of United Nations Theories of Aggression 27–28 (1958).

74. Tuck, supra note 72, 95 (1999).

75. See Steven Forde, Hugo Grotius on Ethics and War, 92 Am. Pol. Sci. Rev. 639, 644–45 (1998); Nussbaum, supra note 10, at 464. For a different understanding of Grotius, see Jon Miller, Hugo Grotius, Stanford Encyclopedia of Philosophy, available at http://plato.stanford.edu/entries/grotius/ (last updated July 28, 2011).

76. Hugo Grotius, On the Law of War and Peace of War and Peace, bk. I, ch. II, sec. 1, para. IV., at 52 (Francis Kelsey trans., Oxford Univ. Press 1925) (1625).

77. Id., bk. I, chap. II, sec. V., at 53.

78. See Miller, supra note 75.

79. G.I.A.D. Draper, Grotius' Place in the Development of Legal Ideas About War, in Hugo Grotius and International Relations 177 (Hedley Bull et al. eds., 1990).

80. Neff, supra note 2, at 59–61, 97–102, 126–29; Tuck, supra note 72, at 18–31, 79–94, 102–06.

81. Grotius, supra note 76, bk. II, ch. I, sec. IX, para. 1.

82. Id. bk. II, ch. XXII, sec. V. One writer cites the latter passage in support of the view that Grotius forbade preventive war; but the text says that a preventive war is permissible if one side concludes that the other has both the power and the intent to attack it. See W.J. Korab-Karpowicz, In Defense of International Order: Grotius's Critique of Machiavellism, 60 Rev. Metaphysics 55, 63 (2006); see also Cornelius M. Murphy, The Grotian Vision of World Order, 76 Am. J. Int'l L. 477, 481 (1982). Colonel Draper, one of the scholars who believes that Grotius had a form of just war doctrine, concedes that its impact on state practice was "minimal." Draper, supra note 79, at 50.

83. Hersh Lauterpacht, The Grotian Tradition in International Law, 23 Brit. Y.B. Int'l L. 47 (1946).

84. Larry May, Studies in the History of Ethics: Grotius and Contingent Pacifism 1 (2006), available at http://www.historyofethics.org/022006/MayContingentPacifism.pdf.

85. Grotius, supra note 76, bk. II, ch. I, sec. II, at 171.

86. Id. bk. II, ch. XX, secs. VII–IX, at 470–78.

87. Id. bk. II, ch. XXIII, sec. XIII, at 565.

88. See David Fisher, Morality and War: Can War Be Just in the Twenty-First Century? 69 (2011).

89. Grotius, supra note 76, bk. II, ch. XXIII, sec. XIII, at 565.

90. See id. bk. III, ch. IV, sec. IV.

91. Id. bk. III, ch. IV, sec. IV.

92. Id. bk. III, ch. IV, sec. II, para. 2 ("[I]t is lawful for Kings to do what they please, because they are exempted from Punishment amongst Men.").

93. See id. bk. II, ch. XXIII, secs. VI–X.

94. Id. bk. II, ch. I, sec. II, para. 1.

95. See id., The Preliminary Discourse, para. IV (contrasting Christian pacifism to doctrine that all war is justified, and indicating that both views are mistaken).

96. See id., The Preliminary Discourse, para. XXVIII ("Of how great Force in Wars is the Consciousness of the Justice of the Cause, Historians everywhere shew, who often ascribe the Victory chiefly to this Reason.... [T]he Equity of the Cause has of itself a certain, and that very great Force towards Action."); Forde, supra note 75, at 645.

97. Yoram Dinstein, War, Aggression, and Self-Defense 62 (2011).

98. A. Claire Cutler, The "Grotian Tradition" in International Relations, 17 Rev. Int'l Stud. 41, 44 (1991).

99. See Ian Clark, Waging War: A Philosophical Introduction 40 (1988). On the transformation and secularization of *jus ad bellum* doctrine in the early modern period, the increasingly anachronistic character of the doctrine, and the origin of the conditions for modern *jus in bello*, see Neff, supra note 2, at 95–102. See also Robert D. Sloane, The Cost of Conflation: Preserving the Dualism of Jus ad Bellum and Jus in Bello in the Contemporary Law of War, 34 Yale J. Int'l L. 47, 60–64 (2009); Martii Koskenniemi, International Law as Political Theology: How to Read Nomos der Erde?, 11 Constellations 492, 496–97 (2004).

100. Geoffrey Parker, Early Modern Europe, in The Laws of War: Constraints on Warfare in the Western World 40, 41 (Michael Howard, George J. Andreapoulos & Mark R. Shulman eds., 1994). For discussion of the articles of war promulgated by both royalist and parliamentary forces in English Civil War of the seventeenth century, see Barbara Donagan, Codes and Conduct in the English Civil War, 118 Past & Present 65, 83–87 (1988). See also Barbara Donagan, Atrocity, War Crime, and Treason in the English Civil War, 99 Am. Hist. Rev. 1137, 1142 (1994).

101. See Neff, supra note 2; Dinstein, supra note 97.

102. See Lynn H. Miller, The Contemporary Significance of the Doctrine of Just War, 16 World Pol. 254, 258 (1964).

103. See Inis L. Claude, Jr., Just Wars: Doctrines and Institutions, 95 Pol. Sci. Q. 83, 90–91 (1980).

104. On the incentives in international affairs to avoid reputational harms, see Andrew T. Guzman, How International Law Works: A Rational Choice Theory (2008).

105. For an account of the origins of Spain's sinister reputation, see Benjamin Keen, The Black Legend Revisited: Assumptions and Realities, 49 Hisp. Am. Hist. Rev. 703 (1969).

106. John U. Nef, War and Human Progress: An Essay on the Rise of Industrial Civilization 139 (1950). On the laws and customs of war regarding the surrender after a siege, see John W. Wright, Sieges and Customs of War at the Opening of the Eighteenth Century, 39 Am. Hist. Rev. 629, 638–44 (1934).

107. Nef, supra note 106, at 139.

108. Carl von Clausewitz, On War 85 (Michael Howard & Peter Paret trans., 1991) ("If, then, civilized nations do not put their prisoners to death or devastate cities and countries, it is because intelligence plays a larger part in their methods of warfare and has taught them more effective ways of using force than the crude expression of instinct.").

109. Id. at 714.

110. See David A. Bell, The First Total War: Napoleon's Europe and the Birth of War as We Know It 8 (2007); J.F.C. Fuller, The Conduct of War 1789–1961, at 26–58 (1992); Gunther E. Rothenberg, The Origins, Causes, and Extension of the Wars of the French Revolution and Napoleon, 18 J. Interdisc. Hist. 771, 773–76 (1988).

111. See David Armstrong, Revolution and World Order: The Revolutionary State in International Society 84–91, 204–19 (1993).

112. Adam Roberts, Land Warfare: From Hague to Nuremberg, in The Laws of War: Constraints on Warfare in the Western World 116, 119 (Michael Howard, George J. Andreapoulos & Mark R. Shulman eds., 1994).

113. See Int'l Comm. of the Red Cross, Instructions for the Government of Armies of the United States in the Field (Lieber Code). 24 April 1863, available at http://www.icrc.org/ihl. nsf/FULL/110?OpenDocument (last visited Mar. 9, 2012). For discussion of the origins and application of the Lieber Code, see Burrus M. Carnahan, Lincoln, Lieber and the Laws of War: The Origins and Limits of the Principle of Military Necessity, 92 Am. J. Int'l L. 213 (1998).

114. The Geneva Convention for the Amelioration of the Condition of the Sick and Wounded of Armies in the Field, Aug. 22, 1864, 22 Stat. 940, available at http://avalon.law.yale.edu/19th_century/geneva04.asp.

115. See Declaration to Prohibit for the Term of Five Years the Launching of Projectiles and Explosives from Balloons, and Other New Methods of a Similar Nature, July 29, 1899, 32 Stat. 1839; Declaration Between the United States and Other Powers Prohibiting the Discharge of Projectiles and Explosives from Balloons, Oct. 18, 1907, 36 Stat. 2439; see also Declaration Renouncing the Use, in Time of War, of Explosive Projectiles Under 400 Grammes Weight, Nov. 29, 1868, 138 Consol. T.S. 297.

116. See Convention Between the United States and Other Powers Respecting the Laws and Customs of War on Land, Oct. 18, 1907, 36 Stat. 2277.

117. Kenneth N. Waltz, Man, The State and War: A Theoretical Analysis 38 (1954).

118. See R. Harrison Wagner, War and the State, 63–65 (2007).

119. Robert G. Gilpin, The Richness of the Tradition of Political Realism, 38 Int'l Org. 287, 303 (1984); see also Reinhart Koselleck, Critique and Crisis: Enlightenment and the Pathogenesis of Modern Society 46–48 (1988).

120. Jonathan Haslam, No Virtue Like Necessity 17 (2002).

121. See Albert O. Hirschman, The Passions and the Interests: Political Arguments for Capitalism Before its Triumph 43–44 (1977).

122. Again, we may cite the example of Cardinal Richelieu. Richelieu's conception of statecraft laid considerable emphasis both on what he called "continuous negotiations" and on the sanctity

of treaties. See Herbert Butterfield, Diplomacy, in Studies in Diplomatic History: Essays in Memory of David Bayne Horn 357, 365 (Ragnhild Hatton & M.S. Anderson eds., 1970); Herbert Butterfield, Raison d'État 16 (1975); G.R. Berridge, Richelieu, in Diplomatic Theory from Machiavelli to Kissinger 71, 75 (G.R. Berridge, Maurice Keens-Soper & T.G. Otte eds., 2001). Richelieu also thought that an enlightened self-interest in maintaining "reputation"—which he saw as a key ingredient of a monarch's power—counseled the strict observance of treaties. Id. at 78.

123. On early formulations of the doctrine of royal absolutism in the works of Jean Bodin and his adherent, King James I of England, see Harold Berman, Law and Revolution, II: The Impact of the Protestant Reformations on the Western Legal Tradition 234–38 (2003). On the weakening of medieval legal and customary restraints on royal power, see Jean Bethke Elshtain, Sovereignty: God, State, and Self 58–64 (2008).

124. See Daniel Deudney, Bounding Power: Republican Security Theory from the Polis to the Global Village 69 (2007).

125. Waltz, supra note 117, at 215.

126. Id. at 215–16.

127. Id. at 216.

128. Thus, in the 1833 account by the nineteenth-century German historian Leopold von Ranke, the ascendancy of seventeenth-century France under King Louis XIV had imperiled the independent development of other European states and cultures. "This arrogated supremacy, which was constantly disturbing the peace, threatened to destroy the foundations of European order and development." See Leopold von Ranke, The Great Powers, in The Theory and Practice of History: Leopold von Ranke 71 (Georg G. Iggers & Konrad von Moltke eds., Wilma A. Iggers & Konrad von Moltke trans., 1973). The solution was found in the balance of power: "The concept of the European balance of power, as it was called, was developed in order that many states might resist the pretensions of the 'exorbitant' court, as it was called." Id. at 73.

129. See Waltz, supra note 117, at 198–99; see also Arthur M. Eckstein, Mediterranean Anarchy, Interstate War, and the Rise of Rome (2006).

130. M.S. Anderson, The Rise of Modern Diplomacy 1450–1919, at 165 (1993). See also id. at 150–66 (tracing evolution of the doctrine).

131. See id. at 165–68.

132. Randall J. Schweller, Unanswered Threats: A Neoclassical Realist Theory of Underbalancing, 29 Int'l Sec. 159, 162 (2004). For an analysis of Rousseau's defense of the balance of power and specifically of his claim that "peace ought to come of itself," see Marc Trachtenberg, The Question of Realism, 13 Sec. Stud. 156, 174–76 (2003).

133. See Immanuel Kant, On the Common Saying: "This May Be True in Theory, but It Does Not Apply in Practice," in Kant: Political Writings 61, 92 (H.S. Reiss ed., 1977).

134. See W.B. Gallie, Philosophers of Peace and War: Kant, Clausewitz, Marx, Engels, Tolstoy 8 (1978).

135. See Paul W. Schroeder, The 19th Century International System: Changes in the Structure, 39 World Pol. 1, 2, 10–11 (1986); Paul W. Schroeder, The Nineteenth Century System: Balance of Power or Political Equilibrium?, 15 Rev. Int'l Pol. 135, 141–42 (1989); Paul W. Schroeder, Did the Vienna Settlement Rest on a Balance of Power?, 97 Am. Hist. Rev. 683, 684–90, 694, 696, 701–02 (1992); Robert Jervis, From Balance to Concert: A Study of International Security Cooperation, 38 World Pol. 58 (1985); Robert Jervis, A Political Science Perspective on the Balance of Power and Concert, 97 Am. Hist. Rev. 716, 718–23 (1992).

136. Richard B. Elrod, The Concert of Europe: A Fresh Look at an International System, 28 World Pol. 159, 161–62 (1976); see also Robert E. Osgood & Robert W. Tucker, Force, Order, and Justice 102–04 (1967).

137. See Edward D. Mansfield, Concentration, Polarity, and the Distribution of Power, 37 Int'l Stud. Q. 105, 116–17 (1992); see also R. Harrison Wagner, Peace, War, and the Balance of Power, 88 Am. Pol. Sci. Rev. 593, 600–01 (1988).

138. See Dominic Lieven, Russia against Napoleon: The True Story of the Campaigns of War and Peace 477, 524 (2008).

139. For modern applications that demonstrate how a rational leader would consider preventive war as a tool in maintaining balance, see Emerson M.S. Niou & Peter C. Ordeshook, Preventive War and the Balance of Power: A Game-Theoretic Approach, 31 J. Conflict Res. 387 (1987), and Emerson M.S. Niou & Peter C. Ordeshook, A Theory of the Balance of Power in International Systems, 30 J. Conflict Res. 685 (1986).

140. See John Mearsheimer, The Tragedy of Great Power Politics 3 (2001).

141. 54 Cong. Rec. S1741, S1742 (Jan. 22, 1917) (address by President Woodrow Wilson). For the Wilsonian vision and its aversion to the use of a "balance of power," see Philip Bobbitt, The Shield of Achilles: War, Peace, and the Course of History 359–60 (2002); see also Thomas J. Knock, To End All Wars: Woodrow Wilson and the Quest for a New World Order 112–15, 195–96 (1992).

142. 58 Cong. Rec. S2336, S2338 (July 10, 1919) (address by President Woodrow Wilson).

143. The war was widely perceived as "a conclusive demonstration that the balance of power system could not provide security for either the powerful or the small nations of the world." Alfred Vagts & Detlev F. Vagts, The Balance of Power in International Law: A History of an Idea, 73 Am. J. Int'l L. 555, 567 (1979). Many jurists—Americans prominently among them—condemned the balance of power in favor of what they saw as a more moral system. Id. at 576–77.

144. See Manfred F. Boemke, Woodrow Wilson's Image of Germany, in The Treaty of Versailles: A Reassessment After 75 Years 603, 610–12, 631 (Manfred F. Boemke, Gerald D. Feldman & Elisabeth Glaser eds., 1998).

145. Marc Trachtenberg, Versailles Revisited, 9 Sec. Stud. 191, 199 (2000).

146. Michael Howard, The Historical Development of the UN's Role in International Security, in United Nations, Divided World 63, 63 (Adam Roberts & Benedict Kingsbury eds., 1993).

147. See, e.g., C. Van Vollenhoven, The Three Stages in the Evolution of the Law of Nations (1919).

148. O'Donovan, supra note 65, at 24.

149. See Evan Luard, A History of the United Nations: Vol. 1, The Years of Western Domination, 1945–1955, at 31–32 (1982); Brett D. Schaefer & Steven Groves, Human Wrongs, in Conundrum: The Limits of the United Nations and the Search for Alternatives 131, 136 (Brett D. Schaefer ed., 2009).

150. See Mark Mazower, No Enchanted Palace: The End of Empire and the Ideological Origins of the United Nations (2009).

151. Julius Stone, Aggression and World Order: A Critique of United Nations Theories of Aggression 98–99 (1958).

152. Anthony Clark Arend & Robert J. Beck, International Law and the Use of Force 33–34 (1993); Inis Claude, Jr., Just Wars: Doctrines and Institutions, 95 Pol. Sci. Q. 83, 94 (1980); David Luban, Just War and Human Rights, 9 Phil. & Pub. Aff. 160, 164–65 (1980).

153. See William V. O'Brien, The Conduct of Just War and Limited War 22 (1981) ("In classic just-war doctrine, offensive wars were permitted to protect vital rights threatened or injured.").

154. Jean Bethke Elshtain, The Third Annual Grotius Lecture: Just War and Humanitarian Intervention, 17 Am. U. Int'l L. Rev. 1, 6 (2001).

155. Id. at 7.

156. The only arguable exception recognized in the Charter is for the case of anticipatory self-defense; and even that exception has been doubted. See, e.g., Louis Henkin, War and Terrorism: Law or Metaphor, 45 Santa Clara L. Rev. 817, 825 (2005). For further discussion, see Robert J. Delahunty & John C. Yoo, Great Power Security, 10 Chi. J. Int'l L. 35, 42 n.23 (2009).

157. See, e.g., Ronald J. Pestritto, Woodrow Wilson and the Roots of Modern Liberalism (2005); Peri Arnold, Remaking the Presidency: Roosevelt, Taft, and Wilson 1901–16 (2011). For the classic work on Wilson's foreign policy, see Thomas J. Knock, To End All Wars: Woodrow Wilson and the Quest for a New World Order (1992); and for the standard biography on Wilson, see John Milton Cooper, Jr., Woodrow Wilson (2009). See also Lloyd E. Ambrosius, Woodrow Wilson and the American Diplomatic Tradition: The Treaty Fight in Perspective (1987).

158. Akira Iriye, The Globalizing of America, 1913–45, at 72 (1993).

159. Walter A. MacDougall, Promised Land, Crusader State: The American Encounter with the World Since 1776, at 132 (1997).

160. Id.

161. Id. at 136.

162. Id. at 138.

163. Id. at 140.

164. Id. at 141.

165. John A. Thompson, Woodrow Wilson and a World Governed by Evolving Law, 20 J. Pol'y Hist. 113, 116 (2008).

166. Woodrow Wilson, The State: Elements of Historical and Practical Politics 30 (Edward Elliott ed., 1918).

167. MacDougall, supra note 159, at 126.

168. Knock, supra note 157, at 9.

169. Michael C. Desch, America's Liberal Illiberalism: The Ideological Origins of Overreaction in US Foreign Policy, 32 Int'l Sec. 7, 12 (2007/2008).

170. Knock, supra note 157, at 21–22.

171. Id. at 48.

172. Id. at 6–7.

173. Woodrow Wilson, The State, reprinted in 6 Papers of Woodrow Wilson 303–04 (Arthur S. Link et al. eds., 1966) (emphasis in original).

174. Knock, supra note 157, at 52.

175. Id. at 53–54.

176. Id. at 149.

177. Id. at 33.

178. Kurt Wimer, Woodrow Wilson and World Order, in Woodrow Wilson and a Revolutionary World, 1913–1921, at 150–51 (Arthur S. Link ed., 1982).

179. On this point, see Jonathan Zasloff, Law and the Shaping of American Foreign Policy: From the Gilded Age to the New Era, 78 N.Y.U. L. Rev. 239, 286 (2003).

180. Lloyd E. Ambrosius, Wilsonianism: Woodrow Wilson and His Legacy in American Foreign Relations 34 (2002).

181. See Robert Wiebe, The Search for Order 1877–1920 (1967). On the management of World War I mobilization as the expression of progressivism, see David M. Kennedy, Over Here: The First World War and American Society (1980).

182. See, e.g., Lloyd Ambrosius, Woodrow Wilson and the American Diplomatic Tradition: The Treaty Fight in Perspective 173–74, 203–04 (1987).

183. Inis Claude, Swords into Ploughshares: The Problems and Progress of International Organization 54–55 (1984).

184. Paul Kennedy, The Parliament of Man: The Past, Present, and Future of the United Nations 16 (2006).

185. MacDougall, supra note 159, at 151.

186. On the drafting of the Atlantic Charter, see Elizabeth Borgwardt, A New Deal for the World 20–28 (2005). See generally The Atlantic Charter (Douglas Brinkley & David R. Facey-Crowther eds., 1994).

187. Kennedy, supra note 184, at 29–36.

188. Mazower, supra note 150.

189. MacDougall, supra note 159, at 154.

190. Franklin Delano Roosevelt, Fireside Chat 27: On the Tehran and Cairo Conferences (Dec. 24, 1943), available at http://millercenter.org/president/speeches/detail/3333; see also Robert A. Divine, Roosevelt and World War II, at 64–65 (1969).

191. Cf. MacDougall, supra note 159, at 156.

192. Robert Hildebrand, Dumbarton Oaks: The Origins of the United Nations and the Search for Postwar Security 71 (1990).

193. See, e.g., Townsend Hoopes & Douglas Brinkley, FDR and the Creation of the UN 178–79 (1997); Stephen Schlesinger, Act of Creation: The Founding of the United Nations 57–58 (2003).

194. UN Charter art. 42, available at http://www.un.org/en/documents/charter/chapter7.shtml.

195. Id.

196. See, e.g., Ian Brownlie, International Law and the Use of Force by States (1963); Thomas Franck, Recourse to Force: State Action against Threats and Armed Attacks (2004).

197. Marc Trachtenberg, The Iraq Crisis and the Future of the Atlantic Alliance, in The Atlantic Alliance Under Stress 201, 205 (David M. Andrews ed., 2005).

198. Id.

199. 1 Foreign Relations of the United States 1945, at 637, available at http://digicoll.library.wisc.edu/cgi-bin/FRUS/FRUS-idx?type=turn&id=FRUS.FRUS1945v01&entity=FRUS.FRUS1945v01.p0699&q1=637.

200. Id.

201. Id.

202. Id. at 677.

203. Trachtenberg, supra note 197, at 220 (quoting United Kingdom, Foreign Office, A Commentary on the Charter of the United Nations 17 (1945)).

204. Id.

205. There have been a few dissenting voices to the now conventional interpretation of the UN Charter. See, e.g., Julius Stone, Aggression and World Order: A Critique of United

Nations Theories of Aggression (1958); Michael Glennon, Limits of Law, Prerogatives of Power: Interventionism after Kosovo (2003). But they are far outnumbered by the view that the Charter prohibits the use of force other than wars in self-defense or supported by the Security Council. See, e.g., Michael Byers, War Law: Understanding International Law and Armed Conflict (2005); Yoram Dinstein, War, Aggression, and Self-Defense (2011); Christine Gray, International Law and the Use of Force (2002); Mary Ellen O'Connell, International Law and the Use of Force: Cases and Materials (2008).

206. See Henry Kissinger, On China (2011).

CHAPTER 4

1. See, e.g., D.W. Bowett, Self-Defense in International Law 187–92 (1958); Myres S. McDougall & Florentino P. Feliciano, Law and Minimum World Public Order: The Legal Regulation of International Coercion 232–41 (1961); Julius Stone, Aggression and World Order: A Critique of United Nations Theories of Aggression 44 (1958); Antonio Cassese, International Law in a Divided World 230–23 (1986); Yoram Dinstein, War and Aggression 191 (4th ed. 2005); Oscar Schachter, The Right of States to Use Armed Force, 82 Mich. L. Rev. 1620 (1984); Ruth Wedgwood, Responding to Terrorism: The Strikes against bin Laden, 24 Yale J. Int'l L. 559, 564–65 (1999).

2. Daniel Webster, Letter to Henry Fox, British Minister in Washington (Apr 24, 1841), in Kenneth Bourne and D. Cameron Watt eds., 1 British Documents on Foreign Affairs: Reports and Papers from the Foreign Office Confidential Print (Part I, Series C) 153, 159 (University Publications of America 1986).

3. See generally Barbara Tuchman, The Guns of August (1962).

4. Thomas Schelling, The Strategy of Conflict 22–28 (1960). Recent work has extended Schelling's original insight into whether acts that promise future military costs create greater instability than "sunk costs" that have already been spent. See, e.g., James Fearon, Signaling Foreign Policy Interests, 41 J. Conflict Resol. 68 (1997); Branislav Slantchev, Military Coercion in Interstate Crises, 99 Am. Pol. Sci. Rev. 533 (2005).

5. Outside the context of the use of force, the International Court of Justice has recognized that imminence cannot be limited purely to matters of timing. In 1997 the I.C.J. addressed whether Hungary was justified in suspending work on a dam, as agreed to by treaty, because of fears of environmental harm to the Danube River. The court considered whether Hungary's suspension of work was justified by a "state of necessity." The ICJ declared that: "Imminence" is synonymous with "immediacy" or "proximity" and goes far beyond the concept of "possibility." As the International Law Commission [has] emphasized..., the "extremely grave and imminent" peril must "have been a threat to the interest at the actual time." That does not exclude, in the view of the Court, that a "peril" appearing in the long term might be held to be "imminent" as soon as it is established, at the relevant point in time, that the realization of that peril, however far off it might be, is not thereby any less certain and inevitable. Case Concerning the Gabcikovo-Nagymaros Project (Hungary/Slovakia), 1997 I.C.J. 7, 41–42 (September 1997) (quoting International Law Commission, Draft Articles on the Int'l Responsibility of States art. 33) (internal citations omitted). In the end, the I.C.J. found that the threats were not in fact imminent, because Hungary only identified uncertain dangers.

6. See, e.g., Paul H. Robinson, 2 Criminal Law Defenses 131(c)(1) (1984).

7. See, e.g., Clare Dalton & Elizabeth M. Schneider, Battered Women and the Law 716–93 (2001).

8. The criminal law of self-defense, for example, has changed its conception of necessity from using force to defend one's honor to self-defense as a mechanistic, unwilling response to attack. See Dan M. Kahan, The Secret Ambition of Deterrence, 113 Harv. L. Rev. 413, 431–35 (1999) (discussing Justice Holmes's reconceptualization of the "true man" doctrine from one in which the law condoned the use of force to protect an interest in honor to one in which the use of force was thought of as a reflexive act of necessity). Criminal law has also changed its conception of what can be defended with deadly force. In New York, an individual may legally use deadly force not just for self-preservation but also to prevent kidnapping, forcible rape, forcible sodomy, or robbery. N.Y. Penal Law § 35.15 (1998); People v. Goetz, 68 N.Y.2d 96, 497 N.E.2d 41 (1986). This is consistent with the thinking of John Locke, who also believed that force could be used to kill thieves as well as to engage in self-preservation. Locke believed that allowing a thief to steal property was akin to allowing him to place a person within his total control, and that this deprivation of freedom was enough to trigger a right of self-defense. See John Locke, The Second Treatise of Government §§ 16–18, in Two Treatises of Government 265, 278–80 (Peter Laslett ed., 1988). See also the helpful discussion in Jeremy Waldron, Self-Defense: Agent-Neutral and Agent-Relative Accounts, 88 Calif. L. Rev. 711, 733–45 (2000) (exploring Locke's position on self-defense).

9. See Schenck v. United States, 249 U.S. 47, 52 (1919) (Holmes, J.).

10. Richard A. Posner, Frontiers of Legal Theory 64 (2001); see also Daniel A. Farber, Free Speech without Romance: Public Choice and the First Amendment, 105 Harv. L. Rev. 554 (1991) (also taking an economic approach to First Amendment Issues).

11. Posner, supra note 10, at 64–65.

12. Legality of the Threat or Use of Nuclear Weapons in Armed Conflict, 1996 I.C.J. 226, 244 (July 8, 1996) (advisory opinion).

13. See generally Julian G. Ku & John Yoo, Taming Globalization: International Law, the Constitution, and the New World Order (2012).

14. Myres McDougal, The Soviet-Cuban Quarantine and Self-Defense, 57 Am. J. Int'l L. 597, 598 (1963).

15. See, e.g., Oceans Law and Policy Department, Naval War College, Annotated Supplement to the Commander's Handbook on the Law of Naval Operations 4–13 § 4.3.2.1 n.32 (1997).

16. See, e.g., United States v. Carroll Towing Co., 159 F.2d 169, 173 (2d. Cir. 1947). For basic discussions of the Learned Hand formula, see William M. Landes & Richard A. Posner, The Positive Economic Theory of Tort Law, 15 Ga. L. Rev. 851, 868–72 (1981); Richard A. Posner, A Theory of Negligence, 1 J. Legal Stud. 29 (1972).

17. For philosophical attempts to wrestle with the difficulties of the concept of proportionality and self-defense, see Jeff McMahan, Killing in War 19–32 (2009); David Rodin, War and Self-Defense 43–48 (2002).

18. Compare McDougal, supra note 14, at 601–03 (quarantine was in accord with notions of self-defense), with Abram Chayes, The Legal Case for US Action on Cuba, 47 Dep't State Bull. 763, 764–65 (1962) (arguing that quarantine was legal but not undertaken under right to use force for self-defense); Quincy Wright, The Cuban Quarantine, 57 Am. J. Int'l L. 546, 563–64 (1963) (suggesting that quarantine was not a lawful act of self-defense against an armed attack).

19. John F. Kennedy, Radio and Television Report to the American People on the Soviet Arms Buildup in Cuba (Oct. 22, 1962), reprinted in Public Papers of President Kennedy 1962, 806, 806–07.

20. Id. at 807.

21. The classic early works on the Cuban Missile Crisis include Robert F. Kennedy, Thirteen Days: A Memoir of the Cuban Missile Crisis (1969); Graham Allison, Essence of Decision: Explaining the Cuban Missile Crisis (1971). The recent release of taped Oval Office meetings during the crisis has provided a deeper understanding of the Kennedy administration's management of the confrontation. See Ernest R. May & Philip Zelikow eds., The Kennedy Tapes: Inside the White House During the Cuban Missile Crisis (2002).

22. On this point, two scholars with different approaches to international law and institutions agree. See, e.g., Abram Chayes, The Cuban Missile Crisis: International Crisis and the Role of Law (1974); Eugene V. Rostow, Until What? Enforcement Action or Collective Self-Defense?, 85 Am. J. Int'l L. 506, 515 (1991). Other scholars argue that the United States had no self-defense justification under the UN Charter. See, e.g., L.C. Green, The Contemporary Law of Armed Conflict 179 (2d. ed. 2000); Quincy Wright, The Cuban Quarantine, 57 Am. J. Int'l L. 546, 548–63 (1963).

23. Norbert A. Schlei, Memorandum to the Attorney General re: Legality under International Law of Remedial Action against Use of Cuba as a Missile Base by the Soviet Union (Aug. 30, 1962), reprinted in 6 Green Bag 2d. 195, 195–96 (2003).

24. See Thomas M. Franck, When, if Ever, May States Deploy Military Force without Prior Security Council Authorization?, 5 Wash. U. J.L. & Pol'y 51, 59 (2001) (characterizing a claim to impose a naval quarantine as anticipatory self-defense); Rostow, supra note 22, at 515 ("Although President Kennedy spoke of the United States action as one of self-defense, his State Department, in presenting the case to the Security Council, the OAS, and the public, sought to justify the American use of force in Cuba primarily under the Rio Treaty and the action of the Organization of American States pursuant to that Treaty. This legal argument is untenable.... The only possible legal basis for the action taken by the United States in the Cuban missile crisis was therefore its 'inherent' right of self-defense, reaffirmed by Article 51 of the Charter.").

25. See, e.g., Adrian Vermeule, Interpretive Choice, 75 N.Y.U. L. Rev. 74, 91 n.68 (2000) (collecting sources); Cass R. Sunstein, Problems with Rules, 83 Calif. L. Rev. 953 (1995); Louis Kaplow, Rules versus Standards: An Economic Analysis, 42 Duke L.J. 557 (1992); Richard A. Epstein, Simple Rules for a Complex World 30–36 (1995).

26. See Vermeule, supra note 25, at 91.

27. Winston Churchill, My Early Life: A Roving Commission 246 (1930).

28. See Marc Trachtenberg, History and Strategy 235–60 (1991).

29. See Timothy L.H. McCormack, Self-Defense in International Law: The Israeli Raid on the Iraqi Nuclear Reactor 297–302 (1996); Anthony D'Amato, Israel's Air Strike against the Osiraq Reactor: A Retrospective, 10 Temple Int'l & Comp. L.J. 259, 262–63 (1996); W. Thomas Mallison & Sally V. Mallison, The Israeli Aerial Attack of June 7, 1981, Upon the Iraqi Nuclear Reactor: Aggression or Self-Defense?, 15 Vand. J. Transnat'l L. 417, 431–33, 444 (1982).

30. S.C. Res. 487, UN SCOR, U.N. Doc. S/RES/487 (June 19, 1981).

31. Statement by the Representative at the United Nations (Kirkpatrick) before the UN Security Council (June 19, 1981), in U.S. Department of State, American Foreign Policy Current Documents 1981, at 689, 690 (1984).

32. UN SCOR, 2288th Meeting, U.N. Doc. S/PV.2288, ¶ 80 (June 19, 1981).

33. UN SCOR, 2674th Meeting, U.N. Doc. S/PV.2674, at 17 (Apr. 15, 1986) (statement of Vernon Walters, U.S. permanent representative to the UN). See also Ronald Reagan, Address to the Nation on the United States Airstrike against Libya (Apr. 14, 1986), in 1 Public Papers of the Presidents of the United States: Ronald Reagan 1986, at 468, 469 (1988).

34. Ronald Reagan, Letter to the Speaker of the House of Representatives and the President Pro Tempore of the Senate of the United States on the United States Air Strike on Libya (Apr. 16, 1986), in 1 id., at 478.

35. Id.

36. See George Bush, Address to the Nation Announcing United States Military Action in Panama (Dec. 20, 1989), in 2 Public Papers of the Presidents of the United States: George Bush 1989, at 1722, 1723 (1990); George Bush, Letter to the Speaker of the House of Representatives and the President Pro Tempore of the Senate on United States Military Action in Panama (Dec. 21, 1989), in 2 id., at 1734.

37. Protection of Nationals–Deployment of US Forces to Panama, U.S. Digest ch. 14, § 1, reprinted in Marian Nash Leich, Contemporary Practice of the United States Relating to International Law, 84 Am. J. Int'l L. 545, 548 (1990). The United States also justified its actions as self-defense resulting from the armed attacks against U.S. citizens. See U.N. Doc. S/21035 (Dec. 20, 1989) (letter from Thomas R. Pickering, U.S. Permanent Representative to the United Nations) (promising to "use only the force necessary to assure the safety of Americans.").

38. Compare Abraham D. Sofaer, The Legality of the United States Action in Panama, 29 Colum. J. Transnat'l L. 281, 290 (1991) (concluding that ousting Noriega was the only way to "end the attacks on US nationals"), with Louis Henkin, The Invasion of Panama under International Law: A Gross Violation, 29 Colum. J. Transnat'l L. 293, 312–13 (1991) (concluding that invasion "was a clear violation of international law."); Ruth Wedgwood, The Use of Armed Force in International Affairs: Self-Defense and the Panama Invasion, 29 Colum. J. Transnat'l L. 609 (1991) (lack of attempt to protect Americans other than through invasion undermined legal justification of self-defense); Tom J. Farer, Panama: Beyond the Charter Paradigm, 84 Am. J. Int'l L. 503 (1990) (neither the UN Charter nor any other international legal text or agreement recognizes a legal right of invasion to protect nationals); Ved P. Nanda, The Validity of United States Intervention in Panama Under International Law, 84 Am. J. Int'l L. 494 (1990) (invasion of Panama cannot be defended as legal under UN Charter, OAS Charter, or principles of customary international law).

39. See William J. Clinton, Letter to Congressional Leaders on the Strike on Iraqi Intelligence Headquarters (June 28, 1993), in 1 Public Papers of the Presidents of the United States: William J. Clinton 1993, at 940, 940–41 (1994).

40. William J. Clinton, Letter to Congressional Leaders Reporting on Military Action against Terrorist Sites in Afghanistan and Sudan (Aug. 21, 1998), in 2 Public Papers of the Presidents of the United States: William J. Clinton 1998, at 1464 (2000). See also William J. Clinton, Remarks in Martha's Vineyard, Massachusetts on Military Action against Terrorist Sites in Afghanistan and Sudan (Aug. 20, 1998), in id., at 1460 (noting the existence of "compelling information" that the terrorists were planning more attacks against U.S. citizens and that the groups affiliated with bin Laden were seeking chemical and other dangerous weapons).

41. Wedgwood, supra note 1, at 565.

42. For a discussion of the legality of the U.S. strikes, compare id. at 564 (concluding that the attacks were justified), with Jules Lobel, The Use of Force to Respond to Terrorist Attacks: The Bombing of Sudan and Afghanistan, 24 Yale J. Int'l L. 537, 557 (1999) (concluding that the attacks "represent the assertion of imperial might and arrogance in opposition to international law.").

43. George Shultz, Low-Intensity Warfare: The Challenge of Ambiguity, 86 Dep't State Bull. 15, 17 (Mar. 1986).

44. Id.

45. See Abraham D. Sofaer, Terrorism, the Law and the National Defense, 126 Mil. L. Rev. 89, 116–21 (1989); W. Hays Parks, Memorandum of Law: Executive Order 12333 and Assassination, Army Lawyer 4, 7–8 (Dec. 1989).

46. S.C. Res. 1441, U.N. Doc. S/Res/1441 (2002).

47. See, e.g., John Yoo, International Law and the War in Iraq, 97 Am. J. Int'l L. 563 (2003).

48. Commission on the Intelligence Capabilities of the United States Regarding Weapons of Mass Destruction, Report to the President of the United States 3 (2005), available at http://www.gpoaccess.gov/wmd/pdf/full_wmd_report.pdf.

CHAPTER 5

1. John Stuart Mill, The Contest in America 31 (1862).

2. See George P. Fletcher & Jens D. Ohlin, Defending Humanity 5–29 (2008).

3. Id. at 6.

4. Id. at 13.

5. See George P. Fletcher, Rethinking Criminal Law 811 (2000).

6. George P. Fletcher, Basic Concepts of Criminal Law 134 (1998).

7. Model Penal Code § 3.04 (1985).

8. Fletcher, Basic Concepts, supra note 6, at 134–35.

9. See, e.g., id. at 134.

10. David Rodin, War and Self-Defense 118 (2002).

11. Hugo Grotius, The Rights of War and Peace, bk. 22, ch. I, ¶ III (1625).

12. Id. ¶ XVI.

13. Emmerich de Vattel, The Law of Nations, bk. 2, ch. 4 (1758).

14. See Santa Clara Cnty. v. S. Pac. R.R. Co., 118 U.S. 394 (1886).

15. See, e.g., Posadas de Puerto Rico Assocs. v. Tourism Co. of Puerto Rico, 478 U.S. 328 (1986).

16. Citizens United v. Fed. Election Comm'n, 558 U.S. 310 (2010).

17. See, e.g., Republic of Austria v. Altmann, 541 U.S. 677 (2004) (retroactivity of Foreign Sovereign Immunities Act); Alden v. Maine, 527 U.S. 706 (1999) (state sovereign immunity).

18. David Luban, Just War and Human Rights, 9 Phil. & Pub. Aff. 160, 166 (1980); Thomas Nagel, Mortal Questions 64 (1979).

19. Michael Walzer, Just and Unjust Wars 41 (1977).

20. John Rawls, A Theory of Justice 98 (1972).

21. Thomas Nagle, War and Massacre, in War and Moral Responsibility 3 (Marshall Cohen et al. eds., 1974).

22. Jeff McMahan, Killing in War 6 (2009).

23. Fletcher & Ohlin, supra note 2, at 20.

24. See generally Ingrid Detter, The Law of War (2d ed. 2000); L.C. Green, The Contemporary Law of Armed Conflict (2000).

25. See George P. Fletcher, Basic Concepts of Criminal Law 134 (1998).

26. Fletcher, Rethinking Criminal Law, supra note 5, at 867.

27. United States v. Peterson, 483 F.2d 1222, 1229 (D.C. Cir. 1973).

28. For critical analysis, see Alex J. Bellamy & Paul D. Williams, Providing Peacekeepers: The Politics, Challenges, and Future of United Nations Peacekeeping Contributions (2013); Virginia Page Fortna, Does Peacekeeping Work?: Shaping Belligerents' Choices after Civil War (2008); Dennis Jett, Why Peacekeeping Fails (2001); William Shawcross, Deliver Us from Evil: Peacekeepers, Warlords, and a World of Endless Conflict (2000).

29. Thomas Franck, Recourse to Force: State Action against Threats and Armed Attacks 98 (2004).

30. Id.

31. See Antonio Cassese, Return to Westphalia?: Considerations on the Gradual Erosion of the Charter System 515–16 (1986).

32. Chaim D. Kaufman & Robert A. Pape, Explaining Costly International Moral Action: Britain's Sixty-Year Campaign against the Atlantic Slave Trade, 53 Int'l Org. 631 (1999).

33. S.C. Res. 1674, U.N. SCOR, 5430th Meeting, ¶ 4, U.N. Doc. S/RES/1674 (April 28, 2006).

34. Central Intelligence Agency, World Factbook, Korea, South, https://www.cia.gov/library/publications/the-world-factbook/geos/ks.html (last updated Oct. 31, 2013).

35. Central Intelligence Agency, World Factbook, Korea, North, https://www.cia.gov/library/publications/the-world-factbook/geos/kn.html (last updated Oct. 28, 2013).

36. See generally Joseph S. Nye, Jr., The Paradox of American Power: Why the World's Only Superpower Can't Go It Alone 137–71 (2002); Global Public Goods: International Cooperation in the 21st Century (Inge Kaul, Isabelle Grunberg & Marc A. Stern eds., 1999); Todd Sandier, Global Challenges: An Approach to Environmental, Political, and Economic Problems (1997); Charles P Kindleberger, International Public Goods without International Government, 76 Am. Econ. Rev. 1 (1986); Robert O. Keohane, After Hegemony: Cooperation and Discord in the World Political Economy 49–64, 107–08 (1984).

37. A classic explanation can be found in Mancur Olson, Jr., The Logic of Collective Action: Public Goods and the Theory of Groups 13–16 (1965).

38. See Robert Cooter & Thomas Ulen, Law and Economics 42 (3d ed. 2000) (defining public goods).

39. See, for example, Daniel A. Farber & Philip P. Frickey, Law and Public Choice: A Critical Introduction 23–24 (1991) (discussing collective action problems); Cooter & Ulen, supra note 38, at 42 (assessing the effect of public goods and free-riders on the political process).

40. See generally Andrew Guzman, How International Law Works (2003); see also Kal Raustiala, The Architecture of International Cooperation: Transgovernmental Networks and the Future of International Law, 43 Va. J. Int'l L. 1, 27 (2002); David P. Fidler, A Globalized Theory of Public Health Law, 30 J. L. Med. & Ethics 150, 156 (2002); Jonathan B. Wiener, Something Borrowed for Something Blue: Legal Transplants and the Evolution of Global Environmental Law, 27 Ecology L.Q. 1295, 1298 (2001).

41. See Mancur Olson, Jr., & Richard Zeckhauser, An Economic Theory of Alliances, 48 Rev. Econ. & Stats. 266, 278 (1966).

42. Joseph S. Nye, Jr., The American National Interest and Global Public Goods, 78 Int'l Aff. 233, 243 (2002).

43. Olson, Jr. & Zeckhauser, supra note 41, at 269.

44. See Olson, Jr., supra note 37, at 132–67; Robert D. Cooter, The Strategic Constitution 151–54 (2000).

45. The Federalist No. 78, at 524 (Alexander Hamilton) (Jacob E. Cooke ed., 1961).

46. Franck, supra note 29, at 167–68 (quoting Russian Ambassador Sergei Lavrov).

47. S.C. Res. 1244, U.N. SCOR, U.N. Doc. S/RES/1244, at 7 (1999).

48. Franck, supra note 29, at 54.

49. S.C. Res. 1368, U.N. SCOR, U.N. Doc. S/RES/1368 (2001).

50. See, e.g., William H. Taft IV & Todd F. Buchwald, Preemption, Iraq, and International Law, 97 Am. J. Int'l L. 557 (2003); John Yoo, International Law and the War in Iraq, 97 Am. J. Int'l L. 563 (2003); Ruth Wedgwood, The Fall of Saddam Hussein: Security Council Mandates and Preemptive Self-Defense, 97 Am. J. Int'l L. 576 (2003).

51. S.C. Res. 1483, U.N. SCOR, U.N. Doc. S/RES/1483, at 2 (2003) (recognizing the "authorities, responsibilities, and obligations" under international law of the United States and the United Kingdom as "occupying powers"); S.C. Res. 1500, U.N. SCOR, U.N. Doc. S/RES/1500, at 2 (2003) (establishing the United Nations Assistance Mission for Iraq); S.C. Res. 1511, U.N. SCOR, U.N. Doc. S/RES/1511 4 (2003) (recognizing the authority of the Iraqi Governing Council).

52. See, e.g., Scott Sagan & Kenneth Waltz, The Spread of Nuclear Weapons: An Enduring Debate (3rd ed. 2012).

53. The level of civilian Iraq casualties remains a controversial issue. See, e.g., Costs of War, http://costsofwar.org/article/iraqi-civilians (Brown University researchers estimate 123,000–134,000 civilians killed); Gilbert Burnham et al., Mortality after the 2003 Invasion of Iraq: A Cross-Sectional Cluster Sample Survey, 368 The Lancet 1421 (Oct. 21, 2006), available at http://brusselstribunal.org/pdf/lancet111006.pdf (Johns Hopkins researchers estimate 601,027 civilian casualties as of 2006).

54. Amy Belasco, Cong. Research Serv., RL33110, The Costs of Iraq, Afghanistan, and other Global War on Terror Operations Since 9/11 (Mar. 29, 2011), available at http://www.fas.org/sgp/crs/natsec/RL33110.pdf.

55. See, e.g., Charles P. Kindleberger, The World in Depression, 1929–1939, at 11, 289 (2d ed. 1986); Charles P. Kindleberger, Dominance and Leadership in the International Economy: Exploitation, Public Goods, and Free Rides, 25 Int'l Stud. Q. 242, 253 (1981). See also Robert Gilpin, War and Change in World Politics 231–34 (1981).

56. See, e.g., Robert Keohane, supra note 36, at 31–46; Duncan Snidal, The Limits of Hegemonic Stability Theory, 39 Int'l Org. 579, 614 (1985).

57. Compare Andrew Guzman, How International Law Works (2008), with Jack Goldsmith & Eric Posner, The Limits of International Law (2005).

58. See Thomas W. Pogge, An Egalitarian Law of Peoples, 23 Phil. & Pub. Aff. 195, 223 (1994) (suggesting that those in developed nations do care about the victims of tragedy in other countries); Amartya Sen, Humanity and Citizenship, in War and Moral Responsibility 111, 117 (Marshall Cohen et al. eds., 1974) (suggesting that harming someone for whom one has affection is equivalent to harming the person who holds that affection); Charles Jones, Patriotism, Morality, and Global Justice, in Nomos XLI: Global Justice 125, 142 (Ian Shapiro & Lea Brilmayer eds.,

1999) (suggesting that there is a "duty to concern [one]self with the safety and rights of … victims, even when those victims were noncompatriots.").

59. See generally Hans Morgenthau, Politics Among Nations (1948); George Kennan, American Diplomacy, 1900–1950 (1951).

CHAPTER 6

1. See John Yoo, International Law and the War in Iraq, 97 Am. J. Int'l L. 563 (2003) (discussing events leading up to invasion of Iraq).

2. See, e.g., Independent Inquiry into the United Nations Oil-for-Food Programme, The Management of the United Nations Oil-for-Food Programme, Volume I: The Report of the Committee (Sept. 7, 2005), available at http://news.bbc.co.uk/2/shared/bsp/hi/pdfs/08_09_05_volume1.pdf; Independent Inquiry into the United Nations Oil-for-Food Programme, The Management of the United Nations Oil-for-Food Programme, Report on Programme Manipulation (Oct. 27, 2005), available at http://news.bbc.co.uk/2/shared/bsp/hi/pdfs/27_10_05_summary.pdf.

3. U.S. Institute of Peace, American Interests and UN Reform: Report of the Task Force on the United Nations 35–36 (2005).

4. Kofi Annan, Op-Ed., Our Mission Remains Vital, Wall St. J., Feb. 22, 2005, http://online.wsj.com/article/0,,SB110903523113160474,00.html.

5. For a general indictment of the United Nations, see Joshua Muravchik, The Future of the United Nations: Understanding the Past to Chart a Way Forward 17–72 (2005). For more hopeful outlooks on the UN, see, e.g., Paul Kennedy, The Parliament of Man: The Past, Present, and Future of the United Nations (2006); Mary Ann Glendon, A World Made New: Eleanor Roosevelt and the Universal Declaration of Human Rights (2001).

6. Harold Hongju Koh, Op-Ed., A Better Way To Deal With Iraq, Hartford Courant, (Oct. 20, 2002), http://articles.courant.com/2002-10-20/news/0210200607_1_united-nations-authorization-iraq-mideast-peace-process.

7. See CBS News, Interview with Hillary Clinton, Secretary of State, in Washington, D.C. (Mar. 8, 2011), available at http://www.cbsnews.com/2100-500202_162-20040981.html. (Secretary Clinton: "[W]e believe it's important that [intervention in Libya] not be an American, or a NATO, or a European effort. It needs to be an international one…. The British and French governments are going to the United Nations with a draft resolution that would authorize international action. I think it's very important that there be a UN decision on whatever might be done."); see also NPR Interview with Bob Woodward, Associate Editor, Washington Post, in Washington, D.C. (Mar. 22, 2011), available at http://www.npr.org/2011/03/22/134768734/Sussing-Out-An-Emerging-Obama-Doctrine. (Neal Conan: "[I]n contrast to his predecessor, [Obama] waited for the Arab League to call for a no-fly zone in Libya and followed the lead of France and Britain to get approval from the United Nations Security Council.").

8. Hearing to Receive Testimony on the Situation in Syria Before the S. Comm. on Armed Servs., 112th Cong. (2012) (statement of Leon Panetta, Sec'y of Def.), available at http://www.armed-services.senate.gov/imo/media/doc/12-07%20-%203-7-12.pdf.

9. See, e.g., W. Michael Reisman, Acting Before Victims Become Victims: Preventing and Arresting Mass Murder, 40 Case W. Res. J. Int'l L. 57 (2008). For a recent survey of various views, see Conor Foley, The Thin Blue Line: How Humanitarianism Went to War 150–59 (2008).

10. S.C. Res. 1674, U.N. Doc. S/RES/1674 (2006).

11. See United Nations, Report of the Secretary-General, In Larger Freedom: Towards Development, Security and Human Rights for All, U.N. Doc. A/59/2005, at 33, ¶¶ 124–126 (2005).

12. Id. ¶ 122.

13. Id. ¶ 124.

14. Id. ¶ 125.

15. United Nations, Report of the High-Level Panel on Threats, Challenges, and Change, A More Secure World: Our Shared Responsibility, U.N. Doc. A/59/565, at 63 (Dec. 2, 2004), available at http://daccess-dds-ny.un.org/doc/UNDOC/GEN/N04/602/31/PDF/N0460231.pdf.

16. Id. at 66.

17. In Larger Freedom, supra note 11, ¶ 126.

18. A More Secure World, supra note 15, at 67.

19. David Caron, The Legitimacy of the Security Council, 87 Am. J. Int'l L. 552, 573 (1993); Thomas G. Weiss, The Illusion of UN Security Council Reform, Wash. Q. 147, 149 (Autumn 2003).

20. Michael J. Glennon, The UN Security Council in a Unipolar World, 44 Va. J. Int'l L. 91, 94–95 (2004).

21. Weiss, The Illusion of UN Security Council Reform, supra note 19, at 153, 156.

22. Thomas M. Franck, The Use of Force in International Law, 11 Tul. J. Int'l & Comp. L. 7, 17 (2003).

23. Anne-Marie Slaughter, Op-Ed., The Will to Make it Work, Wash. Post, Mar. 2, 2003.

24. See, e.g., Jeffrey Mankoff, Russian Foreign Policy: The Return of Great Power Politics 107–08 (2009) (Russia); Jon B. Alterman & John W. Garver, The Vital Triangle: China, the United States, and the Middle East 29–30 (2008) (China); Jack Covarrubias & Tom Lansford, Strategic Interests in the Middle East 39–40 (2007) (France).

25. S.C. Res. 1441, UN SCOR, 57th Sess., 4644th mtg., U.N. Doc. S/RES/1441 (Nov. 8, 2002), available at http://daccess-dds-ny.un.org/doc/UNDOC/GEN/N02/682/26/PDF/N0268226.pdf.

26. Michael Doyle, Striking First: Preemption and Prevention in International Conflict (2008); Jack S. Levy, Preventive War and Democratic Politics, 52 Int'l Stud. Q. 1, 4 (2008); Colin S. Gray, The Implications of Preemptive and Preventive War Doctrine 9–13 (2007); W. Michael Reisman & Andrea Armstrong, The Past and Future of the Claim of Preemptive Self-Defense, 100 Am. J. Int'l L. 525, 526 (2006).

27. Winston S. Churchill, The Second World War: The Gathering Storm 320 (1948).

28. The National Security Strategy of the United States of America 14–15 (2002), available at http://www.state.gov/documents/organization/63562.pdf.

29. Dan Reiter, Preventive War and Its Alternatives: The Lessons of History 2 (2006). See also Phillip Bobbitt, Terror and Consent: The Wars for the Twenty-First Century 433–37 (2008); Doyle, supra note 26, at 25–29; Robert Jervis, Why the Bush Doctrine Cannot Be Sustained, 120 Pol. Sci. Q. 351 (2005).

30. Walter MacDougall, Promised Land, Crusader State: The American Encounter with the World Since 1776, at 213 (1997).

31. Hugo Slim, Killing Civilians: Method, Madness, and Morality in War 20 (2008).

32. Concerns such as these appear to underlie the UN General Assembly's 2005 call for rigid adherence to the Charter's use-of-force rules. See G.A. Res. 60/1, ¶¶ 77–80, 138–39, U.N. Doc. A/RES/60/1 (Oct. 24, 2005).

33. See generally Jeremy Rabkin, Law without Nations?: Why Constitutional Government Requires Sovereign States (2005).

34. George C. Herring, From Colony to Superpower: U.S. Foreign Relations Since 1776, at 948 (2008).

35. John G. Stoessinger, Why Nations Go to War 311 (2005).

36. Arthur Schlesinger, Jr., Commentary, The Immorality of Preventative War, L.A. Times, Aug. 15, 2002, at B15.

37. John Lewis Gaddis, Surprise, Security, and the American Experience 16–22 (2005).

38. Marc Trachtenberg, Preventive War and US Foreign Policy, in Preemption: Military Action and Moral Justification 40, 66 (Henry Shue & David Rodin eds., 2007).

39. Hew Strachan, Preemption and Prevention in Historical Perspective, in Preemption: Military Action and Moral Justification 23, 23 (Henry Shue & David Rodin eds., 2007).

40. Gray, supra note 26, at 23–27.

41. Trachtenberg, supra note 38, at 60–61; see also Robert J. Delahunty, Paper Charter: Self-Defense and the Failure of the United Nations Collective Security System, 56 Cath. U. L. Rev. 871, 912–13 (2007).

42. Gray, supra note 26, at 23; Strachan, supra note 39, at 23.

43. Gray, supra note 26, at 25.

44. See Daniel Walker How, What Hath God Wrought: The Transformation of America, 1815–1848, at 731–91 (2007).

45. Gray, supra note 26, at 26.

46. See Levy, supra note 26, at 18.

47. See, e.g., Robert A. Pape, Empire Falls, Nat'l Interest, Jan. 22, 2009, http://www.nationalinterest.org/Article.aspx?id=20484.

48. See Paul K. MacDonald & Joseph M. Parent, Graceful Decline? The Surprising Success of Great Power Retrenchment, 35 Int'l Sec. 7 (2011). Randall L. Schweller, Unanswered Threats: Political Constraints on the Balance of Power 22–23 (2006) ("[T]he nature and success of the established powers' responses to rising powers has varied not only from one historical epoch to another but on a case-by-case basis within the same era"); Douglas Lemke, Investigating the Preventive Motive for War, 29 Int'l Interactions 273, 288 (2003) ("[T]he preventive motive is not statistically linked to the probability of war…. Is war the only preventive option states might have in the face of relative decline? Almost certainly not.").

49. See Walter Russell Mead, God and Gold: Britain, America, and the Making of the Modern World 346–56 (2007).

50. See, e.g., Andrew J. Bacevich, The Limits of Power: The End of American Exceptionalism (2008); Chalmers Johnson, The Sorrows of Empire: Militarism, Secrecy, and the End of the Republic (2004).

51. See, e.g., Int'l Comm'n on Intervention & State Sovereignty, The Responsibility to Protect § 4.16 (2001), http://responsibilitytoprotect.org/ICISS%20Report.pdf.

52. See, e.g., Christopher Greenwood, Essays on War in International Law 16 (2007). On the difficulties of defining proportionality, see, e.g., Thomas M. Franck, On Proportionality of Countermeasures in International Law, 102 Am. J. Int'l L. 715, 719–34 (2008) (surveying

international law relating to proportionality as a requirement of *jus ad bellum*); id. at 734 (noting that international law "has not as yet generated a textured, mature jurisprudence conducive to the credible weighing of a military wrong against concomitant countermeasures.").

53. Paul M. Kennedy, The Parliament of Man: The Past, Present, and Future of the United Nations (2006).

54. See John Mearsheimer, The Tragedy of Great Power Politics 3 (2001).

55. Id. at 336. See also Edward Vose Gulick, Europe's Classical Balance of Power: A Case History of the Theory and Practice of One of the Great Concepts of European Statecraft 9 (1955).

56. For a survey of the writing by international relations scholars on the Concert of Europe and an independent evaluation of its effectiveness, see Dan Lindley, Promoting Peace with Information: Transparency as a Tool of Security Regimes 55–85 (2007).

57. Eugen Weber, The Hollow Years: France in the 1930s, at 11 (1994).

58. Although generally not exposed to the hazards of the front, civilians as well as combatants suffered fearfully from the war. One of the main causes of such suffering was the (questionably legal) British naval blockade of Germany. One calculation finds that the British blockade was responsible for 726,766 deaths in Germany between 1915 and 1918. Michael Glover, The Velvet Glove: The Decline and Fall of Moderation in War 125 (1982).

59. For a searching account of the Wilsonian vision and its aversion to the use of a "balance of power" to maintain peace, see Philip Bobbitt, The Shield of Achilles: War, Peace, and the Course of History 359–60 (2002). Bobbitt argues that the concepts of "collective security" and "balance of power" are not inherently incompatible, but that the underlying predicates of the Wilsonian vision—the nationality principle and democratic self-governance—create a contradiction between the two.

60. Emily O. Goldman, Sunken Treaties: Naval Arms Control Between the Wars 8–17 (1994).

61. See Marc Trachtenberg, Versailles Revisited, 9 Sec. Stud. 191, 198–99, 201 (Spring 2000), reviewing Manfred Boemeke, Gerald Feldman, and Elisabeth Glaser, The Treaty of Versailles: A Reassessment after 75 Years (1998).

62. See id. at 197–98.

63. See Mearsheimer, The False Promise of International Institutions, 13 Int'l Sec. 3 (1994); Sebastian Rosato, Europe's Troubles: Power Politics and the State of the European Project, 35 Int'l Sec. 45 (2011).

64. Walter Russell Mead, God and Gold: Britain, America, and the Making of the Modern World 355 (2007).

65. See generally Steven E. Lobell, Britain's Paradox: Cooperation or Punishment Prior to World War I, 27 Rev. Int'l Stud. 169 (2001) (analyzing Britain's readiness to accommodate U.S. rise to global power in pre-World War I period); see also William R. Thompson, The Evolution of Great Power Rivalry: The Anglo-American Case, in Great Power Rivalries 201, 208–16 (William R. Thompson ed., 1999) (surveying possible causes of end of Anglo-American rivalry before World War I). For a suggestive analysis of nineteenth-century British decline and its implications for the United States, see Aaron L. Friedberg, The Weary Titan: Britain and the Experience of Relative Decline, 1895–1905 (1988).

66. See Guide to International Relations and Diplomacy 130–32 (Michael Graham Fry, Erik Goldstein & Richard Langhorne eds., 2002). See generally G.D. Clayton, Britain and the Eastern Question: Missolonghi to Gallipoli (1971).

67. Michael W. Doyle, Ways of War and Peace: Realism, Liberalism, and Socialism 168 (1997).

68. Paul W. Schroeder, Did the Vienna Settlement Rest on a Balance of Power?, 97 Am. Hist. Rev. 683, 698 (1992). See also id at 699–702; Paul W. Schroeder, The 19th-Century International System: Changes in the Structure, 39 World Pol. 1, 12–13 (1986).

69. See., e.g., Robert Jervis, A Political Science Perspective on the Balance of Power and the Concert, 97 Am. Hist. Rev. 716, 720–22 (1992) (commenting on Schroeder).

70. See generally Arthur M. Weisburd, Use of Force: The Practice of States Since 1945 (1997).

CHAPTER 7

1. Amy Belasco, Cong. Research Serv., R40682, Troop Levels in the Afghan and Iraq Wars, FY2001–FY2012: Cost and Other Potential Issues (July 2, 2009).

2. UK Ministry of Defence, UK Forces: Operations in Afghanistan, available at https://www.gov.uk/uk-forces-operations-in-afghanistan (British troop levels in Afghanistan); UK Ministry of Defence, Operations in Iraq: Facts and Figures, http://webarchive.nationalarchives.gov.uk/20121212174735/http://www.mod.uk/DefenceInternet/FactSheets/OperationsFactsheets/OperationsInIraqFactsandFigures.htm (British troop levels in Iraq).

3. See, e.g., Louis Henkin, The Use of Force: Law and U.S. Policy, in Right v. Might: International Law and the Use of Force 60 (Louis Henkin et al. eds., 1991). See also Thomas M. Franck, Recourse to Force: State Action against Threats of Armed Attacks (2002); Ian Brownlie, International Law and the Use of Force by States (1963).

4. See UN Charter art. 2, para. 4 ("All Members shall refrain in their international relations from the threat or use of force against the territorial integrity or political independence of any state...."); See also Fernando R. Teson, Humanitarian Intervention: An Inquiry into Law and Morality (1997); Sean Murphy, Humanitarian Intervention: The United Nations in an Evolving World Order (1996); Christopher Greenwood, Humanitarian Intervention: The Case of Kosovo, 1999 Finnish Y.B. Int'l L. 141 (2002).

5. See Alberto Alesina & Enrico Spolaore, The Size of Nations (2003).

6. Gerald B. Helman & Steven R. Ratner, Saving Failed States, 89 Foreign Pol'y 3 (1992–93).

7. See, e.g., Robert I. Rotberg, The Failure and Collapse of Nation-States: Breakdown, Prevention, and Repair, in When States Fail: Causes and Consequences 1 (Robert I. Rotberg ed., 2004); Stuart E. Eizenstat et al., Rebuilding Weak States, 84 Foreign Aff. 134, 136–37 (2005); Daniel Thurer, The "Failed State" and International Law, 81 Int'l Rev. Red Cross 731 (1999).

8. Robert I. Rotberg, The New Nature of Nation-State Failure, 52 Wash. Q. 85, 86 (2002). See also James D. Fearon, Why Do Some Civil Wars Last so Much Longer Than Others?, 41 Int'l Org. 275 (2004).

9. International Development Association, Operational Policy and Country Services and Resource Mobilization Department, Operational Approaches and Financing in Fragile States 2 (June 2007).

10. Id. A higher ranking corresponds to a higher degree of state failure. The World Bank considers Liberia, Myanmar, Somalia, and the Territory of Kosovo to be fragile states, but they are unranked in the bottom seventy-five states by institutional assessment—in other words, the violence in those states is sufficiently great to push them into the fragile states category, even though their scores on economic, social, and political policy would rank them higher. I have included them at the end of this listing in alphabetical order. Conversely, there are some states

that would rank here solely in terms of their policy scores, but the World Bank left them off its list of fragile states, presumably because of the absence of serious violent conflict.

11. The Failed State Index 2009, available at http://www.foreignpolicy.com/articles/ 2009/06/22/2009_failed_states_index_interactive_map_and_rankings. Foreign Policy and the Fund for Peace use a 1 to 10 scale to rank nations on several characteristics, including demographic pressures, refugees, group grievances, human flight, uneven development, economic decline, delegitimization of the state, public services, human rights, security apparatus, factionalized elites, and external intervention.

12. Compare Rotberg, supra note 8, at 22–23, with Susan E. Rice & Stewart Patrick, Brookings Institution Index of State Weakness in the Developing World 10–11 (2008).

13. President of the United States, The National Security Strategy of the United States of America iv (Sept. 2002); European Union, European Security Strategy: A Secure Europe in a Better World 4 (2003); United Nations, Report of the Secretary-General, In Larger Freedom: Towards Development, Security, and Human Rights for All (2005).

14. James D. Fearon & David D. Laitin, Neotrusteeship and the Problem of Weak States, 28 Int'l Sec. 13 (2004).

15. See James Risen & Judith Miller, C.I.A. Is Reported to Kill a Leader of Qaeda in Yemen, N.Y. Times, Nov. 5, 2002, at A14; Walter Pincus, U.S. Strike Kills Six in Al Qaeda, Wash. Post, Nov. 5, 2002, at A1; Charles Levinson & Margaret Coker, Al Qaeda's Deep Tribal Ties Make Yemen a Terror Hub, Wall St. J., available at http://online.wsj.com/article/NA_WSJ_PUB: SB10001424052748704320104575015493304519542.html.

16. President of the United States, National Security Strategy of the United States (2002).

17. See Eric Posner, Human Welfare, Not Human Rights, 108 Colum. L. Rev. 1758, 1766–69 (2008; Fernando Teson, The Liberal Case for Humanitarian Intervention in Humanitarian Intervention: Ethical, Legal, and Political Dilemmas 93 (J.L. Holzgrefe & Robert O. Keohane, eds., 2003).

18. Vienna Convention on the Law of Treaties, 1155 U.N.T.S. 331, 8 I.L.M. 679 (1969) (entered into force Jan. 27, 1980).

19. See, e.g., Reparation for Injuries Suffered in the Service of the United Nations, 1949 I.C.J. 174, 179 (noting that the United Nations Organization was itself a party to treaties, including, e.g., the Convention on the Privileges and Immunities of the United Nations, 21 U.S.T. 1418, T.I.A.S. No. 6900, 1 U.N.T.S. 15 (entered into force for the United States Apr. 29, 1970)).

20. See I.I. Lukashuk, Parties to Treaties—The Right of Participation, 135 Rec. des Cours 231, 280–81 (1972); James Crawford, The Creation of States in International Law 394 (1979).

21. Convention on Rights and Duties of States, 49 Stat. 3097, T.S. 881, 165 L.N.T.S. 19, 3 Bevans 145 (entered into force Dec. 26, 1934).

22. See Olivier Roy, Globalized Islam: In Search for a New Ummah 56 (2004); Paul Berman, Terror and Liberalism (2004); Rohan Gunaratna, Inside Al Qaeda: Global Network of Terror 122 (2002).

23. UN Charter arts. 75–85.

24. Helman & Ratner, supra note 6, at 16.

25. See, e.g., James D. Fearon & David D. Laitin, Neotrusteeship and the Problem of Weak States, 28 Int'l Sec. 5 (2004).

26. See, e.g., Simon Chesterman, Just War or Just Peace?: Humanitarian Intervention and International Law 77–80 (2001); Nicholas J. Wheeler, Saving Strangers: Humanitarian

Intervention in International Society 78–138 (2000); Sean D. Murphy, Humanitarian Intervention: The United Nations in an Evolving World Order 102–06 (1996).

27. See e.g., Stephen D. Krasner, The Hole in the Whole: Sovereignty, Shared Sovereignty, and International Law, 25 Mich. J. Int'l L. 1075 (2004).

28. See John Yoo, Politics as Law?: The Antiballistic Missile Treaty, the Separation of Powers, and Treaty Interpretation, 89 Calif. L. Rev. 851, 904–05 (2001).

29. Accordance with International Law of the Unilateral Declaration of Independence in Respect of Kosovo, Advisory Opinion, 2010 I.C.J. 141 (July 22).

30. S.C. Res. 1483, ¶ 4, U.N. Doc. S/RES/1483 (May 22, 2003).

31. S.C. Res. 794 (1992).

32. See, e.g., John Yoo, Iraqi Reconstruction and the Law of Occupation, 11 U.C. Davis J. Int'l L. & Pol'y 7 (2004).

33. See John Yoo, Politics as Laws?: The ABM Treaty, the Separation of Powers, and Treaty Interpretation, 89 Calif. L. Rev. 851 (2001) (American policy on Soviet Union); Edwin D. Williamson & John E. Osborn, A U.S. Perspective on Treaty Succession and Related Issues in the Wake of the Breakup of the USSR and Yugoslavia, 33 Va. J. Int'l L. 261 (1993) (U.S. State Department Office of Legal Adviser views).

34. Helman & Ratner, supra note 6, at 12–18; Robert O. Keohane, Political Authority after Intervention: Gradations in Sovereignty, in Holzgrefe & Keohane, supra note 17, at 275–98; Fearon & Laitin, supra note 14, at 7.

35. Ruth Gordon, Saving Failed States: Sometimes a Neocolonialist Notion, 12 Am. U. J. Int'l L. & Pol'y 903, 907 (1997). See also Ruth E. Gordon, Some Legal Problems with Trusteeship, 28 Cornell Int'l L.J. 301 (1995).

36. Rosa Ehrenreich Brooks, Failed States, or the State as Failure?, 72 U. Chi. L. Rev. 1159, 1159, 1191 (2005). See also Saira Mohamed, Note, From Keeping Peace to Building Peace: A Proposal for a Revitalized United Nations Trusteeship Council, 105 Colum. L. Rev. 809, 830–34 (2005) (surveying sources). See also Christian Eric Ford & Ben A. Oppenheim, Neotrusteeship or Mistrusteeship—The Authority Creep Dilemma in United Nations Transitional Administration, 41 Vand. J. Transnat'l L. 55 (2008).

37. Ashraf Ghani & Clare Lockhart, Fixing Failed States: A Framework for Rebuilding a Fractured World 4, 7, 10 (2008).

38. The literature on the rise of nongovernmental organizations is vast. See, e.g., Peter Willetts, Non-Governmental Organizations in World Politics: The Construction of Global Governance (2011); Ian Hurd, International Organizations: Politics, Law, Practice (2011); Anna-Karin Lindblom, Non-Governmental Organisations in International Law (2006).

39. See Ryan Goodman & Derek Jinks, Toward an Institutional Theory of Sovereignty, 55 Stan. L. Rev. 1749, 1779–80 (2002); Martha Finnemore, Constructing Norms of Humanitarian Intervention, in The Culture of National Security in World Politics 153 (Peter J. Katzenstein ed., 1996).

40. Julian E. Barnes, Report: Afghanistan War Costs Jump, Wall St. J. Washington Wire Blog (September 8, 2010, 8:52 AM), http://blogs.wsj.com/washwire/2010/09/08/afghanistan-war-co sts-jump-congressional-report-shows/.

41. See generally Julian Ku & John Yoo, Taming Globalization: International Law, the U.S. Constitution, and the New World Order (2012).

42. Oliver Williamson, The Mechanisms of Governance (1999).

43. Max Weber, The Theory of Social and Economic Organization 156 (A.M. Henderson & Talcott Parsons trans., 1947).

44. See, e.g., Rosa Ehrenreich Brooks, Failed States, or the State as Failure, 72 U. Chi. L. Rev. 1159, 1173 (2005).

45. See, e.g., Anne-Marie Slaughter, A New World Order 12 (2004); Helen Stacy, Relational Sovereignty, 55 Stan. L. Rev. 2029, 2043 (2003); Kenichi Ohmae, The End of the Nation State: The Rise of Regional Economies 140 (1996).

46. Jeremy Rabkin, The Case for Sovereignty: Why the World Should Welcome American Independence (2004).

47. See Cristina G. Badescu & Linnea Bergholm, The Responsibility to Protect and the Conflict in Darfur: The Big Let-Down, 40 Sec. Dialogue 287 (2009); David B. Kopel, Paul Gallant & Joanne D. Eisen, Is Resisting Genocide a Human Right?, 81 Notre Dame L. Rev. 1275 (2006); Richard Goldstone, The Politics of Sudan, 102 Am. Soc'y Int'l L. Proc. 89 (2008).

48. Kenneth Waltz, A Theory of International Politics (1979).

49. James Morrow, Alliances and Asymmetry: An Alternative to the Capability Aggregation Model of Alliances, 35 Am. J. Pol. Sci. 904 (1991).

50. David Lake, Anarchy, Hierarchy, and the Variety of International Relations, 50 Int'l Org. 1, 2 (1996).

51. See, e.g., Ahmed Rashid, Taliban: Militant Islam, Oil & Fundamentalism in Central Asia, 207–08, 212–13 (2001); Francis Fukuyama, State-Building: Governance and World Order in the 21st Century 101 (2004).

52. See Edwin Williamson & John Osborn, A U.S. Perspective on Treaty Succession and Related Issues in the Wake of the Breakup of the USSR and Yugoslavia, 33 Va. J. Int'l L. 261 (1993).

53. Steven R. Ratner, Drawing a Better Line: Uti Possidetis and the Borders of New States, 90 Am. J. Int'l L. 590 (1996).

54. S.C. Res. 1483, U.N. Doc. S/RES/1483 (May 22, 2003).

55. See Alberto Alesina & Enrico Spolaore, The Size of Nations (2003).

56. Id. at 18–23.

57. The Federalist No. 10, at 63–64 (Jacob E. Cooke ed., 1961) (James Madison).

58. For further discussion, see Ravi Bhavnani & Dan Miodownik, Ethnic Polarization, Ethnic Salience, and Civil War, 53 J. of Conflict Resolution 30 (2009); Badredine Arfi, International Change and the Stability of Multiethnic States: Yugoslavia, Lebanon and Crises of Governance (2005); Sammy Smooha, The Model of Ethnic Democracy: Response to Danel, 28 J. Israeli Hist. 55, 55–56 (2009); Erika Forsberg, Polarization and Ethnic Conflict in a Wide Strategic Setting, 45 J. Peace Res. 283 (2008); Joan Esteban & Debraj Ray, Polarization, Fractionalization and Conflict, 45 J. Peace Res. 163 (2008); Gerald Schneider & Nina Wiesehomeier, Rules that Matter: Political Institutions and the Diversity-Conflict Nexus, 45 J. Peace Res. 183 (2008).

59. Id. at 69, 81–85.

60. See Chaim Kaufmann, Possible and Impossible Solutions to Ethnic Civil Wars, 20 Int'l Sec. 136 (1996); Chaim Kaufmann, When All Else Fails: Ethnic Population Transfers and Partitions in the Twentieth Century, 23 Int'l Sec. 120 (1998). See also Alexander B. Downes, The Holy Land Divided: Defending Partition as a Solution to Ethnic Wars, 10 Sec. Stud. 58 (2001).

61. See Carter Johnson, Partitioning to Peace: Sovereignty, Demography, and Ethnic Civil Wars, 32 Int'l Sec. 140, 151 (2008) (summarizing debate).

62. See, e.g., Nicholas Sambanis & Jonah Schulhofer-Wohl, What's In a Line?: Is Partition a Solution to Civil War?, 34 Int'l Sec. 82 (2009); Thomas Chapman & Philip G. Roeder, Partition as a Solution to Wars of Nationalism: The Importance of Institutions, 101 Am. Pol. Sci. Rev. 677 (2007).

63. W.R. Smyser, From Yalta to Berlin: The Cold War Struggle over Germany 135 (1999).

64. Post-Cold War developments may be largely responsible for European opposition to defense spending increases. See Office of Technology Assessment, Global Arms Race: Commerce in Advanced Military Technology and Weapons 63–82 (June 1991), available at http://ota-cdn. fas.org/reports/9122.pdf; Robert Kagan, Of Paradise and Power: America and Europe in the New World Order 22–23 (2003).

65. U.S. Department of Defense, Fiscal Year 2010 Budget Request, graph on page 2, "Department of Defense Topline: FY2001–2010" (May 2009), available at http://comptroller. defense.gov/defbudget/fy2010/fy2010_BudgetBriefing.pdf (showing that the United States spent $535 billion in 2006, $601 billion in 2007, and $667 billion in 2008 on defense).

66. On Iraq, see Thomas E. Ricks, Fiasco: The American Military Adventure in Iraq 97 (2006). An army briefing noted that postwar reconstruction of Iraq would require around 470,000 troops. Id. at 79. Iraq has an estimated population of 28.9 million. On Kosovo, see North Atlantic Treaty Organization, NATO's Role in Kosovo, http://www.nato.int/cps/en/natolive/topics_48818. htm#evolution (last visited July 5, 2010). Kosovo has an estimated population of 2 million.

67. See James D. Fearon, Rationalist Explanations for War, 49 Int'l Org. 379, 379–81(1995); Robert Powell, Bargaining Theory and International Conflict, 5 Ann. Rev. Pol. Sci. 1 (2002); Kenneth A. Schultz, Do Democratic Institutions Constrain or Inform?: Contrasting Two Institutional Perspectives on Democracy and War, 53 Int'l Org. 233 (1999).

68. Several assumptions underlie this model. There must be a real probability that either group can win and that both groups can estimate this probability. The government and the rebel group in this model are not risk-seeking, in the sense that they would gamble to win a low-probability victory. Additionally, the territory in dispute can be bargained over and divided, rather than transferred as a whole, through side payments, linked deals, or different spheres of influence. Also, neither group can prevail in the first stage of bargaining by completely eliminating the other, so that any armed conflict may result in the loss of the territory, but not the end of the insurgency.

69. See Sebastian Rosato, The Flawed Logic of Democratic Peace Theory, 97 Am. Pol. Sci. Rev. 585, 599 (2003); James D. Fearon, Domestic Political Audiences and Escalation of International Disputes, 88 Am. Pol. Sci. Rev. 577, 578 (1994).

70. See, e.g., Robert Powell, War as a Commitment Problem, 60 Int'l Org. 169 (2006); Robert Powell, The Inefficient Use of Power: Costly Conflict with Complete Information, 98 Am. Pol. Sci. Rev. 231 (2004).

71. James D. Fearon, Rationalist Explanations of War, 49 Int'l Org. 379 (1995); Robert Powell, In the Shadow of Power: States and Strategies in International Politics (1999).

72. S.C. Res. 1483, ¶ 5, U.N. Doc. S/RES/1483 (May 22, 2003).

73. Doris Graber, The Development of the Law of Belligerent Occupation 13 (1949).

74. See, e.g., American Ins. Co. v. 365 Bales of Cotton, 26 U.S. (1 Pet.) 511, 542 (1828); Emmerich de Vattel, The Law of Nations or Principles of the Law of Nature, Applied to the Conduct and to the Affairs of Nations and of Sovereigns 308 (Charles G. Fenwick trans., 1916) (1758).

75. Instructions for the Government of Armies of the United States in the Field, General Order No. 100 § 1, art. 3 (Apr. 24, 1863) [hereinafter Lieber Code].

76. Id. § 1, art. 14.

77. Convention Respecting the Laws and Customs of War on Land § III, art. 43, Oct. 18, 1907, 36 Stat. 2277, T.S. 539.

78. Geneva Convention Relative to the Protection of Civilian Persons in Time of War art. 64, Aug. 12, 1949, 6 U.S.T. 3516, 75 U.N.T.S. 287.

79. Id.

80. See Eyal Benvenisti, The International Law of Occupation 73–74 (1993).

81. See id.

82. All statistics are taken from Jason H. Campbell & Michael E. O'Hanlon, The Brookings Institution, The State of Iraq: An Update (Dec. 22, 2007), http://www.brookings.edu/opinions/2007/1222_iraq_ohanlon.aspx, and Jason H. Campbell & Michael E. O'Hanlon, The Brookings Institution, The State of Iraq: An Update (June 22, 2008), http://www.brookings.edu/opinions/2008/0622_iraq_ohanlon.aspx.

83. See, e.g., Kimberly Kagan, The Surge: A Military History (2009).

84. Testifying before Congress following the announcement of the Afghanistan surge, American commanders acknowledged that their plan was to create "breathing space" for the Afghani central government, the same language used to describe the Iraq surge. See Yochi J. Dreazen & Peter Spiegel, Surge Strategy Borrows from Bush Argument, Wall St. J., Dec. 4, 2009, at A8.

85. A similar but somewhat different explanation is provided by Stephen Biddle et al., Testing the Surge: Why Did Violence Decline in Iraq in 2007?, 37 Int'l Sec. 7 (2012) (synergism between surge and Anbar Awakening produced reduction in conflict).

86. See, e.g., Daron Acemoglu & James A. Robinson, Why Did the West Extend the Franchise?: Democracy, Inequality, and Growth in Historical Perspective, 115 Q. J. Econ. 1167 (2000); Daron Acemoglu & James A. Robinson, A Theory of Political Transitions, 91 Am. Econ. Rev. 938 (2001).

87. Another dynamic that might be at work in successful interventions, though not in Iraq, is that a larger power could force ethnic groups to cooperate temporarily. One study has found ethnic violence to be far more exceptional than might be expected. See James D. Fearon & David D. Laitin, Explaining Interethnic Cooperation, 90 Am. Pol. Sci. Rev. 715–35 (1996). This study proposes that conflicts between ethnic groups result from inabilities to maintain a cooperative equilibrium because of a downward cycle of a loss of trust. Cooperation over time, imposed by an intervening power, might reintroduce trust between fighting groups that would create the conditions for a permanent political settlement.

CHAPTER 8

1. Daniel J. Hughes ed., Von Moltke on the Art of War 45 (1995).

2. See Robert J. Delahunty & John Yoo, Great Power Security, 10 Chi. J. Int'l L. 35, 43 (2009) (citing Kalevi J. Holsti, The State, War, and the State of War 24 (1996)).

3. Bethany Lacina & Nils Petter Gleditsch, Monitoring Trends in Global Combat: A New Dataset of Battle Deaths, 21 Eur. J. Population 145, 157 & tbl.3 (2005).

4. Marc Lacey, 10 Years Later in Rwanda, The Dead Are Ever Present, N.Y. Times (Feb. 26, 2004), http://www.nytimes.com/2004/02/26/world/10-years-later-in-rwanda-the-dead-are-ever-present.html (estimating 800,000 killed in the Rwandan genocide); Jeffrey Gettleman, The World's Worst War, N.Y. Times (Dec. 15, 2012), http://www.nytimes.com/2012/12/16/sunday-review/congos-never-ending-war.html (estimating more than 5 million dead from the war in Congo);

Editorial, No More Delay on Darfur, N.Y. Times (Apr. 19, 2007), http://www.nytimes. com/2007/04/19/opinion/19thu2.html (estimating at least 200,000 killed in Darfur, Sudan as of April 2007).

5. See Paul Collier et al., World Bank, Breaking the Conflict Trap: Civil War and Development Policy 17 (2003). Some, however, dispute this ratio. See, e.g., Kristine Eck, Human Security Report Project, Human Security Report 2005, 75 (2005) (calling the 90 percent civilian death rate a "myth").

6. United Nations Development Programme, Human Development Report 2005 156 (2005) (calling the "conflict in the eastern part of the Democratic Republic of the Congo…the site of the deadliest conflict since the Second World War").

7. See UN Charter art. 2, para. 4. The exceptions are (1) "in self-defence if an armed attack occurs against a Member of the United Nations" and (2) if the Security Council authorizes the use of force "to maintain or restore international peace and security." Id. at arts. 42, 51.

8. See Countries at the Crossroads: Libya, Freedom House (2011), http://www.freedomhouse. org/report/countries-crossroads/2011/libya.

9. Freedom House started rating nations in 1973, covering 1972. Gadhafi had already been in power by then, and Libya would continue to receive a "not free" rating each year hence, until 2013, when it received its first "partly free" rating. See Freedom in the World Country Ratings 1972–2011, http://www.freedomhouse.org/sites/default/files/FIW%20All%20Scores%2C%20 Countries%2C%201973-2012%20%28FINAL%29.xls; Libya: Freedom in the World 2013, Freedom House (2013), http://www.freedomhouse.org/report/freedom-world/2013/libya.

10. Steven Greenhouse, Libya Declares End to Chad War, N.Y. Times (May 27, 1988), http://www.nytimes.com/1988/05/27/world/libya-declares-end-to-chad-war.html; Roger Cohen, Chad Wins World Court Decision in Territorial Dispute With Libya, N.Y. Times (Feb. 04, 1994), http://www.nytimes.com/1994/02/04/world/chad-wins-world-court-decision-in-territorial-dispute-with-libya.html.

11. Associated Press, Qaddafi Announces Pullback of Troops on Egypt's Border, N.Y. Times (Mar. 29, 1988), http://www.nytimes.com/1988/03/29/world/qaddafi-announces-pullback-of-troops-on-egypt-s-border.html.

12. Jeffrey Gettleman, Libyan Oil Buys Allies for Qaddafi, N.Y. Times (Mar. 15, 2011), http://www.nytimes.com/2011/03/16/world/africa/16mali.html.

13. Brian Davis, Qaddafi, Terrorism, and the Origins of the U.S. Attack on Libya 19-20, 34-44, 78-81 (1990).

14. Steven Erlanger, 4 Guilty in Fatal 1986 Berlin Disco Bombing Linked to Libya, N.Y. Times (Nov. 14, 2001), http://www.nytimes.com/2001/11/14/world/4-guilty-in-fatal-1986-berlin-disco-bombing-linked-to-libya.html.

15. David Cutler, Timeline: Key Dates in Lockerbie Bombing Case, Reuters (Aug. 12, 2009), http://www.reuters.com/article/2009/08/13/us-britain-lockerbie-events-timeline-sb-idUSTRE57C02I20090813.

16. See Bush Official: Libya's Nuclear Program A Surprise, CNN.com (Dec. 19, 2003), http://www.cnn.com/2003/WORLD/africa/12/19/libya.nuclear/.

17. Libya Declares Chemical Weapons, BBC (Mar. 5, 2004), http://news.bbc.co.uk/2/hi/africa/3535177.stm.

18. See David D. Kirkpatrick & Mona El-Naggar, Qaddafi's Son Warns of Civil War as Libyan Protests Widen, N.Y. Times (Feb. 20, 2011), http://www.nytimes.com/2011/02/21/world/africa/21libya.html.

19. Simon Denyer, Defections, Protests Hit Libyan Regime, Wash. Post (May 30, 2011), http://www.washingtonpost.com/world/middle-east/defections-protests-hit-libyan-regime/2011/05/30/AGLGJzEH_story.html.

20. Kareem Fahim & David D. Kirkpatrick, Qaddafi Massing Forces in Tripoli as Rebellion Spreads, N.Y. Times (Feb. 23, 2011), http://www.nytimes.com/2011/02/24/world/africa/24libya.html.

21. See Profile: Khamis Gaddafi, BBC (Sept. 4, 2011), http://www.bbc.co.uk/news/world-africa-14723041.

22. See Martin Chulov, Libya Rebels Isolate Gaddafi, Seizing Cities and Oilfields, The Guardian (Feb. 24, 2011), http://www.theguardian.com/world/2011/feb/24/libya-rebels-control-gaddafi-oilfields.

23. Jack Farchy & Roula Khalaf, Gold Key to Financing Gaddafi Struggle, FT.com (Mar. 21, 2011), http://www.ft.com/intl/cms/s/0/588ce75a-53e4-11e0-8bd7-00144feab49a.html.

24. Sylvia Poggioli, Gadhafi's Military Muscle Concentrated in Elite Units, NPR.org (Mar. 10, 2011), http://www.npr.org/2011/03/10/134404618/gadhafis-military-muscle-concentrated-in-elite-units; Profile: Khamis Gaddafi, BBC (Sept. 4, 2011), http://www.bbc.co.uk/news/world-africa-14723041.

25. Yaroslav Trofimov, Libyan Rebels Flee Key Post, Retreat to Benghazi, Wall St. J. (Mar. 15, 2011), http://online.wsj.com/article/SB10001424052748704662604576202821789052208.html.

26. See Yaroslav Trofimov, Strikes Blunt Benghazi Attack, Wall St. J. (Mar. 21, 2011), http://online.wsj.com/article/SB20001424052748703292304576212874038683848.html.

27. Charles Levinson, Gadhafi's Compound Falls, Wall St. J. (Aug. 24, 2011), http://online.wsj.com/article/SB10001424053111903327904576525652544535820.html.

28. Margaret Coker, Gadhafi's Death Ushers in New Era, Wall St. J. (Oct. 20, 2011), http://online.wsj.com/article/SB10001424052970204618704576642661915994024.html.

29. See Emily O'Brien & Andrew Sinclair, New York University, Center on International Cooperation, The Libyan War: A Diplomatic History February–August 2011, 10–11 (2011), available at http://cic.es.its.nyu.edu/sites/default/files/libya_diplomatic_history.pdf.

30. S.C. Res. 1973, U.N. Doc. S/RES/1973 (Mar. 17, 2011).

31. E.g., Charles McDermid, Arming Libya's Rebels: A Debate in Doha, Time (Apr. 14, 2011), http://content.time.com/time/world/article/0,8599,2065124,00.html ("Belgian Foreign Minister…[told] reporters[,] 'The U.N. resolution speaks about protecting civilians, not arming them.'").

32. Paula Newton, NATO Approves Expanded Role In Libya, CNN (Mar. 27, 2011), http://www.cnn.com/2011/WORLD/africa/03/27/libya.nato/index.html.

33. Chris Buckley, China Intensifies Condemnation of Libya Air Strikes, Reuters (Mar. 21, 2011), http://www.reuters.com/article/2011/03/21/us-china-libya-idUSTRE72K0LX20110321.

34. See Press Release, Security Council, Security Council Approves "No-Fly Zone" over Libya, Authorizing "All Necessary Measures" to Protect Civilians, By Vote of 10 in Favour with Abstentions, UN Press Release SC/10200 (Mar. 17, 2011) (Brazil, China, Germany, India, Russia abstaining); Jo Ling Kent, Leaders at BRICS Summit Speak Out Against Airstrikes in Libya, CNN (Apr. 14, 2011), http://www.cnn.com/2011/WORLD/asiapcf/04/14/china.brics.summit/index.html (Brazil, Russia, India, China, and South Africa issuing a joint statement against the use of force in Libya).

35. Barack Obama, Remarks by the President in Address to the Nation on Libya to the National Defense University (Mar. 28, 2011), available at http://www.whitehouse.gov/the-press-office/2011/03/28/remarks-president-address-nation-libya.

36. Rod Nordland, Latest Syrian Defectors Are from Higher Ranks, N.Y. Times (June 25, 2012), http://www.nytimes.com/2012/06/26/world/middleeast/syrian-military-defections-reported.html.

37. Ben Hubbard, Momentum Shifts in Syria, Bolstering Assad's Position, N.Y. Times (July 17, 2013), http://www.nytimes.com/2013/07/18/world/middleeast/momentum-shifts-in-syria-bolstering-assads-position.html.

38. See, e.g., Security Council Fails to Adopt Resolution on Syria, July 19, 2012, UN News Centre, available at http://www.un.org/apps/news/story.asp?NewsID=42513#.Ugf84hZOTwx.

39. See Pieter D. Wezeman, Arms Transfers to Syria, in Stockholm International Peace Institute Yearbook 2013: Armaments, Disarmament and International Security 269–70 (2013), available at http://www.sipri.org/yearbook/2013/files/sipri-yearbook-2013-chapter-5-section-3.

40. Alan Cowell, War Deaths in Syria Said to Top 100,000, N.Y. Times (June 26, 2013), http://www.nytimes.com/2013/06/27/world/middleeast/syria.html.

41. United Nations High Commissioner on Refugees, 2013 UNHCR Country Operations Profile—Syrian Arab Republic, available at http://www.unhcr.org/pages/49e486a76.html.

42. NPR Staff and Wires, At Least 17 Killed in Syria Protests, NPR (July 15, 2011), http://www.npr.org/2011/07/15/138166584/at-least-17-killed-in-syria-protests (citing Amnesty International).

43. For one review of Syria's motives in invading Lebanon during the latter's civil war, see MERIP Staff, Why Syria Invaded Lebanon, Middle East Research and Information Project Reports 3–10 (Oct. 1976).

44. Thomas E. Ricks, General: Iraqi Insurgents Directed from Syria, Wash. Post (Dec. 17, 2004), http://www.washingtonpost.com/wp-dyn/articles/A5886-2004Dec16.html.

45. Eben Kaplan, Nuclear Questions Aimed at Syria, Council on Foreign Relations (Sept. 26, 2007), http://www.cfr.org/missile-defense/nuclear-questions-aimed-syria/p14307.

46. Kareem Fahim, Still More Questions Than Answers on Nerve Gas in Syria, N.Y. Times (June 10, 2013), http://www.nytimes.com/2013/06/11/world/middleeast/still-more-questions-than-answers-on-nerve-gas-in-syria.html.

47. Joby Warrick & Babak Dehghanpisheh, Syrian Army Weakening as Rebels Make Gains, Wash. Post (Dec. 04, 2012), http://articles.washingtonpost.com/2012-12-04/world/35625028_1_syrian-army-syrian-opposition-rebels.

48. Michael R. Gordon & Mark Landler, Rebels' Losses in Syria Complicate Options for U.S. Aid, N.Y. Times (June 10, 2013), http://www.nytimes.com/2013/06/11/world/middleeast/as-rebels-lose-ground-in-syria-us-mulls-options.html.

49. Adam Entous, Legal Fears Slowed Aid to Syrian Rebels, Wall St. J., July 15, 2013, at A1.

50. John A. Tirpak, The Syria Question, Air Force Magazine (March 2013), available at http://www.airforcemag.com/MagazineArchive/Pages/2013/March%202013/0313syria.aspx.

51. Matthew Hurley, The Bekaa Valley Air Battle, June 1982: Lessons Mislearned?, Airpower J. (Winter 1989), available at http://www.airpower.au.af.mil/airchronicles/apj/apj89/win89/hurley.html.

52. Ilya Arkhipov, Putin Endorses Permanent Russian Navy Presence in Mediterranean, Bloomberg, June 6, 2013, available at http://www.bloomberg.com/news/2013-06-06/putin-endorses-permanent-russian-navy-presence-in-mediterranean.html.

53. See, e.g., Ruslan Pukhov, Why Russia is Backing Syria, N.Y. Times, July 6, 2012.

54. Julian Ku, China and the Future of International Adjudication, 25 Md. J. Int'l L. 154 (2012).

55. See, e.g., Alan J. Kuperman, A Model Humanitarian Intervention?: Reassessing NATO's Libya Campaign, 38 Int'l Sec. 105 (2013).

56. Central Intelligence Agency, World Factbook: North Korea https://www.cia.gov/library/publications/the-world-factbook/geos/kn.html (last visited Aug. 28, 2013).

57. Id.

58. Id.

59. Central Intelligence Agency, World Factbook: South Korea, https://www.cia.gov/library/publications/the-world-factbook/geos/ks.html (last visited Aug. 28, 2013).

60. See Office of the Secretary of Defense, U.S. Department of Defense, Military and Security Developments Involving the Democratic People's Republic of Korea 2012 (Feb. 15, 2013), available at http://www.defense.gov/pubs/Report_to_Congress_on_Military_and_Security_Developments_Involving_the_DPRK.pdf.

61. See Directorate of Intelligence, Rangoon Bombing Incident—The Case against the North Koreans (Oct. 19, 1983), available at http://www.foia.cia.gov/sites/default/files/document_conversions/89801/DOC_0000408056.pdf.

62. Bill Powell, South Korea's Case for How the *Cheonan* Sank, Time (Aug. 13, 2010), http://content.time.com/time/world/article/0,8599,2010455,00.html (describing the official investigation by South Korea, the United States, UK, Australia, and Sweden).

63. Dafna Linzer, Low Yield of Blast Surprises Analysts, Wash. Post. (Oct. 10, 2006), http://www.washingtonpost.com/wp-dyn/content/article/2006/10/09/AR2006100901246.html.

64. David Chance & Jack Kim, North Korea Nuclear Test Draws Anger, Including from China, Reuters (Feb. 12, 2013), http://www.reuters.com/article/2013/02/12/us-korea-north-idUSBRE91B0482013012 (describing also North Korea's third nuclear test in 2013).

65. Office of the Secretary of Defense, Military and Security Developments Involving the Democratic People's Republic of Korea 19 (2012), available at http://www.defense.gov/pubs/Report_to_Congress_on_Military_and_Security_Developments_Involving_the_DPRK.pdf.

66. Id. at 16.

67. Id. at 8.

68. Id. at 12, 19.

69. Id. at 18.

70. USKF Public Affairs, President Visits Soldiers on Demilitarized Zone, Army.mil (Mar. 27, 2012).

71. Office of the Coordinator for Counterterrorism, U.S. Department of State, Country Reports on Terrorism 2011 (July 31, 2012), available at http://www.state.gov/j/ct/rls/crt/2011/195547.htm.

72. Id.

73. Id.; Michael Peel, Iran, Russia and China Prop Up Assad Economy, Financial Times (June 27, 2013), http://www.ft.com/intl/cms/s/0/79eca81c-df48-11e2-a9f4-00144feab7de.html ("Mr[.] Jamil [Syria's Deputy Prime Minister for the Economy] said Syria had an unlimited credit line with Tehran for food and oil-product imports.").

74. Fredrik Dahl, Iran Expands Nuclear Capacity, Delays Sensitive Reactor: IAEA, Reuters (Aug. 28, 2013), http://www.reuters.com/article/2013/08/28/us-iran-nuclear-iaea-idUSBRE97R0LZ20130828.

75. Transcript of the 2012 Republican Primary Debate in Spartansburg, South Carolina, Wash. Post (2012), http://www.washingtonpost.com/wp-srv/politics/2012-presidential-debates/republican-primary-debate-november-12-2011/.

76. Id.

77. Id.

78. Id.

79. Barack Obama, Remarks at AIPAC Policy Conference (Mar. 04, 2012), available at http://www.whitehouse.gov/the-press-office/2012/03/04/remarks-president-aipac-policy- conference-0.

80. Press Release, The White House, Statement by the President on the Announcement of Additional Sanctions on Iran (Nov. 21, 2011), http://www.whitehouse.gov/the-press-office/2011/11/21/statement-president-announcement-additional-sanctions-iran.

81. Charlie Savage, Cheney Says He Urged Bush to Bomb Syria in '07, N.Y. Times (Aug. 24, 2011), http://www.nytimes.com/2011/08/25/us/politics/25cheney.html.

82. See UN Charter art 2., para. 4.

83. See UN Charter, chap. VII (arts. 39–51).

84. See id.

85. China Backs Statement Opposing War Resolution, PBS (Mar. 6, 2003), http://www.pbs.org/newshour/updates/iraq_03-06-03.html ("Chinese officials on Thursday announced their support for a joint statement released Wednesday by France, Germany and Russia vowing to block a United Nations resolution authorizing the use of force on Iraq.").

86. See Ernest R. Ray, John F. Kennedy and the Cuban Missile Crisis, BBC (Feb. 17, 2011), http://www.bbc.co.uk/history/worldwars/coldwar/kennedy_cuban_missile_01.shtml.

87. There was disagreement as to whether this was a misinterpretation of Ahmadinejad's remarks, but the official English version of his website used such language. See Internet Archive of the Official Website of the Presidency of the Islamic Republic of Iran, President Says Zionist Regime of Israel Faces Deadend (June 3, 2008), http://web.archive.org/web/20110716100837/http://www.president.ir/en/?ArtID=10114 ("President Mahmoud Ahmadinejad said here Monday that the Zionist Regime of Israel faces a deadend and will under God's grace be wiped off the map.").

88. Clifford Krauss, Argentina Arrests 8 Iranians and Ousts 7 in Anti-Jewish Bombings, N.Y. Times (May 17, 1998), http://www.nytimes.com/1998/05/17/world/argentina-arrests-8-iranians-and-ousts-7-in-anti-jewish-bombings.html.

89. Charlie Savage & Scott Shane, Iranians Accused of a Plot to Kill Saudis' U.S. Envoy, N.Y. Times (Oct. 11, 2011), http://www.nytimes.com/2011/10/12/us/us-accuses-iranians-of-plotting-to-kill-saudi-envoy.html.

90. Peter Kenyon, Iran Can Disrupt Key Waterway, But for How Long?, NPR (Feb. 14, 2012), http://www.npr.org/2012/02/14/146866084/iran-can-disrupt-key-waterway-but-for-how-long.

91. E.g., Associated Press, Iranian Attack Damages Tanker, N.Y. Times (Dec. 24, 1987), http://www.nytimes.com/1987/12/24/world/iranian-attack-damages-tanker.html (reporting on an Iranian vessel attacking a Norwegian tanker).

92. See generally Samuel P. Huntington, The Soldier and the State: The Theory and Politics of Civil-Military Relations (1985).

93. See Geneva Convention Relative to the Protection of Civilian Persons in Time of War art. 28, Aug. 12, 1949, 6 U.S.T. 3316, 75 U.N.T.S. 308.

Index